D   V. Barrett has been a school teacher, a government
in   igence analyst and a journalist. He has written for the
I   endent and the Guardian amongst other newspapers and
is a regular contributor to Fortean Times. His many books,
mainly on aspects of religious and esoteric belief and history,
include The New Believers and A Brief History of Secret
Societies. He has a PhD in Sociology of Religion from the
London School of Economics.

Highlights from the series

A BRIEF GUIDE TO

SECRET RELIGIONS

DAVID V. BARRETT

ROBINSON   RUNNING PRESS
PHILADELPHIA · LONDON

Constable & Robinson Ltd
3 The Lanchesters
162 Fulham Palace Road
London W6 9ER
www.constablerobinson.com

First published in the UK by Robinson,
an imprint of Constable & Robinson, 2011

A copy of the British Library Cataloguing in Publication
Data is available from the British Library

UK ISBN 978-1-84901-595-0

1 3 5 7 9 10 8 6 4 2

First published in the United States in 2011
by Running Press Book Publishers

US Library of Congress Control number: 2010928994
US ISBN 978-0-7624-4103-7

Running Press Book Publishers
2300 Chestnut Street
Philadelphia, PA 19103-4371

Visit us on the web!
www.runningpress.com

Printed and bound in the UK

This book is dedicated
to those who question
to those who seek
to those who choose

CONTENTS

What I Believe . . .

Quotations from followers of New Age, Hermetic and Neo-Pagan religions

ACKNOWLEDGEMENTS

First of all I would like to thank the leaders, staff and members of the vast majority of the movements in this book for their cooperation, their willingness to answer my questions and their permission to quote them. Thanks also to the writers and copyright holders of all the books, essays, lyrics, magazines, booklets and websites I have quoted.

The staff at the British Library, the British Library of Political and Economic Science, the Wellcome Library and Inform, the research centre for new religious movements at the London School of Economics, have, as always, been helpful and efficient. The website http://www.sacred-texts.com is also a splendid resource for any writer on religion.

Most sociologists and anthropologists see participant observation as an invaluable research tool. By spending time with members of movements one can gain not just knowledge but understanding, not just facts but insight. Over the last decade or more the London esoteric scene has made me welcome and has included me in many of its activities, knowing that I am a researcher and writer and not a member of any esoteric movement myself. Over the same period I have benefited greatly from listening to and questioning other researchers and speakers, and also from questions, comments and criticisms from the audience when I have been the speaker, both at academic seminars and conferences and in meetings in upstairs rooms in pubs. All of these have been immensely valuable; I owe a lot to them.

The seminars include Inform conferences and many post-graduate seminars at the London School of Economics, and also at Goldsmiths College, King's College, Senate House and the School of Oriental and African Studies, all parts of the University of London. The meetings include, in alphabetical order, London Earth Mysteries, the Moot with No Name, Pagan Federation conferences and open rituals, Research into Lost Knowledge Organisation, Secret Chiefs, Skeptics in the Pub, the South East London Folklore Society, Talking Stick and UnConvention.

There are also a number of people, many of them friends and colleagues and a few I have never met, whom I would like to thank by name. Between them, in conversation and by email, they offered invaluable suggestions and criticisms on my text, and/or were willing to give up their time to talk to or email me about their beliefs and practices for the 'What I Believe' panels. In alphabetical order: Dolores Ashcroft-Nowicki, Geraldine Beskin, Dr Jenny Blain, Dr William Bloom, Philip Carr-Gomm, Chic and Tabatha Cicero, Ina Cüsters-van Bergen, Terry Dobney, Ken Eakins, Dr Dave Evans, Jack Gale, Dr Graham Harvey, Professor Ronald Hutton, Stuart Inman, Professor Jean La Fontaine, Gareth J. Medway, Mani Navasothy, Dr Paul Newman, Dr Christina Oakley Harrington, Phil Parkyn, Jon Randall, Dr William S. Redwood, Emma Restall Orr, Steve Wilson, Dr Michael York and Oberon Zell-Ravenheart. My thanks also to Howard Watson for his excellent copy-editing of the text.

Between them they have helped make this book much better than it would otherwise have been, but they are not responsible for any remaining faults.

INTRODUCTION

For anyone who writes about the variety of religious movements it is dispiriting that a decade into the new millennium it is still necessary to point out that Wiccans are not Satanists.

Journalists writing an attention-grabbing story equating witches with black magic with Satanism either haven't done their homework, or don't care – why let the facts get in the way of a good story?

Fundamentalist Christians who do the same have a different reason: any belief which is not of Christ must necessarily be of the Devil – 'He that is not with me is against me' (Matthew 12:30) – so all Neo-Pagans are by definition Satanists, whether they think they are or not. The fact that the same 'logic' would also apply to Buddhists and followers of every other religion is usually ignored.

Christians in particular shy away from the word 'occult' as though it must have devilish connotations. In fact, the word simply means 'hidden' or 'secret' (see p. 13), and since many of the traditional occult teachings are now widely available – indeed, many of the esoteric or occult schools now have websites explaining their purpose – the term no longer really applies.

This book is in many ways a companion volume to my *A Brief History of Secret Societies*,[1] hence the similar title, *A Brief Guide to Secret Religions* – though most of the movements in it would say that they are not secret at all; they publish books, magazines and leaflets, they have websites and many openly publicise their meetings.[2] But they are all 'alternative religions', outside the mainstream, and many of them keep their beliefs and practices to themselves.

One of the book's main aims is to dispel many of the popular misconceptions about New Age, Hermetic and Neo-Pagan beliefs and their believers.

I entitled an earlier book on new religious movements *The New Believers*[3] because, wherever possible, I sought to understand these religions by talking to their believers, not just by listing their beliefs. I take the same approach with this book, which is in part based on one chapter of that one, updated and very much expanded.[4] In addition to presenting the objective facts about the origins, history, beliefs and practices of the movements I try to give an indication of what their members, followers, believers or practitioners think about their own religion – or, as many would call it, their path. This is a form of the phenomenological approach to religious studies that I first encountered many years ago when studying for my first degree: in essence, in terms taken from cultural anthropology, a well-rounded description of a religious movement depends both on *emic* accounts, based on what the members themselves say about their own beliefs, and on *etic* accounts, the scholar's own observation and analysis.[5]

As with all my books I aim to bring a scholarly approach to the content, while avoiding the dryness of far too many scholarly books; this book is written for anyone with an interest in these religions, whatever their academic background.

The monotheistic religions in general have problems with religious pluralism; they believe that there is not only one god but one truth, and that each one of them alone has it. In contrast, esoteric religions, again in general, tend to think in terms of paths; someone may choose one path for himself, but will not only respect the right of other people to choose their own paths, but also accept the validity of those other paths. Many occultists and Neo-Pagans are polytheists, but even those who focus on one god are most likely to be henotheists, following one god but happily accepting the existence of others.

Esoteric religions do not enjoy the same respect from others that mainstream religions usually do. In religiously conservative America a Republican Senate candidate in the 2010 mid-term elections felt that she had to begin a political advertisement with the words 'I'm not a witch' because in 1999 she had said in a TV chat show, 'I dabbled into witchcraft.'[6] One suspects that she would not have felt the need to say, 'I'm not a Methodist.' Even in Britain's largely secular society today there is still a great deal of prejudice against all forms of esoteric religion. As this book was being completed two British newspaper columnists attacked Neo-Pagans in the same month. One, a tabloid journalist, called Druidry 'a cult' and described the granting of basic social rights to Pagans as 'totally barking mumbo-jumbo'[7] (see p. 323). The other, writing a blog for a broadsheet newspaper, spoke without any explanation of 'the overlap between paganism and various forms of Satanism'[8] (see p. 248, p. 280).

It is partly to counter such inflammatory remarks that this book has been written. It covers a large number of movements and a large number of beliefs. It does not assume that any one of them is right and all the others are wrong; that is the antithesis of most esoteric thinking, particularly in Britain and Europe. It does not judge the spiritual truth of any of the movements – though it may sometimes question their histories.

The book does not set out to be an encyclopedic directory of all esoteric movements; that would be impractical and unwieldy, if not impossible to do. Neither is it an apologia for the groups included, though some might have wished it to be so.

It is instead an overview of a wide range of esoteric movements, describing their origins and history, their beliefs and practices, and sometimes their controversies. One of the themes running throughout the book, for example, is the uncertain provenance of many groups and the uncertain backgrounds of some of their founders (see p. 183–4, p. 197, p. 300–1). The book aims to help readers to distinguish between factual history and mythic history in a number of cases.

Although the song 'The Age of Aquarius', from the 1967 musical *Hair!*, promised the Sixties ideal of peace and love, with harmony and trust,[9] the reality of New Age, Hermetic and Neo-Pagan movements has often been anything but, with schisms, accusations, recriminations, lawsuits and sometimes outright deceptions. These are all part of the colourful tapestry woven by esoteric movements not just in the last few decades but over more than a century – though they are, of course, not unique to esoteric religions.

Schisms and offshoots are frequent, perhaps partly because of the nature of both the beliefs and the believers, challenging the orthodox, the mainstream in religion.

The originators of these movements were often highly individual and highly unorthodox in both their spiritual thinking and their personalities. Indeed, amongst the founders and leaders there were some remarkable people – warts and all – such as Helena P. Blavatsky, Annie Besant, Samuel Liddell 'MacGregor' Mathers, Aleister Crowley, Elizabeth Clare Prophet, Sir George Trevelyan, Gerald Gardner and many more, not to mention those still living. They were women as often as men; nobility and Nobel laureates; artists and educators; social rebels and social reformers. Many were mavericks. It is perhaps not too surprising that a number of them had somewhat inflated egos, and attracted strong feelings both for and against themselves. They were innovators; they stood out against the conventional, the accepted and acceptable.

In the root sense of the term they could be called heretics: they *chose* their beliefs (see p. 12).

The same applies to the leaders of schismatic offshoots or variants – and also to the vast majority of esoteric adherents today; compared to mainstream religions, very few people grow up within an esoteric movement. Esoteric believers tend to be 'seekers'; they have often tried several other paths before settling on the one they currently espouse. Partly because of this element of individual, personal choice of path, of belief and practice and of level of commitment, and partly because of the decentralised nature of much esoteric religion, it often falls into what sociologists call 'privatised religion', in contrast to the communal religious activity of much of mainstream religion. Many practise their spiritual activity on their own. When it is communal, in most cases esoteric religion is 'small group religion'.

The book covers a variety of aspects of what might loosely be called alternative spirituality. It includes entries on significant people (G. I. Gurdjieff) and historical movements (Theosophy); it includes many individual organisations, some of which are religions (Church Universal and Triumphant), some philosophies (Template Network), some esoteric schools (Servants of the Light) and some more open communities (Findhorn); it includes movements (Druidry) which themselves include individual groups (Order of Bards, Ovates and Druids), in a way like denominations within a religion. It also includes some specific topics, both in the text (Kabbalah, Tarot) and as panels of quotations (Magic, Initiation, Ritual).

The quotation panels throughout the book titled 'What I Believe', are an opportunity for people to speak out from the page about their personal beliefs; but they also illustrate the diversity of beliefs in the esoteric world. As Church of All Worlds founder Oberon Zell once said: 'Ask two Pagans a question and get three different answers.'[10]

For these panels I approached a dozen or so people and asked each of them for the impossible: 'In a sentence, what do *you* mean by "magic", "initiation", "ritual", "gods and spirits" . . .' Many of them are friends or acquaintances; some are, or have been, academics; some are authors; some are leaders of groups; some are long-term believers; but all are practitioners, followers of their chosen paths, and between them they cover a wide range of esoteric and Neo-Pagan beliefs. Their views are certainly not definitive, and quite possibly not representative; that was not the intention. They are personal, individual comments, and as such they epitomise the ethos of alternative spirituality: the individual, personal quest for the divine, for empowerment, for self-realisation, for meaning.

In two places I touch on aspects of Christianity which are relevant to the book. First, the entry on Independent Episcopal Churches and the Apostolic Succession in Part One explores the connections between traditional Christianity and Theosophy and related groups and ideas (see p. 56); second, there is a brief discussion on millennial expectations and their disconfirmation, which draws parallels between prophecies of the return of Christ on specific dates and prophecies of other returning messiahs, saviours or alien beings (see p. 114–7).

A more general connection, unfortunately outside the scope of this book, is the growing acceptance of a variety of esoteric beliefs by some of the more theologically and socially liberal Christian Churches, particularly perhaps Unitarianism, and even by some individual churches within the Anglican/ Episcopalian denominations.

Structure of the Book
For convenience the book is divided into three parts: New Age Movements; Hermetic, Occult or High Magic Groups; and Neo-Paganism.

This division is largely for convenience; it should not be taken to suggest that these are three completely separate areas of esoteric religion with clear-cut boundaries between them. They are not. Wicca, for example, draws on many of the same roots as several Hermetic movements; its influences include the Hermetic Order of the Golden Dawn, Freemasonry and Rosicrucianism. New Age movements and Neo-Pagan movements both have a focus on spiritual healing, particularly perhaps reiki. Some leaders in both Neo-Paganism and schools of occult science are qualified neuro-linguistic programming practitioners. Movements and members in all three parts of the book may have an active interest in astrology and in Tarot.

Another example is a small group, the Rosicrucian Order Crotona Fellowship, which was influential on Peter Caddy, one of the founders of the Findhorn Community (see p. 92 in Part One), and also on Gerald Gardner, the founder of Wicca (see p. 289–90 in Part Three). The Rosicrucians themselves are examined in Part Two.

Throughout the book cross-references show the many connections between movements – including between the two late nineteenth-century organisations which typify Parts One and Two, the Theosophical Society and the Hermetic Order of the Golden Dawn (see p. 23 and p. 195).

The grouping into three parts is useful but to some extent arbitrary. Other authors might equally validly place certain movements in a different part, or have more categories, or fewer, or none at all.

Part One is to some extent dominated by groups influenced to a greater or lesser degree by Theosophy, broadly speaking a synthesis of Western (Judaeo-Christian) and Eastern (Hindu, Buddhist or Sufi) thought. But in addition to the specific groups considered in this part there are millions of individual people who do not belong to any movement, but who have some interest in what are loosely called New Age ideas. The Mind, Body, Spirit shelves in many bookshops will contain books on healing, spiritual environmentalism, crystals, channelling, Tarot, astrology, mythology, the Goddess, reincarnation and esoteric Christianity, to name but a few subjects, stacked side by side – in addition to Rosicrucianism, the Hermetic Order of the Golden Dawn, Wicca, Druidry and other areas covered in Parts Two and Three of this book. Some book-buyers may only be interested in one particular subject, but most will probably have an interest in several, which will overlap in different ways for different people.

There are also many today who use reiki, aromatherapy, reflexology, acupuncture, homeopathy, herbal remedies, yoga, meditation and a host of other alternative medical or psychological methods. The New Age (or Aquarian) ideology that encompasses all of these interests, ideas and therapies, and that has now almost entered the mainstream, overlaps strongly with the development of Neo-Pagan religious movements over the past three or four decades.

Part Two covers the wide range of Hermetic or occult groups which have developed over the last century or so. They have many differences, but also have a number of things in common. Some could be described as mystical, magical Judaeo-Christianity; others may have their roots in that, but are now something quite different. Many are, in one way or another, Gnostic, in that they emphasise secret spiritual knowledge, restricted to a select few – their own members.

Their beliefs and practices can be described as occult (hidden), esoteric (within, i.e. only for the initiated) or Hermetic (after the ancient Greek/Egyptian god Hermes Trismegistus, but also implying 'sealed', as in an hermetic seal); they also usually include both magic and mysticism. They are highly complex, and progressive, in that the teachings build upon each other in steps.

This part also includes examinations of Satanism, both what it isn't and what it is, and of the 'Satanic Ritual Abuse' phenomenon of the 1980s and 1990s, and what we can learn from it.

Part Three examines a variety of Neo-Pagan religions in Britain and the United States. Few Neo-Pagan movements today claim to be continuations of historically early nature-based religions. With a few exceptions they accept that very little of actual substance is known of pre-Christian beliefs in the West, and that scholarly books in the first half of the twentieth century that described a hidden tradition of Pagan beliefs, preserved through the centuries and reappearing today, were badly flawed. Today's Neo-Pagans, particularly Wiccans and Druids, have consciously created new religions drawing on mythology, with a strong focus on nature, the turning of the year and the cycle of birth, reproduction, maturity and death. Many emphasise the polarity between female and male divine principles; many are pantheist, polytheist or henotheist.

Heathenry is included in the Neo-Pagan part of the book despite several major differences. Unlike Wicca and Druidry, Heathenry, or the Northern Tradition, is a resurgence in the present day of Norse/Germanic religious beliefs that were supplanted by Christianity over a millennium ago. But like Neo-Paganism it is a religion of the people and of the land.

A short Coda explores whether the Church of Scientology could be considered as an esoteric movement on a number of criteria. It is specifically *not* suggesting that the Church of Scientology is in any way occult; this is an exercise in comparative religion.

Magic

One term which Neo-Pagan, Hermetic and to some extent New Age movements have in common is 'magic', a word which immediately summons up Dennis Wheatley-type images, giving opponents an easy rod with which to beat such movements.

Magic in the sense of casting spells to harm people, or to make people do things against their will, is not part of any esoteric religion. For a Neo-Pagan magic might mean healing someone of a headache by drawing power into them; or it might mean encouraging plants to grow healthily. Blessing a new child, or a home, or any positive activity, perhaps by dedicating it to a goddess and/or a god, might also be called magic. But in all esoteric religion magic is more a reworking of the inner person than of the outer world. The alchemical transformation of base metals to gold was always an analogy for the transformation of the soul.

All magic involves the will and the imagination, or controlled visualisation; a person pictures what she desires to occur, realistically or symbolically, and wills it to be. Part of the work of many esoteric schools is training in visualisation techniques and in concentration of the will.

Does magic actually work? The short answer has to be 'Yes', so far as those who use it are concerned. Whether a sceptical observer could be persuaded is another matter, and is perhaps irrelevant. If someone believes that magic works, then magic does work, at least for that person. Magic has been beautifully described as 'a creative and potentially valuable self-delusion'.[11]

Looking at the examples of magic just mentioned, there can be little doubt that healing sometimes appears to work, and whether it is through a Christian's prayers and the Holy Spirit's action, or through a Neo-Pagan asking her goddess, or through a channelling of natural power, or through psychosomatic means, the headache is still gone – or not. So far as encouraging plants to grow healthily is concerned, some people naturally have 'green fingers', which could be seen as a form of magic – certainly by those people who are unable to keep a plant alive for more than a week. And blessing a child, a home or a new enterprise is as common in Christian circles as it is in esoteric ones. The most common greeting between Neo-Pagans is 'Blessed be'.

As for the transformation of the soul, so that someone becomes more spiritual and a better person, and so has a positive effect on the world around them: prayer, devotion, contemplation, meditation, mysticism, miracles and magic could all be seen as different names for much the same inter-related causes, processes and effects.

Definitions

In religion, and perhaps especially in esoteric religion, definitions can be a minefield. In a previous book I devoted a whole chapter to the question often asked of specialists in new religious movements (NRMs): 'Is it a cult or a real religion?'[12] Obviously that depends on what you mean by 'a religion', 'a cult' and even, if you are a philosopher or a physicist, 'real'. For anyone new to the subject this might seem like the medieval question of how many angels can dance on the head of a pin, but it is a question with far more practical, real-world implications.

Every now and then someone will suggest legislating to make 'cults' illegal. Some years ago I recorded a discussion for the BBC with a Member of Parliament who wanted to do just that, or at least, to draw up a register of them so they could be regulated.[13] In order to do that, of course, someone has to decide which religious movements are 'cults' and which are acceptable religions. But who decides? And on what criteria? Are they to be judged on their beliefs as well as their practices? Just within Christianity there are books denouncing the Jehovah's Witnesses, Mormons, Christadelphians and others because their beliefs are not conventional Christian beliefs; do we label these religions 'cults' because of that? If so, what about the Evangelical church down the road that features dancing in the aisles, spiritual healing and, more controversially, the casting out of demons?

If this is problematic with Christian movements, it is far more so with New Age, Hermetic and Neo-Pagan movements, the subject of this book. Neo-Pagans still have the problem of being lumped together with Satanists, and when they ask for the same rights as members of other religions – to be able to celebrate their sacred days, for example, or to have the same charitable status enjoyed by other religions – they are ridiculed in the press, as seen above.

This book deliberately avoids the word 'cult'. The word has a wide variety of meanings, from the pre-Christian mystery cults of the Middle East to the Catholic usage of the cult of a saint or a place, such as the cult of Mary or the cult of Medjugorje, as well as a century's worth of assorted academic definitions by anthropologists and sociologists of religion. But in popular usage the word is always pejorative, and often preceded, in tabloid newspaper headlines, by adjectives such as 'sex', 'dangerous' or 'evil'. In that sense we all know what a cult is: 'A cult is a religion I don't like.' It is a word that often says more about its user than about the movements being discussed.[14]

The following terms are defined in the sense that they are used in this book.

Alchemy was popularly believed to be about the transmutation of base metals into gold; this was symbolic of the transmutation of the base nature of man to the godly nature of the transformed man.

Arcane, meaning mysterious, comes from the Latin for something that is shut up, or locked in a chest.

'As above, so below' refers to the mirroring of the macrocosm (the world, the cosmos, the God without) and the microcosm (the individual man, the soul, the God within).

Christ spark is a term sometimes used to refer to the spark of the divine flame, or the fragment of God, within each human being.

Esoteric comes from the Greek for 'inner' or 'within', and applies to something taught to or understood by the initiated only.

Exoteric, from the Greek for 'outside' or 'the outward form', applies to knowledge available to the uninitiated.

Frater and **Soror,** the Latin for Brother and Sister, are used in some esoteric societies to refer to initiated members.

Gnostic, Gnosis, from the Greek, refer to spiritual knowledge and understanding, often within an initiatory religious movement, and to a personal relationship with the divine, not mediated through a priest.

Heresy and Heretical beliefs are always defined as such by the establishment Church (of whatever religion), usually as a means of identifying and enforcing their control over spiritual dissidents. The word actually comes from the Greek *hairesis* meaning 'choice'; heretics choose what they wish to believe rather than being told by others what they must believe.

Hermetic comes from the name Hermes Trismegistus, Hermes the thrice-greatest, the mythical author of the fourth or fifth century CE occult Greek and Egyptian texts which lay behind fifteenth to seventeenth century alchemists and Hermetic Philosophers; he was named after the Greek messenger of the gods, equivalent to the Roman Mercury. It has also come to mean 'closed' or 'sealed', as in an hermetic seal.

Immanent, Immanence (from the Latin *manere*, 'remain') refer to the indwelling nature of God; cf. Transcendent/Transcendence.

Initiate, as a noun or a verb, comes from the Latin for 'beginning', and in religion refers to the admission of someone into secret knowledge or into a level within a movement: initiation.

Magic, Mage, Magus, Magician come from the Greek for 'art' as in 'skill' – artful rather than artistic.

Matter of Britain refers mainly to the Arthurian cycle of stories and the quest for the Grail, but more loosely includes folk tales, folk history and folk customs of Britain.

Myth, used in this book in its technical sense rather than its everyday sense, means a story where the importance rests on the message it carries, rather than on whether or not it is historically factual. Use of the word does *not* imply that a story never actually happened; in its scholarly usage the masonic tale of Hiram the Architect, the stories about King Arthur and incidents in the life of Jesus are all myths. The phrase 'the Jesus myth' includes not just the New Testament account, but also the centuries of popular accretions, such as the three wise men, not numbered in the Bible.

Mythic history, Ritual history and **Foundation myths** are stories told about the origins of movements or about the early lives of their founders in order to grant authority; sometimes they are claimed as factual truth despite their folkloric or hagiographic nature.

Occult comes from the Latin for 'hidden'; it is used in that sense in both astrology and astronomy today, without any devilish connotations.

Rite, Ritual, from the Latin, mean a solemn or religious ceremony or observance.

Transcendent, Transcendence (from the Latin *trans*, 'beyond', and *scandere*, 'climb') refer to God being 'out there somewhere', beyond human apprehension; see also Immanent/Immanence.

Western Mystery Tradition usually includes study of the Kabbalah and Tarot, and the spiritual alchemical teachings of the Hermetic Philosophers. Depending on the particular emphasis of a school it can include the study of the Arthurian cycle, or Greek, Roman and Egyptian mythology.

The capitalised word 'Church' refers to an organisation, not to a church building. The abbreviations CE and BCE (Common

What I Believe . . .
Why I Follow My Particular Path

I follow this path because it is one of the very few paths that I've ever found that embraces both the enchantment of the mystery that one encounters in childhood in the imaginative realm, and carries that on into adulthood, and simultaneously doesn't weigh it down with a dogmatic overload and ask a great deal of belief in specific articles of faith about the nature of the universe; it leaves that open.

Dr Christina Oakley Harrington, Wiccan priestess
Owner of Treadwells esoteric bookshop, London,
former university lecturer in History and
Religious History

Mainstream religions are clogged with historical dogma and people-managing machinations, and tend to keep and see the humans as separate from the deities. The Pagan path not only portrays nature as divine so that I can go anywhere and be with the divine, but also takes me deeper within where the gods and goddess already are a part of me – which in itself is highly empowering!

Mani Navasothy, Wiccan High Priest
and founder of Hern's Tribe
Physicist

This path is a challenge, because mainstream religion is often dogmatic, it tells me what I need to do, or not. It gives priests the power to say to me if I am condemned or not, and that is taking my personal responsibility away.

This path makes me responsible for myself, and when I can take responsibility then I can also help other people to go through the same process.

Ina Cüsters-van Bergen, Magister,
Hermetic Order of the Temple of Starlight

It works. It makes sense to me.
Steve Wilson, Thelemite
Civil Servant

I follow it because I choose to. It's very much a personal
involvement with the Powers That Be . . . It's an attempt to
be in tune with nature, to be aware of the value of the
seasons of the year, to be a part of something that is ineffably
ancient and hopefully will go on for many, many long times,
and it's a religion that allows me to make mistakes, to be
lonely, it's not going to throw hellfire and brimstone at me,
my mistakes are my mistakes, they were there all the time,
but the more you put in the more you get out of it. You
constantly have fresh chances with it.
Geraldine Beskin, third-generation esoteric witch
and eclectic occultist
Co-owner of the Atlantis Bookshop, London

Paganism is the religious path that makes the most sense
to me, as it doesn't require dismissal/rejection of
rational thinking/reasoning, empirical evidence/'Truth',
objective or subjective reality, scientific discoveries,
personal understanding and insights, etc. 'Religion'
literally means 're-linking', and Paganism as a religious
path is one that acknowledges, integrates, and reconciles
all perspectives, eschewing only the erroneous and
invidious notion of there being only 'One True Right and
Only Way'.
Oberon Zell-Ravenheart, Co-founder,
Church of All Worlds

Era and Before the Common Era) are the now standard scholarly replacements for AD (*Anno Domini*, in the Year of our Lord), and BC (Before Christ).

All emphases in quotations are as in the original unless otherwise stated. Words in [square brackets] are my interpolations. American quotations have been anglicised in spelling and punctuation for consistency.

I have tried wherever possible to give citations to published works, but at times it has been necessary to cite webpages. Like all researchers and writers I am well aware of both the transient nature of webpages, and also the complete lack of quality control over what appears on the internet. On the subject of religions, especially new religions, and esoteric religions even more so, the amount of unmitigated rubbish online far outweighs well-researched and scholarly material. 'It must be true; I read it on a website' does *not* score any scholarly points.

In a number of places I have cited the websites of movements or organisations on the grounds that what they say about themselves online is likely to be just as accurate or inaccurate as what they might say about themselves in their own booklets and leaflets – which can in any case be just as transient as websites. In other cases I have cited online sources where, having some knowledge of the source, I would have been quite content to cite them if their words had appeared in print. This, of course, is a judgement call, but one which, on occasion, has been unavoidable. I can only ask readers to accept that every website I have cited has been carefully considered.

Most of the notes are simply citations, but a few add further comments to the text.

NOTES TO INTRODUCTION

1 Barrett 2007a.
2 An alternative title for this book was *Mystical and Magical Religions: A Brief Guide to New Age, Hermetic and Neo-Pagan Movements*.
3 Barrett 2001.

4   Some of the entries in this book are based in part on entries in my previous books on new religious movements, Barrett 2001 and Barrett 1996. In all cases they have been updated with fresh information from the movements concerned and other sources, but where ten- or fifteen-year-old quotations about origins, history, beliefs or practices are still valid some have been retained.

5   The terms *emic* and *etic* were coined by linguist Kenneth L. Pike in 1954 and have been used in a variety of different ways in different disciplines over the past half-century.

6   Christine O'Donnell, Republican Senate candidate for Delaware; see http://blogs.reuters.com/faithworld/2010/10/06/tea-party-candidate-says-im-not-a-witch/.

7   Melanie Phillips, 'Druids as an official religion? Stones of Praise here we come', *Daily Mail*, 4 October 2010, http://www.dailymail.co.uk/debate/article-1317490/Druids-official-religion-Stones-Praise-come.html.

8   Damian Thompson, 'The BBC sucks up to Pagans', *Daily Telegraph* website, 31 October 2010, http://blogs.telegraph.co.uk/news/damianthompson/100061559/the-bbc-sucks-up-to-pagans/.

9   James Rado, Gerome Ragni and Galt MacDermot, 'The Age of Aquarius' from *Hair!*

10   Oberon Zell in correspondence with the author, 14 June 1995.

11   Ronald Hutton commenting on Tanya Luhrmann's *Persuasions of the Witch's Craft* (1989) in Hutton 1999: 375.

12   Barrett 2001: 19–27.

13   4 November 1995 for the *Sunday* programme on BBC Radio 4. So far as I know this was never broadcast; I returned from the studio to learn that Yitzhak Rabin, Prime Minister of Israel, had been assassinated; understandably this filled the news programmes the following day.

14   A cult cannot be defined as a religion that abuses; abuses can and do occur in all religions, including the most historic and mainstream.

Part One:
New Age Movements

The term 'New Age' is sometimes used pejoratively, even with derision, to suggest airy-fairy, lightweight mystical spirituality. New Age books and New Age music are casually dismissed as bland and inoffensive; critics speak of 'New Age psychobabble'. To avoid this less than flattering image may be one reason for the increasing use of alternative terms such as 'holistic'.

It is a mistake to associate New Age ideas just with the Age of Aquarius, 1960s hippies and channelling, crystals and pyramids. Today's New Age movements have a long tradition, going back just as far as the modern occult movement and much further than any Neo-Pagan movements, and overlapping with both in history, people and ideas. Spiritual healing, Tarot, astrology, meditation and visualisation, for just a few examples, may all be found in both New Age and the other two types of esoteric religion and philosophy covered in this book.

American scholar of new religions J. Gordon Melton says that the New Age movement: 'can be defined by its primal experience of transformation. New Agers have either experienced or are diligently seeking a profound personal transformation from an old, unacceptable life to a new, exciting future.'[1] Melton identifies healing and the holistic health movement as 'possibly the largest identifiable segment of the movement'.

New Age writer Eileen Campbell accepts this but takes a broader view: 'Usually "New Age" is used to denote a whole range of interests including health and well-being, the many forms of therapy or self-help, the practice of an esoteric or spiritual tradition, concern for the rest of humanity and the environment, and respect for Nature and feminine wisdom.'[2]

Paul Heelas of Lancaster University speaks of 'an eclectic hotch-potch of beliefs' stemming from esoteric or mystical Buddhism, Christianity, Hinduism, Islam, Taoism and assorted Pagan teachings, with practices including: 'Zen meditations, Wiccan rituals, enlightenment intensive seminars, management trainings, shamanic activities, wilderness events, spiritual therapies, forms of positive thinking'.[3]

William Bloom, one of the most respected New Age teachers and writers, explains it this way:

> I see the New Age phenomenon as the visible tip of the iceberg of a mass movement in which humanity is reasserting its right to explore spirituality in total freedom. The constraints of religious and intellectual ideology are falling away.
>
> The New Age movement represents several very different dynamics, but they thread together to communicate the same message: *there is an invisible and inner dimension to all life – cellular, human and cosmic. The most exciting work in the world is to explore this inner reality.*[4]

More than the other two strands of esoteric spirituality in this book, New Age may be seen as a movement in itself, both spiritually and socially. Within this movement there are numerous religions and even more groups, small and large, exploring aspects of spirituality; but encompassing all of these the New Age is a spiritual social trend, even a paradigm shift in social consciousness. This is not just an individual, personal quest; when Heelas calls it 'Self-spirituality' he does not mean that it is a selfish or self-centred path, but that 'the Self itself is sacred'[5] – that New Age spirituality often assumes the immanence of divinity. As with the ideal stated in the Rosicrucian manifestos (see p. 179–80), one's own personal spiritual development should affect the world around one. To quote Melton again: 'As ever-greater numbers of individuals were transformed, the larger goal, the transformation of society, would follow. The emergence of this new social and cultural situation was the real New Age.'[6]

Speaking of his own realisation in the early 1970s Bloom writes: 'There, in my meditation, alongside my own path of change, I became increasingly certain that the sense of a global transformation, a shift in the mass consciousness of humanity, was neither romantic nor naïve.'[7]

The decade of the 1980s, which for many, particularly in Thatcher's Britain and Reagan's America, epitomised the self-first greed culture and, perhaps not coincidentally, an increase in both cynicism and world-weariness, may have dented the optimism in a coming New Age to some extent; but a decade into the new millennium New Age movements seem as strong as ever.

Although many date the modern beginnings of New Age religion to the 1960s and 1970s – Melton pinpoints it as 'circa 1971' – several movements happy to be identified as New Age go back long before that; Sir George Trevelyan (see p. 96) was teaching New Age courses in the 1950s, and Guy Ballard's I AM Movement (see p. 65) and the Emissaries (see p. 82) both date to the 1930s. But the roots of many of today's New Age religions, philosophies and groups can be traced back over a hundred years, to the last quarter of the nineteenth century.

THEOSOPHY

The Theosophical Society is associated with a number of names, in particular its first two leaders, Madame Blavatsky and Annie Besant. Important in its own right in its day, it is more significant now for the many other movements that owe it a massive debt, and for two of the most important esoteric teachers of the twentieth century, Rudolf Steiner (see p. 34) and Jiddu Krishnamurti (see p. 31), both of whom had connections with Theosophy.

Madame Blavatsky

Helena Petrovna Blavatsky (1831–91, often known as HPB) claimed psychic abilities even as a small child in her native Russia. The surname Blavatsky came from her husband, whom she married at the age of seventeen; he was forty. The marriage was never consummated, and she left her husband after a few months, though they never divorced and she kept his name.

Like several other modern founders of movements, such as G. I. Gurdjieff, L. Ron Hubbard, Raymond Armin (Leo) and others, HPB travelled to the Far East, and claimed to have studied with the Secret Masters in Tibet for a while. The years 1848–58, when she was travelling and studying, she later called 'the veiled time' of her life; it is difficult to verify her various accounts of this period, but it is part of the 'foundation myth' of the movement. She went to Cairo, and founded the Société Spirite. She was well practised in the late nineteenth-century arts of table-tapping, clairvoyance and levitation; both then and later in her life she was accused of fraudulent mediumship.

In 1873 she emigrated to New York, and the following year met Colonel Henry Steel Olcott (1832–1907), who had similar esoteric interests. In 1875 they founded the Theosophical Society, along with William Q. Judge (1851–96). Olcott was its first president, but it was Blavatsky who would provide its teachings, initially in her first book *Isis Unveiled* (1877) which told of the Masters and their secrets. Originally the Theosophical Society was based on areas of the Western Mystery Tradition, and HPB's Hidden Masters or Secret Chiefs came from an Egyptian Order.

By 1878 the Society was faltering, and HPB and Olcott travelled to India in the hope that the source of Hinduism and Buddhism might revive it. The Society's headquarters were moved to Adyar, near Madras, where HPB continued to receive communications from the Masters on the spirit level. (The main branch of the Theosophy Society today is sometimes known as the Adyar group.)

In 1885 she moved to Germany where she wrote her second book, *The Secret Doctrine*. This set out the Theosophical beliefs on the evolution of the universe and mankind, and on reincarnation; it also attempted to build bridges between religion and science, and between the occult traditions of the East and the West. She wrote two more books, *The Key to Theosophy* and *The Voice of the Silence*, before her death in 1891; *The Theosophical Glossary* was published posthumously in 1892. She claimed that parts of her books were 'dictated' by the Masters Koot Hoomi (sometimes spelt Kuthumi) and El Morya, though critics have accused her of plagiarising other people's books.

The purpose of the Theosophical Society was originally 'to collect and diffuse a knowledge of the laws which govern the universe', but its aims are most commonly stated as:

> To form a nucleus of the universal brotherhood of humanity, without distinction of race, creed, sex, caste or colour.

To encourage the study of comparative religion, philosophy and science.

To investigate the unexplained laws of nature and the powers latent in man.[8]

The word Theosophy comes from the Greek *theos*, god, and *sophia*, wisdom, and hence means Divine Wisdom.[9] Some of its concepts have been around for over 2,000 years, going back as far as Pythagoras. In its general sense the word is used to describe mystical philosophies that seek to explore the relationship between mankind and the Universe or God.

To understand the strong appeal that the Theosophical Society had to intellectuals in its heyday it is necessary to see it in its historical setting. In 1859 Charles Darwin's *On the Origin of Species* had introduced Western society to the theory of evolution, and had driven an apparently immovable wedge between science and religion (the reverberations are still echoing through American courts, where in some states Fundamentalist Christians have successfully fought for rulings that evolution cannot be taught in schools unless Creationism be taught alongside). Science had stripped God of his role as Creator; intellectuals were torn between being godless scientists or irrational believers.

With Darwin's ideas exciting Western intelligentsia, Theosophy neatly took the concept of evolution and projected it forwards instead of backwards. Not only was the human race still evolving, but each individual person, progressing from life to life through reincarnation, was evolving to a far higher state. The Masters had long held secret knowledge, which was now available to all, to help us progress more rapidly until we too could become Masters.

In its essence the Theosophical Society teaches that there is some truth in all religions, as man attempts to find ways to approach the absolute; it draws together spiritual teachings from the East, including reincarnation, with elements of the Western Mystery Tradition, including Neo-Platonism,

Kabbalah and Hermeticism, and presents them in a Western context. There is no creed, no single belief statement, but members, through their study, grow in spiritual wisdom.

Add to this the allure of the mysterious East, the thrill of HPB's spiritualist manifestations and the ideas of social reform, and the whole package became a powerful and very attractive mixture at the end of the nineteenth century. The Theosophical Society was a child of its time – and some of its teachings have provoked controversy.

Speaking through HPB the Masters provided a body of teachings that have led to accusations of racism. There are seven root races of which the Aryans, the European peoples who originated in India, are the fifth; but the pure Aryans (the word means 'noble'), in the words of one commentator, 'lost their original purity through miscegenation with less pure races'.[10] There is little doubt that racist interpretations of Blavatsky's teachings take them into areas that she did not intend, but on the other hand she did make specific statements such as, 'The Semites, especially the Arabs, are later Aryans – degenerate in spirituality and perfected in materiality'.[11]

However HPB may be criticised today for expressing some of the social attitudes of her time, and whatever the allegations of fraud and plagiarism levelled against her in her lifetime, she holds a vital place in the history of esoteric religion in the West. Eastern religions scholar Andrew Rawlinson sums up Madame Blavatsky:

> An extremely unusual woman, who lived most of her life outside the normal confines of 19th-century society, and who had the courage and capacity to explore what was new and 'difficult' . . .
> Someone who genuinely held Eastern spirituality in high esteem at a time when hardly any Westerners did . . .
> Blavatsky has a unique place in the great process by which Eastern teachings – and, by extension, spiritual psychology as a world-view – have come to the West.[12]

The Theosophical Society not only opened up esoteric Eastern spiritual teachings to the West, but in so doing it provided the basis for much of esoteric and New Age spirituality of the next century and more.

Dr Anna Kingsford

There was a small but important split in the Theosophical Society in 1884. Dr Anna Kingsford (1846–88) was one of the first women to train as a doctor, an ardent feminist (she edited *The Lady's Own Paper: a Journal of Taste, Progress and Thought* in 1872–3) and a fervent anti-vivisectionist and vegetarian. She was a writer on astrology and mystical Christianity, who had a close spiritual relationship for many years with fellow writer Edward Maitland; they called their teachings Christian Pantheism. In 1882 they published a series of lectures entitled *The Perfect Way, or the Finding of Christ.*

In May 1883 Kingsford was recruited to be president of the Theosophical Society's London branch, even though she was not a member of the Society; Maitland became vice-president. With their esoteric Christian beliefs Kingsford and Maitland were not in sympathy with the Eastern emphasis of Madame Blavatsky's teachings, including the Mahatmas, or Hidden Masters. Before even meeting her Blavatsky disliked Kingsford intensely, calling her 'the divine Whistle-breeches', though they later became more friendly.[13]

To avoid doctrinal conflict, instead of Kingsford being re-elected as London president, the following year Henry Steel Olcott, Blavatsky's co-founder of the Theosophical Society, suggested that she should form a subsidiary group, the Hermetic Lodge of the Theosophical Society. As soon as this had been founded, in April 1884, the Hermetic Society became a separate organisation. The same year Kingsford and Maitland translated the writings of Hermes Trismegistus under the title *The Virgin of the World.*

The Hermetic Society is a little known but important link between the Theosophical Society and the Hermetic Order of the Golden Dawn (see p. 199–200), which was founded the month of Kingsford's death; two of the Golden Dawn's founders, William Wynn Westcott and 'MacGregor' Mathers, regularly attended and were speakers at Hermetic Society meetings. They took into the Golden Dawn Kingsford's emphasis on men and women working together in their esoteric studies.[14] It has also been suggested that her writings influenced the Golden Dawn's Hermetic interpretation of the Tarot.[15] The esoteric historian A. E. Waite, co-creator of the Rider-Waite-Smith Tarot, was also a member of the Hermetic Society.

A further link with the Golden Dawn was the Esoteric Section of the Theosophical Society, formed in 1888 ostensibly in response to a demand for 'the deeper study of esoteric philosophy',[16] though R. A. Gilbert comments: 'Aware now of both the existence and growing appeal of the Golden Dawn, Madame Blavatsky responded to its perceived threat by announcing the formation of a new body: the Esoteric Section of the Theosophical Society.'[17] The Irish poet W. B. Yeats, already a member of the Theosophical Society, joined, but perhaps because of the Esoteric Section's prohibition on any form of practical magic – its 'preliminary memorandum' states that the student 'will not be taught how to produce physical phenomena, nor will any magical powers be allowed to develop in him'[18] – he left two years later, joining the Golden Dawn. The Esoteric Section, which had a strictly abstemious and ascetic membership code, did not survive much longer.

Golden Dawn founder William Wynn Westcott also joined the Esoteric Section of the Theosophical Society. He wrote: 'I was selected as the Hermetist who should endeavour to cast oil on troubled waters and to be a bond of union and peace between the two societies, and the Soc. Ros. in Anglia'[19] (see p. 196). This quotation probably says more about Westcott than about what his role actually was.

Annie Besant

Another major name associated with Theosophy is Annie Wood Besant (1847–1933). She was a great intellect; a free-thinker and a radical, she was a colleague of the political activist and atheist Charles Bradlaugh, a member of the Fabian Society and a supporter of both workers' rights and Home Rule for Ireland. She was a feminist campaigner, and was once unsuccessfully prosecuted for selling a leaflet on birth control. She was very prominent in Co-Masonry which, unlike United Grand Lodge Freemasonry, is open to women; and she took the Boy Scout movement, founded by Robert Baden-Powell in 1907, to India.

Her lasting legacies in India were in education and politics. She founded several schools, one of which is now the University of Benares. She also founded the Indian Home Rule League, and became president of the Indian National Congress. More than most spiritual leaders she took the ideals of her beliefs and applied them in the real world – so exemplifying a stated aim of Freemasonry, and before that of the Rosicrucian manifestos, that the outcome of personal spiritual development should be to bring good to the world.

Besant was introduced to Theosophy when she wrote a review of *The Secret Doctrine*; she met HPB in 1889 and became a supporter of Theosophy, turning her London home into the UK headquarters.

After HPB's death in 1891 Besant and William Q. Judge took joint control of the Theosophical Society, until they fell out in 1894. By this time, even though Judge had been there since the beginning, Besant had established a power base in just five years, and took over the British, Indian and some of the American organisations. In 1895 Judge split away to found the Theosophical Society in America; elected president for life, he died the following year, and was succeeded by Katherine Tingley (1847–1929). Confusingly, the American Section of the Theosophical Society (Adyar), the smaller American group loyal to Besant, renamed itself the Theosophical Society in America (Adyar) in 1934.

Judge's group renamed itself several times, eventually becoming simply the Theosophical Society (headquarters, Pasadena, California). It also suffered from a number of schisms resulting in, for example, the Theosophical Society of New York (1899), the Temple of the People (1899), the United Lodge of Theosophists (1909), the Blavatsky Association (1923) and others. Of these, the Temple of the People is a small community at Halcyon, California, which lives by Theosophical principles, though most of the hundred residents work outside the community;[20] the United Lodge of Theosophists spreads the original writings of Blavatsky and Judge rather than later revised versions, without dogma or organisation.[21]

HPB had been a mystic, at times a flamboyant show-woman and possibly on occasion a fraud, though most esotericists believe she had genuine psychic powers. Besant had no great psychic abilities, at least at first, but as well as being a great intellect she was an excellent administrator; she was responsible both for the continued growth and influence of the Theosophical Society and for something of an improvement in the respect given to it. But the changes that she brought to Theosophy did not meet with the approval of all members.[22]

Besant became closely associated with a former Anglican clergyman, the Rev Charles W. Leadbeater (1854–1934); together they changed the emphasis of the Theosophical Society more towards esoteric Christianity than esoteric Buddhism. She wrote a number of influential books, including *Esoteric Christianity*, *Introduction to Yoga* and a translation of the Buddhist scripture the *Bhagavad Gita*; she also co-wrote several books with Leadbeater. They conducted investigations into the astral and mental planes, life after death and past lives, and performed occult experiments into the nature of matter.

Leadbeater wrote a number of significant books of his own, and in 1916 became one of the earliest members and a bishop of the Liberal Catholic Church (see p. 58). This was a successful offshoot from the tiny Old Catholic Church which had been founded in Britain by Bishop Arnold Harris Mathew in 1908; today a number of esoteric leaders, many with a Theosophical background, are clergy of the Liberal Catholic Church.

Jiddu Krishnamurti

It was Leadbeater who in 1908 first discovered the fourteen-year-old Jiddu Krishnamurti (1895–1986; Jiddu is the surname). The boy apparently had a remarkable aura; Leadbeater announced that he would become the Maitreya, the long-prophesied fifth Buddha (Gautama was the fourth), the living incarnation of a Master and the new World Teacher. Besant and Leadbeater promoted Krishnamurti, initiating him into the Great White Brotherhood in 1910, and founding a separate organisation for him to head, the Order of the Star in the East, in 1911. Krishnamurti wrote of his acceptance by the other Masters of the Great White Brotherhood in his book *At the Feet of the Master*, written when he was still just fourteen, though many believe the book was actually 'ghosted' by Leadbeater.

Krishnamurti became increasingly uncomfortable with the role that had been thrust upon him, and in 1929 he disbanded the Order of the Star in the East, resigning from the Theosophical Society the following year. He continued teaching throughout his long life, but insisted that the Truth could not be apprehended through any religion or organisation; it must always be an individual, personal discovery through complete self-knowledge. Despite this, and the fact that he never wanted any followers, there are now several schools around the world presenting his teachings.

The diversity of ideas that the Theosophical Society encompassed was both its strength and its weakness. There were many who disliked Madame Blavatsky's showmanship, though her demonstration of psychic or spiritualist abilities, genuine or not, undoubtedly attracted many others. Later there were some, including Rudolf Steiner, who were put off by Annie Besant's championing of the young Krishnamurti as the coming World Teacher – but again, the publicity brought Theosophy to a wider audience. There were many, including Colonel Olcott, who thought the most important parts of Theosophy were its social and educational aspects, and its scholarly work in bringing Eastern texts to the attention of the West.

With the exit of Krishnamurti the Theosophical Society lost much of its impetus. There are still Theosophical Societies in Britain, the United States and around the world, with groups or lodges in many major cities; in 2009 they claimed about 1,000 members in Britain, nearly 4,000 in the United States, 12,700 in India and over 28,000 worldwide.[23] But the fire of a century ago has largely gone out of the movement, at least in the West; it appears to consist of little more than study groups, custodians of interesting libraries, whose impressive buildings now host meetings of a variety of other spiritual groups. The occultist Gerald Suster wrote, perhaps unkindly, that 'although the Theosophical Society is still in being, these days it is the preserve of those who prefer tepid tea to tough thought'.[24]

Arguably far more important than the present state of the Theosophical Society itself is its legacy in both individual people and later movements. Krishnamurti became a widely respected mystic and teacher. Rudolf Steiner, once head of the German Theosophical Society, went off to found Anthroposophy (see p. 34). P. D. Ouspensky (see p. 45–6) was influenced by Theosophical teachings. As mentioned, the poet and mystic W. B. Yeats was a member for a few years, before moving on to the Hermetic Order of the Golden Dawn (see p. 195). Annie Besant's daughter Mabel Besant-Scott, on failing to succeed her mother as leader of the Theosophical Society, co-founded a mystical order within Co-Masonry called the Rosicrucian Order Crotona Fellowship, named after Crotone or Crotona in southern Italy where Pythagoras founded his school around 530 BCE. In its short existence this was to have a major influence on both Gerald Gardner, creator of Wicca (see p. 289–90), and Peter Caddy, co-founder of the Findhorn Foundation (see p. 92). There were many other influential members of the Theosophical Society.

Beyond that, many of the esoteric movements that are thriving today, including the Church Universal and Triumphant (see p. 70) and the Sant Mat-derived religion Eckankar,[25] have borrowed liberally from Theosophical teachings, particularly in respect of the Great White Brotherhood. (The word 'white' does not refer to race, but to the aura of white light which apparently surrounds the Ascended Masters.) The idea of the Secret Masters was not original to the Theosophical Society, but it greatly fleshed out and popularised the concept. The Master Koot Hoomi, in particular, not only gave HPB much of the content of her books, but later inspired Alice Bailey (see p. 37) in the writing of her own books of mystical teaching, and also Robert and Earlyne Chaney, who founded the Astara Foundation in California in 1951; this was a school of the ancient mysteries and a centre for psychic research, 'dedicated to elevating the spiritual consciousness and health of humankind',[26] and perhaps one of the closest of all the Theosophical Society's successors to the original.

ANTHROPOSOPHY

Rudolf Steiner (1861–1925) had an interest in both esoteric wisdom and social reform for some years before he joined the Theosophical Society (see p. 23). His unusual intelligence was recognised early; he was only twenty-two when he was invited to edit the scientific works of Goethe for a standard edition. He began giving lectures for the Theosophical Society around 1900 and became general secretary of the German organisation when it was founded in 1902. In 1904 Annie Besant made him the leader in Germany and Austria of the Esoteric School of the Theosophical Society, a linked but separate organisation.

Steiner also belonged for a short time to the Rite of Memphis and Misraim, a quasi-masonic occult order – or at least was granted some of the degrees within it by its German leader, Theodor Reuss. Persistent claims that Steiner may also have belonged briefly to the Ordo Templi Orientis (see p. 212), which in its original (pre-Crowley) form was a quasi-Rosicrucian occult society founded by Reuss in Germany in 1906, have been fairly comprehensively disproved by German writer Peter-R. Koenig, author of *The OTO Phenomenon*.[27]

Two causes contributed to Steiner leaving the Theosophical Society. In 1912 he expelled a particularly troublesome member, only to have his decision overruled by Annie Besant. But he had already been moving away from the Theosophical Society's beliefs and practices for some time. Besant's championing of Krishnamurti as the coming World Teacher (see p. 31) was the last straw, and in 1913 he broke away, setting up his own Anthroposophical Society, and taking many of the German Theosophists with him.

Loosely, Theosophy means God-wisdom; Anthroposophy means man-wisdom. Steiner probably took the name from the title of a book by the Rosicrucian Thomas Vaughan, *Anthroposophia Teomagica*, published in 1650. Vaughan, twin brother of the metaphysical poet Henry Vaughan, had been a priest and a scholar of medicine and alchemy.

Steiner believed that we have great spiritual depths within us, and that through study and meditation we can achieve spiritual growth on four levels: the senses, imagination, inspiration and intuition. While Theosophy had taught that man was evolving towards higher powers, Steiner taught that mankind used to have God-like powers, but we have lost them – but with Christ's help we may attain these higher spiritual levels again.

Steiner was a mystic, but he also applied his mystical experiences and beliefs in very practical ways. In the spirit of the Rosicrucian manifestos (see p. 179–80) he linked science and religion. He had innovative ideas in agriculture, architecture and education. He introduced the Biodynamic movement, in some ways a forerunner of today's organic farming; he was opposed to chemical fertilisers, and championed natural times for sowing and harvesting. In architecture he preferred curves to straight lines. He designed the Goetheanum, built near Basel in Switzerland between 1913 and 1919, which had two interlocking domes, the larger one bigger than the dome of St Peter's Basilica in Rome. The original Goetheanum was destroyed by fire in 1922. Steiner designed a second one in Dornach, Switzerland; completed after his death, this is the headquarters of the Anthroposophical Society.

Steiner is perhaps best known for the Steiner Schools which promote child-centred education, with teachers helping to open up and awaken what is within each individual child, at the child's pace. Music, craft and arts are an essential part of the curriculum. There are around a thousand Steiner Schools, often called Waldorf Schools, largely in Europe and the United States.

The Anthroposophical Society is closer to mystical Christianity than is Theosophy; Steiner was never happy with the Hindu and Buddhist underpinnings of Theosophy, or with its focus on Madame Blavatsky's messages from Koot Hoomi and other Secret Masters from Tibet. In addition to the Anthroposophical Society Steiner helped found a small, non-dogmatic Christian denomination, the Christian Community, which has perhaps 15,000 members worldwide, two-thirds of these in Germany.

Rudolf Steiner illustrates well the interconnectivity of esoteric movements. He was involved with the Theosophical Society for over a decade. As well as being in touch with Theodor Reuss, founder of the Ordo Templi Orientis, he was a major early influence on Max Heindel, whom he met in 1907; Heindel later wrote *The Rosicrucian Cosmo-Conception* and founded the Rosicrucian Fellowship (see p. 190), one of the most significant modern Rosicrucian movements. Steiner was also a great influence on Dr Robert Felkin, leader of Stella Matutina, one of the successors to the Hermetic Order of the Golden Dawn (see p. 206–7). They met around 1910, and Felkin was so impressed by Steiner that he sent one of his members to study under him and bring his teachings back to Britain where they were incorporated into the secret teachings of the inner order of Stella Matutina.

ALICE BAILEY

Alice Bailey (1880–1949) was born to an Evangelical Christian family in Manchester, UK, and as a young woman worked for the YMCA in India, where she met her first husband. They moved to the United States and he trained as an Episcopalian priest. When the marriage broke down she moved to California where she joined the Theosophical Society, quickly becoming editor of their magazine *The Messenger*. In 1919 she met the American secretary of the Society, Foster Bailey, whom she later married.

From 1919 she claimed she was contacted by several Masters, including Koot Hoomi and Djwhal Khul, whom she called 'the Tibetan'; the Masters lived in Shambhala, usually thought of as a mythical city or kingdom in or near Tibet. (Shambhala has since become a staple of New Age teaching.) She began channelling messages from them and writing books from their messages. Many esoteric organisations enter a 'post-prophetic' phase after the death of their founder, and most Theosophists believed there would be no more messages from the Masters after Helena Blavatsky's death in 1891. Annie Besant, Blavatsky's successor in the Theosophical Society, clearly saw Bailey as a threat and fired her and Foster Bailey from their posts; the couple left California for New York, and eventually left the Society. They married in 1921.

In 1922 they founded the Lucis Trust to publish Alice Bailey's books (she wrote twenty in all, mostly channelled messages from the Masters) and the magazine *The Beacon*, and in 1923 they founded the Arcane School to teach their followers. At the heart of their work was meditation to help radiate spiritual energy into the world and prepare for the coming New Age. Meditation is particularly powerful each month at the time of the full moon, and at three special festivals in spring and early summer: Easter (Christ's resurrection), Wesak (Buddha's birthday) and Goodwill (in June).[28]

In her autobiography Alice Bailey wrote of herself that 'a rabid, orthodox Christian worker' had 'become a well-known occult teacher'.[29]

Bailey's teachings were basically Theosophical, with an emphasis on meditation, reincarnation, the ancient wisdom of the Masters and the imminent coming of the Maitreya Buddha, who could be seen as the second coming of Christ, or as another avatar of Krishna, or as the Jewish Messiah, or as the Muslim Imam Mahdi. In being identified as all of these, Maitreya can be given the spiritual authority of all of these religious traditions, and thus can be made to appeal to people from Hindu, Buddhist, Jewish, Christian and Muslim backgrounds. Some have seen Bailey's teaching on the Maitreya as a replacement for Theosophy's reluctant world teacher, Krishnamurti (see p. 31). The idea of the Maitreya was later taken up and developed by a number of religious leaders including L. Ron Hubbard (see p. 357), Raël (see p. 128–9) and especially Benjamin Creme (see p. 41).

As with Madame Blavatsky there have been criticisms of Alice Bailey for implied racism and anti-Semitism in some of her writings, which discuss 'root races' such as the Lemurians, the Atlanteans and Aryans – though her use of the word 'Aryan' is not the same as white supremacist usage of the term. However, she did describe different races as different stages of the evolution of mankind, and notably called Jews 'the most reactionary and conservative race in the world'. At the same time she criticised whites for their treatment of blacks, and Gentiles for their treatment of Jews. Whatever she may have meant by her comments on different races, some of her writings have influenced right-wing elements in the New Age movement.

After Alice Bailey's death in 1949 her movement splintered into several offshoots, including the School for Esoteric Studies (founded in 1956); the Arcane School itself continued under her husband until his death in 1977, and then under his second wife Mary Bailey. A 32nd Degree Freemason, Foster Bailey wrote an influential book on the esoteric heart of masonry, *The Spirit of Masonry* (1957). The School still promotes Bailey's teachings through correspondence courses from its three headquarters in New York, London and Geneva:

> The purpose of the esoteric training given in the Arcane School is to help the student grow spiritually toward acceptance of discipleship responsibility and to serve the Plan by serving humanity. Esotericism is a practical way of life.
>
> The function of the School is to assist those at the end of the probationary path to move forward on to the Path of discipleship, and to assist those already on that path to move on more quickly and to achieve greater effectiveness in service.[30]

The current president of the Arcane School says:

> The training of the Arcane School has changed over the years to meet the need of students who seek training in group discipleship for the purposes of service to humanity. Lessons are periodically revised to reflect the creative contribution of the many servers who are actively engaged in service in all departments of human living. However, the basic note and fundamental purpose of the School have remained unchanged and, we hope, continue to reflect the vision of its founder, Alice Bailey, and the spiritual Hierarchy which it is intended to serve.[31]

Bailey has had a tremendous influence, often unrecognised, on New Age philosophy, on spiritual UFO movements and to some extent on Neo-Paganism. People and groups influenced by her include Guy Ballard's I AM Religious Activity (see p. 65), which she trenchantly dismissed as 'cheap comedy',[32] and through them the Church Universal and Triumphant (see p. 70), George King's Aetherius Society (see p. 119), Benjamin Creme's teaching on Maitreya (see p. 41) and many others. She is responsible for the Great Invocation (given to her by 'the Tibetan', Djwhal Khul), which is spoken, usually by groups of three people, while visualising the movement of spiritual energy. It was first published around 1936, and was revised in 1940 and 1945, in what became the standard version:

> From the point of Light within the Mind of God
> Let light stream forth into the minds of men.
> Let Light descend on Earth.
>
> From the point of Love within the Heart of God
> Let love stream forth into the hearts of men.
> May Christ return to Earth.
>
> From the centre where the Will of God is known
> Let purpose guide the little wills of men –
> The purpose which the Masters know and serve.
>
> From the centre which we call the race of men
> Let the Plan of Love and Light work out.
> And may it seal the door where evil dwells.
> Let Light and Love and Power restore the Plan on Earth.

Because of the worldwide spread of the Great Invocation, used by many very different movements in many different cultures and languages, the Lucis Trust has allowed slight variations in the wording, with 'Christ' replaced by 'the Coming One', 'the minds of men' by 'human minds', etc.[33]

The Findhorn community (see p. 92) began using the Great Invocation in the 1970s, and through them it spread into many other New Age groups in the last decades of the twentieth century.

BENJAMIN CREME, MAITREYA AND SHARE INTERNATIONAL

Christ is alive and well and living among the Pakistani community around Brick Lane, London, according to Scottish-born artist Benjamin Creme (b.1922). This was Creme's message in 1982, as perceived by Evangelical Christians, who were greatly offended by it. In fact, Creme was speaking of Maitreya, the most senior of the Masters or the Great White Brotherhood who, in recent religious mythology, have usually been based in Tibet or the Himalayas. Maitreya had 'over-shadowed' Jesus, making him the Christ; now he would be returning in his own right.

Creme's teachings are based largely on Alice Bailey's developments from Theosophy (see p. 37). Creme studied the works of Blavatsky, Leadbeater and Bailey, amongst many others, in his youth. In 1957 he joined the Aetherius Society (see p. 119), but left them in 1959 after disagreements.

He was contacted by a Master in 1959 and told of the Maitreya's imminent return, and of his own importance in spreading the word. Little happened until 1972, when he received further messages. In 1974 he began to set up an organisation of followers; with them he learnt to transmit spiritual energy. Later that year, Maitreya himself spoke through him; Creme began to publish books containing messages from Maitreya. He is the editor of *Share International* magazine, which contains information about Maitreya and teachings that are partly Theosophical and partly New Age. Creme's organisation, also called Share

International, was previously known as the Tara Centre (in Los Angeles) and the Tara Press (in London).

In 1982 Creme announced that Maitreya was living anonymously in the Asian community in East London, and would reveal himself to the world shortly; the media must be ready. Sensing a good offbeat story a number of journalists searched the Brick Lane area, but no one could point them to the returned Christ. Creme lost both credibility and supporters, and gained some serious enemies among Evangelical Christians. An Evangelical book, *The Hidden Dangers of the Rainbow* (1983), attacked all New Age and esoteric movements – especially Creme and the Maitreya – as a Satanic conspiracy; it was one of the first of several such books in which conservative Evangelicals attacked the New Age, and did much to promote the illogical belief that members of New Age movements, Neo-Paganism, Wicca and esoteric religious movements are all Satanists (see p. 248, p. 280).

According to Creme:

> On 31 July 1985, largely through the efforts of one freelance journalist who had actually seen Maitreya in His local area in 1984 and who was convinced of the truth of Creme's information, an internationally representative group of 22 influential journalists met in an Indian restaurant in London's East End, hoping that Maitreya or an envoy would approach them there.[34]

They were to be disappointed.

In an unusual twist on the urban myth about the vanishing hitch-hiker, Creme claims that Maitreya has hitched lifts with Evangelical Christians, told them they would shortly see Christ, then vanished from their cars.[35]

His most publicised appearance, however, was said to be at a healing meeting in Nairobi, Kenya. He was supposedly seen by 6,000 people, photographed, and reported in the *Kenya Times* and on CNN and BBC news. Since 1992, says Creme, Maitreya has appeared – and disappeared – in front of many groups of Christians, Jews, Muslims, Hindus and Buddhists 'from Mexico City to Moscow, from Geneva to Johannesburg; in North Africa and the Middle East, India and Pakistan'.[36] At several of these meetings he spoke to the assembled people for 15–20 minutes before vanishing again. In July 1994, claims Creme, he finally turned up in London, addressing a group of 300–400 Christians for 17 minutes.

These appearances (none of them independently documented) are all a prelude to the Day of Declaration, when Maitreya will appear on radio and TV all over the world, and speak to everyone, simultaneously, in his or her own language.[37]

Maitreya's message (as with the Aetherius Society, the Raelian Movement and other New Age movements which claim contact with either Ascended Masters or extraterrestrials) is simple: 'Share and save the world . . . Take your brother's need as the measure for your action and solve the problems of the world. There is no other course.'[38]

In January 2010 Benjamin Creme announced that: 'the Master of all the Masters, for the first time in human history, himself physically came on a well-known television programme on a major network in the United States, but undeclared as Maitreya, just as one of us'.[39] Creme would not say on which programme, or on which network, the Maitreya had spoken, but his followers soon identified him as a thirty-seven-year-old liberal economic activist, Dr Raj Patel, a British-born academic in the United States.[40] When he started receiving emails asking if he was truly the Maitreya, Patel had to search online to find out who the Maitreya is. Taking the spiritual misidentification in good humour he posted a blog entitled 'Call me Brian', including a clip from the famous Monty Python film, *The Life of Brian*, and finishing with, 'Sadly, I'm not the Messiah. I'm just a very naughty boy.'[41] Despite this some of Creme's followers claimed that the very fact that Patel denied he was the Maitreya proved that he was. According to the *New York Times* one 'seemed amazed when told that Mr. Patel did not believe he was the messiah and had never heard of Mr Creme. "See how deep the spiritual world is," he said.'[42]

G. I. GURDJIEFF

Georgei Ivanovitch Gurdjieff (c.1866–1949) was one of the most colourful and controversial gurus of the last century. Gurdjieff was a powerfully charismatic teacher, a clever businessman and an unpredictable, even volatile personality; he has also been called a charlatan and a showman. Born of a Greek father and Armenian mother in Alexandropol near the Russian–Turkish border, he spent some years wandering in the East. 'Gurdjieff spent most of his time with the Seekers of Truth in the Caucasus and Central Asia, though he also went to Egypt and Tibet,' says Tilo L. V. Ulbricht of the Gurdjieff Society.[43] In Tibet he claimed to have studied under teachers of ancient wisdom and learned, among much else, the techniques of hypnotism and yoga.

'Unlike Blavatsky,' says Ulbricht, 'he never spoke of "Masters". He did find a monastery, whose whereabouts he had to vow not to reveal, where the tradition of sacred dances had been preserved. It may have been in Afghanistan.'

It should be noted that a number of authorities present Gurdjieff's early travels more as myth than as history. His biographer, James Moore, an active Gurdjieff follower since 1956, comments wryly: 'we are chasteningly reliant on Gurdjieff's own four impressionistic accounts, which – in the nature of myth – are innocent of consistency, Aristotelian logic and chronological discipline. Notoriously problematical are "the missing twenty years" from 1887 to 1907'.[44] In Moore's very thorough biography Gurdjieff's first forty-five years take up only thirty-one pages. Andrew Rawlinson, a scholar of Eastern and esoteric religions, describes any attempt to discern the actual facts of Gurdjieff's early life from his own writings as 'problematic', 'because Gurdjieff the teacher undoubtedly takes precedence over Gurdjieff the autobiographer; or perhaps it would be more accurate to say that the two are really indistinguishable. Hence it is more or less impossible to tell if anything that he says is straight fact or straight teaching, or not-so-straight-fact or not-so-straight-teaching (or a mixture of all four).'[45]

It should be noted that Madame Blavatsky and L. Ron Hubbard, amongst other founders of religious movements, share similar early life stories; these become the foundation myths of their religions.[46] In some cases the religions go to great lengths to portray these accounts as factual (see p. 262–3).

On his travels, at times working for a railroad company, Gurdjieff set up stores, restaurants and cinemas and traded in expensive carpets, making a small fortune; at the same time he was seeking deep philosophical and religious wisdom, and gathering a band of like-minded seekers around him. By the time he had moved to Moscow, and later to St Petersburg, he was lecturing on what he had learnt. But Russia, being in the middle of a revolution, was not the safest place for a wheeler-dealer and unorthodox philosopher; he moved to France, where in 1922 he bought an estate, the Prieuré des Basses Loges near Fontainebleau, setting up his Institute for the Harmonious Development of Man. He moved to Paris in 1933.

One of his earliest followers, whom he met in Moscow in 1915, was the Russian mathematician Piotr D. Ouspensky (1878–1947), who earlier had been greatly influenced by Theosophy. Ouspensky established the largest Gurdjieff-derived school, in Surrey, England. He later wrote a book, *In Search of the Miraculous: Fragments of an Unknown Teaching*,[47] to some extent clarifying Gurdjieff's teachings. What made for a powerful synthesis between the two is that

Gurdjieff was intuitive and unpredictable, encouraging the unexpected and the out-of-balance, while Ouspensky was rational, logical and methodical, and looked for a systematic approach. Outside observers suggest that Ouspensky's contribution lay in codifying Gurdjieff's seemingly disconnected teachings into a cohesive spiritual system.

Many movements today with some sort of background in Gurdjieff's teachings are actually Gurdjieff–Ouspensky (G–O) inspired. This rankles with the Gurdjieff Society: 'The teaching, including the ideas, came from Gurdjieff . . . Groups who couple the names Gurdjieff and Ouspensky base themselves on the ideas presented by Ouspensky in his book, and his lectures after he left Gurdjieff, and actually have no direct connection with Gurdjieff's teaching at all. Ouspensky was only with Gurdjieff for a few years.' In fact, Gurdjieff treated Ouspensky so badly in 1922 that the latter forbade his students even to mention Gurdjieff's name;[48] the two were never reconciled.

Gurdjieff's own books are *Beelzebub's Tales to his Grandson*, *Meetings with Remarkable Men* and *Life is Only Real when I Am*.

Amongst many other things, Gurdjieff has been criticised for imposing quite unsuitable exercises – most of them exhausting and some actually dangerous – on his followers. The writer Katherine Mansfield, for example, went to Fontainebleau suffering from tuberculosis; critics allege that he ordered her to ignore her illness and made her sleep above the cowshed; she died shortly afterwards, aged only thirty-five. The Gurdjieff Society paints a different picture:

> It was known that Katherine Mansfield was dying of TB when she asked to come to the institute. Although foreseeing un-favourable publicity, Gurdjieff was impressed by her sincerity and allowed her to come. He did not order her to ignore her illness. He suggested that she sleep above the cowshed because he believed the atmosphere would relieve her pain. Alexander de Salzmann painted the ceiling and walls of her room with beautiful murals. In the letters she wrote before her death . . . she says how kindly she was cared for, and allowed to participate to

the extent that she wished, and how there, for the first time in her life, she had found inner peace.

As so often there is probably some truth in both versions of the story.

After his death Gurdjieff's teachings were continued by one of his closest followers, Madame Jeanne de Salzmann, who died in 1990 aged 101, having established or consolidated Gurdjieff Foundations or Societies in London, Paris, New York, California, Caracas and Sydney.

Gurdjieff's teachings could be described as a sort of esoteric Christianity, or as a blending of the West and the East, or as a combination of religious thought and philosophical psychology (or perhaps psychological philosophy). They are a hugely complex mixture of almost science-fictional cosmological mythology, esoteric number theory, sacred dance – and spiritual development from sleep to wakefulness.

The two main states of consciousness are to be either awake or asleep, though most people, Gurdjieff said, more or less sleepwalk their way through their waking life. He put forward two other states of being: self-consciousness and objective consciousness. Like some more recent personal development movements Gurdjieff's philosophy points out that most of us are not really in touch with ourselves, with the entirety of our inner being, our 'I', and so are cut off from anything approaching full use of our abilities. Ouspensky likened this to people living in the basement of a house, without ever realising there are other floors upstairs. Life passes us by, and we are mere observers of it, like an audience at a play, rather than being actively involved in our life-production as participants, scriptwriters and directors. Even if one changes the analogy to make us the actors, we are confined to a script, having grown into roles imposed on us by upbringing and strengthened by unthinking habit. Our several 'brains', our Instinctive, Moving, Emotional and Intellectual Centres, are out of kilter with each other.

We can only be woken up by performing arduous physical exercises, which break our deeply ingrained habits. As Rawlinson writes: 'But in order to wake people up, you have to shake them – and this explains Gurdjieff's reputation for being unpredictable and "difficult".'[49] Gurdjieff made his followers perform tasks well below their intellectual or social level; part of his teaching on esoteric development was unquestioning submission to a teacher – a Man Who Knows.

One of the most important practical aspects of Gurdjieff's teachings was sacred dance. Tilo Ulbricht writes:

> The sacred dances . . . express the laws of the universe, they demand such a fine attention from those who practise them that all their faculties need to work together in harmony. Being able to execute well the postures required, in their correct sequence, rhythm and tempo, is very hard, but still only a stage: then, how to be so calm and collected inside, that the body, meant to be a temple for the spirit, serves as an instrument for a higher force. This is an extraordinary call to obey and submit consciously, and in that akin to the deepest religious experience.[50]

Gurdjieff's methods also included rhythmic exercises to music and breathing exercises. The emphasis on music came from a new interpretation of Pythagoras's esoteric teaching on the music of the spheres and the numerical or numerological significance of rhythm and the functions of parts of the body.

By performing these exercises one can reach a higher level of consciousness, become truly self-aware and tap one's reserves of spiritual and psychic power. Perhaps from Pythagoras, Gurdjieff developed a Law of Seven to do with music, and a Law of Three to do with the working of the universe (active, passive and neutral), the human body (carnal, emotional and spiritual) and food. He devised a symbol called the enneagram, a circle divided by nine points, which join up to illustrate his teachings.

Many of his followers, including Ouspensky, deserted him, but most of them continued to follow what he taught: the message without the man. Today's movements which follow

Gurdjieff's teachings – sometimes called the Fourth Way School or the Way of the Sly Man, combining and moving on from the three old ways of the fakir (physical), the monk (emotional) and the yogi (intellectual) – tend to concentrate more on their mystical aspects rather than on the punishing physical exercises he required. Gurdjieff's Fourth Way of spirituality has also influenced much New Age thinking, though his biographer is utterly dismissive of these 'thousand contemptible modern parodies'.[51]

SUBUD

Subud began in Java, Indonesia, in 1924, when Muhammad Subuh Sumohadiwidjojo (1901–87), a clerk in a local treasurer's office, unexpectedly had a series of powerful religious experiences, in which he felt the inner power of God. By the 1930s he had realised that he should pass on this experience to others, and in 1933 he set up Subud, which is not related to his name but is an abbreviation of the Sanskrit words Susila, Buddhi and Dharma, meaning 'to follow the Will of God, with the help of the Divine Power that works both within us and without'.[52]

Over the next twenty years Subuh worked quietly, spreading Subud slowly in Indonesia. Eventually some Europeans came into contact with Subud.

G. I. Gurdjieff, in common with other esoteric teachers, had spoken of One who is to come; for some it was the Maitreya, but for Gurdjieff it was the Prophet of Consciousness, the Ashiata Shiemash. A group of Gurdjieff's followers invited Subuh to England in 1956, believing him to be the Prophet foretold by Gurdjieff. First in Britain, then in the United States and Australia, Subud spread rapidly; by the turn of the century there had been 'significant growth' in Eastern Europe, the former Soviet Union, parts of Africa and South America.

Muhammad Subuh, known to his followers as Bapak (an affectionate and respectful Indonesian term for 'father'), died in 1987.

Subuh discovered not only that he could enable others to receive the spiritual energy he had first encountered in 1924, but that those who had received it from him could pass it on to others. (This is similar to the Toronto Blessing in Evangelical Christianity, which also seems to be passed on by personal contact; the effects are also remarkably similar.)[53] The basis of Subud is the *latihan kejiwaan*, Indonesian for 'spiritual exercise', usually just known as the latihan, or exercise 'in which one surrenders to, opens up one's inner feeling to and comes into contact with the power of God':[54] 'Although in Western culture the word exercise refers usually to an activity performed with the aid of the heart and mind, the latihan is rather an inner experience which involves movement originating from deep inside the soul of the individual (which is hindered rather than helped by the willful guidance of heart and mind).'[55] Some three months after first attending Subud meetings, a new member stands in a group with several others, including some experienced 'Helpers', and the latihan occurs. The first time is known as the 'opening'.

The experience of 'contact with the divine force of life'[56] is different for different people; this is part of the basis of Subud. Some will experience joy, others peace; some will laugh, others cry; some feel an inner vibration, others a quiet simplicity; some will dance, others will pray. Every one of these is equally valid.

The latihan lasts for about thirty minutes, and is usually done twice a week with the group. Once members are experienced, they can do an additional latihan once a week on their own, at home: 'The effects of the latihan vary greatly. People usually have a feeling of well-being and relaxation after doing latihan. In the longer term, the process for some may bring a peaceful, gradual development in their acceptance of themselves and others and their experience of constant inward wholeness. For others it may initiate dramatic changes in their lives.' The experience of latihan is apparently not always pleasant; the power of God is acting directly on the inner person, and may well be clearing out the faults within: 'O

What I Believe . . .
Meditation and Visualisation

Meditation should refer to the various stages of
attempting to completely quieten the mind to allow
space for something more spiritual to happen.
Steve Wilson, Thelemite
Civil Servant

People say 'I find meditation really, really hard' – so
don't try so hard, and don't try to do it for half an
hour. If you manage to do it for a minute you're doing
very well, and be more content with that, but don't
give up because you're not good at it for half an hour.
It's actually keeping at it is the important thing; you
won't make progress otherwise, really.

To be able to visualise is terribly important. The
subconscious only being able to deal with images,
that's where you can get the flow of stuff through
from somewhere else, that is creative and useful in
your magical work.
Geraldine Beskin, third-generation esoteric
witch and eclectic occultist
Co-owner of the Atlantis Bookshop, London

Meditation: sometimes a simple and very therapeutic method of
relaxation, a means of stilling the mind, a means of accessing
other realms of being, a means of casting a spell. Visualisation
may come into this, using the technique of pathworking, which
originally applied to the various paths on the kabbalistic Tree of
Life but nowadays has a broader context of going on a visualised
journey for a magical purpose.
Jack Gale, Magician
Retired school teacher

You can use the Tarot images in meditation. Because
the Tarot cards are connected to the paths of the Tree
of Life; so the Tarot cards are in effect symbolic keys
that give access to those paths. As guided visualisation
they create changes in your life.
**Ina Cüsters-van Bergen, Magister, Hermetic
Order of the Temple of Starlight**

Meditation is the ability to sink comfortably into a
state of compassionate witnessing.

Visualisation is part of a package of mental abilities
which include sensing and imagining.
**Dr William Bloom
Author and educator in a holistic and modern
approach to spirituality**

Visualisation is an important key to all magical and ritual
work. If you cannot even 'see' something clearly in your
mind's eye, how could you make it come real in front of you?
**Mani Navasothy, Wiccan High Priest and founder of
Hern's Tribe
Physicist**

To my mind visualisation, which is absolutely core in the Western
Mystery Tradition, is deeply over-rated, as we come further to
appreciate that human beings apprehend and communicate through a
lot of different senses. We now appreciate that many people are very
auditory, many people are very kinaesthetic, and the great god of
visualisation I think has come rightly off its pedestal.
**Dr Christina Oakley Harrington, Wiccan priestess
Owner of Treadwells esoteric bookshop, London, former
university lecturer in History and Religious History**

people experience suffering and difficulties at some stage as the purification begun by the latihan takes its course.'

The Subud organisation says firmly that it is not a religion in its own right; it has no priests, no rituals, no dogmas or doctrines. 'Subud is not foreign. It did not "originate" in the East and it did not "come" to the West . . . It comes from the Spirit of God, which is nowhere a stranger,' said Subuh.[57] Members are actively encouraged to continue to belong to the religion they came from. Because they are directly in touch with the Power of God, or the Holy Spirit, or the Great Life Force, they become brothers and sisters together, irrespective of whether they are Christians, Muslims, Buddhists, Hindus or anything else.

> Therefore, in the latihan of Subud we do not have a teaching; there is nothing we have to learn or do, because all that is required of us is complete surrender . . .
>
> So this divine power, which works in us during the latihan, will bring to each person what is already in himself . . . the latihan of two people can never be the same, because everyone is different from everyone else. It is clear, then, that there cannot be a theory or spiritual teaching in Subud because each person is different. Whatever he needs and whatever he receives will differ from what somebody else needs and receives . . .
>
> Every person will find for himself the right way towards God, and what may be the right way for one may be completely wrong for another . . . You must become your own self and you must develop your inner self if you want to find the way to God. You must not follow or imitate anyone else, because you must find your own way to God . . . it is God who will lead you towards himself and what really happens in the latihan is that you will be introduced to your real inner self – to the real I.[58]

The World Subud Association exists in part 'to enable people who practice the latihan to understand its benefits and use it in their daily lives.' In addition: 'Because the latihan heightens awareness and concern for the needs of others, it is also the aim of the Subud movement that these activities of Subud members should benefit local communities and humanity more generally.'[59] Like a number of other religious movements from the Quakers to the Bahá'í Faith to Soka Gokkai, and esoteric movements including Theosophy (see p. 23) and Anthroposophy (see p. 34), Subud is very strong on the brotherhood of all mankind. It has a number of subsidiary organisations working in welfare, education, health and the arts. Susila Dharma International Association (SDIA), the social welfare arm of Subud, is accredited as a non-governmental organisation (NGO) to the United Nations Economic and Social Council (ECOSOC) and UNICEF, and (in 2010) is involved in forty-seven development projects in over twenty-five countries, including education, community health, sustainable livelihoods and environmental protection. The work is funded by voluntary donations from members, who are also actively encouraged to set up businesses that will donate a portion of their profits to support Subud, particularly in its charitable work.

Like most of the movements in this book Subud does not evangelise or actively recruit new members. People might read about it, or know someone who is a member, and so decide to find out more about it. There are around 13,000 members in 77 countries; the UK has the largest membership at around 1,100, in some 55 groups around the country.

INDEPENDENT EPISCOPAL CHURCHES AND THE APOSTOLIC SUCCESSION

Leaders of some esoteric movements, such as the Servants of the Light (see p. 231), are also priests or bishops in small non-mainstream Christian Churches such as the Liberal Catholic Church. This has little in common with the Church it developed from, the Old Catholic Church, and even less in common with the Roman Catholic Church, though technically its origins go back to that. It is included in this part of the book because of its early connection with the Theosophical Society, and particularly with the Rev Charles W. Leadbeater (see p. 30).

Small denominations like the Liberal Catholic Church, known as independent or autocephalous (self-heading) Episcopal Churches, take their authority from the concept of Apostolic Succession.

The Apostolic Succession is the supposedly unbroken line of laying-on-of-hands from Christ to his apostles, through all the bishops of the last 2,000 years, to every bishop today. The Roman Catholic Church takes its succession back through Peter, who they claim as 'the first pope' or Bishop of Rome – perhaps more of a foundation myth than an historical fact (see p. 13) – but there are several very early Christian Churches, mainly around the Mediterranean, which trace their succession back to other apostles.

A bishop has the sacramental power and authority to confirm believers, to ordain priests and, crucially, to consecrate (or ordain) new bishops. A new bishop is consecrated through the laying on of hands by one or more existing bishops in a solemn ceremony – though if several bishops are taking part, all trying to lay their hands on the new bishop at the same time, it can become something of a melee. Once he has the Apostolic Succession a bishop can pass it on to others, even if he has left or has never been in the Catholic Church or any other mainstream Episcopal denomination; it is a spiritual matter, not dependent on organisational loyalty. This leads to the strange situation where the Catholic Church accepts such consecrations outside its authority as 'valid but illicit'.

The Anglican/Episcopalian Church believes its bishops have a valid Apostolic Succession, though some Catholics dispute this for a variety of both historical and theological reasons, as a result of which the Anglican line of Apostolic Succession dating back to the Reformation has on occasion been strengthened from the Old Catholic line (see below). The Orthodox Churches also have Apostolic Succession. So do numerous other Churches or denominations, some of them very small – and also many individuals, known as *episcopi vagantes* or Wandering Bishops.

The Old Catholic Church, a small but well-established denomination mainly in the Netherlands and Germany, was founded by Roman Catholic clergy who disagreed with the doctrine of papal infallibility instituted by the first Vatican Council in 1869–70. They did not have any bishops, but the Jansenists (a largely Dutch denomination who split from Rome in the mid-seventeenth century) did, and 'were thus able to transmit the Apostolic Succession to the Old Catholic Churches of Germany and Switzerland when these became separate from the Roman Church . . . Thus, although the various Old Catholic Churches were excommunicated by the popes of the day, the validity of their sacred orders has never been seriously contested by theologians.'[60]

In 1908 a British former Roman Catholic priest, Arnold Harris Mathew, persuaded the Old Catholic Church in Utrecht that a significant number of Catholic priests in Britain were willing to reject the authority of the pope, and hence there was a need for the founding of the Old Catholic Church there under his leadership. He was duly consecrated a bishop.

Mathew quickly found that, rather than disaffected Catholics, the majority of his clergy and members were Theosophists; he also began having second thoughts and decided to return to the fold of Rome. So that he would not leave his new Church without a bishop, in 1914 he consecrated Frederick Samuel Willoughby (founder of what became St Chad's College, Durham University) as his successor. In 1915 and 1916 Willoughby (who was also having doubts) consecrated three new bishops, one of whom, the Theosophist James Ingall Wedgwood, became Presiding Bishop of the Church. In 1917 the Church decided that it had moved so far from its origins in the Old Catholic Church that it should take a new name, and it became first the Liberal Christian Church, then in 1918 the Liberal Catholic Church.

In 1915 Wedgwood had visited Australia in his role as Grand Secretary of the Order of Universal Co-Masonry; there he met Charles W. Leadbeater, a leading Theosophist and a former Anglican priest, and initiated him into Freemasonry (see p. 30). In 1916 Wedgwood, now a bishop, returned to Australia and accepted Leadbeater into what was then still called the Old Catholic Church, then consecrated him as a bishop. Together they set about revising the Mass and compiling the liturgy of the Church. In 1923 Wedgwood resigned following a sex scandal and Leadbeater became Presiding Bishop. In 1926 the Liberal Catholic Church consecrated its pro-cathedral church in Caledonian Road, London (now replaced by a pro-cathedral church in Putney, south London), and began to spread around the world.

In 1941 there was a split over beliefs and authority in the Liberal Catholic Church in the United States, resulting in two separate organisations there, both calling themselves the Liberal Catholic Church. Worldwide these are known as the

Liberal Catholic Church International (LCCI) and the Liberal Catholic Church (LCC); both exist in Britain. 'The main differences are that the LCCI ordains women and openly gay people to all orders and a commitment to theosophy is optional rather than compulsory,' says Elizabeth Stuart, LCCI arch-bishop of Great Britain and Ireland.[61]

There was a further worldwide split in the LCC in 2003, largely over the ordination of women, resulting in 'tradition-alist' and more 'liberal' groups in most countries, causing yet further confusion.

In Britain, the origin of the whole Liberal Catholic community, there are now at least three different Churches: the Liberal Catholic Church International, Province of Great Britain and Ireland, which has one bishop and four active priests; the Liberal Catholic Church, which has three bishops and a number of priests; and the Liberal Catholic Church in the British Isles, founded in 2005, and accepting women priests. The leader of the much smaller Liberal Catholic Church Grail Community (founded in 1989), based in Devon, Bishop Roy Bannister, died in September 2010. A further small offshoot known as the Young Rite was founded in 2006.

There is no formal connection between any of the Liberal Catholic Churches and the Theosophical Society, but many Liberal Catholic clergy and members hold broadly Theosophical beliefs, for example on reincarnation, which distinguish them from mainstream Christianity.

As a general rule independent Episcopal Churches tend to be liberal in both their theology and their social attitudes, for example towards sexual orientation. At the same time they tend to be very traditional in their religious practice, preferring a rich liturgy and splendid vestments.

It has often been observed that the high church Anglo-Catholic wing of the Church of England has large numbers of gay clergy: 'Evidence is becoming increasingly strong that the level of homosexuality in Anglo-Catholicism, especially amongst clergy, is above the general level . . . There is the need for scientific enquiry, but until it has been carried out, individual observations and the results of limited surveys all add up to the one conclusion.'[62] This has certainly been the case with the Liberal Catholic Church; three of its first four presiding bishops, Willoughby, Wedgwood and Leadbeater, were caught up in homosexual scandals.

The Open Episcopal Church was founded in 2001 by Jonathan Blake, a former Anglican priest, and Richard Palmer, formerly a bishop in the Liberal Catholic Church, who had consecrated Blake as a bishop in 2000. The intention was 'to provide an episcopal church which operated in a comprehensively inclusive manner'.[63] Amongst others it attracted clergy and members of the mainstream denominations who were unhappy with their Churches but wished to stay within an Episcopal framework. It hit the news in 2003 with the consecration of the first female bishop in Britain, Elizabeth Stuart, Professor of Christian Theology at the University of Winchester, and an authority on gay and lesbian theology.

It has also suffered numerous internal conflicts and schisms in its short existence, with Palmer eventually leaving over leadership issues to found the Reformed Liberal Catholic Church (Old Catholic), and other bishops also leaving for different reasons – one, an Evangelical, disagreeing with the liberal direction of the Church, and another, Elizabeth Stuart, leaving in 2006 to become archbishop of the British province of the Liberal Catholic Church International.[64]

Despite these defections the Open Episcopal Church in 2010 has 5 bishops and 20 priests, and claims 17,000 members in Britain 'who have been baptised by our clerics and who have requested and received sacramental and Christian ministry from us'. According to Bishop Jonathan Blake, 'The majority of our ministry is not intended to replicate the ministry or provision of other denominations in building up settled congregations. Rather our work is evangelistic and rooted in a concept of the universal nature of the Church abiding throughout society.' For this reason 'the majority of services are taken in the homes of members of the public, in their gardens or their choice of location including pubs, clubs, hotels, church halls, schools, beauty spots etc'.[65]

Blake says of the Open Episcopal Church, 'Despite its early fissiparous history the Church has been stable and united since 2006.' But it is clear that small Episcopal Churches, like esoteric movements, have a tendency to splinter. There are probably several reasons for this. One is obviously that there is no ultimate hierarchical authority and no well-established administrative structure; another is that the sort of people who choose to belong to a small heterodox movement, especially at or near leadership level, are by definition unlikely to be the sort of people who will meekly submit to authority (see p. 4). As a webpage on the Liberal Catholic Church comments:

> Due to differences, division and disagreement, the Liberal Catholic Church has split – into several groups – each still working to the Liberal Catholic tenets, but each feeling its need to work freed from the restraints that group felt it was under . . .
> It is a church which encourages open minds and free thinking: in a catholic setting this was never going to be easy and the divisions should not be a surprise.[66]

One website lists over 220 different independent Episcopal denominations, mainly in the United States, in addition to around a dozen Old Catholic Churches in the Union of Utrecht.[67]

Not all independent Episcopal Churches have Theosophical or other esoteric beliefs; some are orthodox Christian – with either a small or a capital 'O'.

As well as small Churches that trace their Episcopal roots back to the Roman Catholic Church there are many, in Britain, the United States and around the world, with roots in the Orthodox tradition, either the Eastern Orthodox (largely Russian and Greek) or Oriental Orthodox (Coptic, Armenian, etc.). In Britain there has been a British Orthodox Church since 1866, but in the 1990s it split, with its most senior bishop and many members linking with the Coptic Orthodox Church of Alexandria, while the remaining bishops formed the British Eparchy of the Celtic Orthodox Church, under a French primate; they were joined by several priests who left the British Orthodox Church. In 2008 the last remaining bishop of the Celtic Orthodox Church left his Church to become a lay monk in the Russian Orthodox tradition, leaving the state of his Church unclear. The British Orthodox Church has around fifteen clergy across the British Isles.

Small Churches outside the major denominations are much more a part of the religious scene in the United States than in Britain; some of the American independent Episcopal Churches are well established small denominations. To take just one example, the Catholic Apostolic Church of Antioch Malabar Rite (usually abbreviated to the Church of Antioch) has over thirty churches across the United States. Founded in 1959 it takes its Apostolic Succession from several sources, including the Liberal Catholic Church, but also from several much older Eastern or Oriental Orthodox traditions; the Malabar Christians of India claim to be descendants of a first-century Church established by the apostle Thomas, though historically it is more likely that they came from sixth-century Syrian Nestorian Christians. It is both theologically and socially liberal, with no gender or sexual orientation restrictions on its clergy. Its second archbishop, from 1986 to 2005, was a matriarch rather than a patriarch.

As well as the links between esoteric movements and the Liberal Catholic Church, leaders of the Ordo Templi Orientis (OTO, see p. 212) are associated with one strand or another of the Gnostic Catholic Church. This had very different origins.

A nineteenth-century French occultist, Jules Doinel (1842–1903), claimed to have found a manuscript written by a martyr of the Cathar religion[68] who died in 1022. Doinel had a series of visions and claimed that forty long-dead Cathar bishops encouraged him to revive Gnostic beliefs and re-establish the

Gnostic Church. He founded the Nouvelle Église Gnostique Universelle in 1890, though he resigned from it in 1895, converting to Roman Catholicism; he spent the next two years collaborating with Leo Taxil (pseudonym of Gabriel Jogand-Pagès) in the creation of scurrilous attacks on Freemasonry, exposed by the English writer on Freemasonry and Rosicrucianism and senior member of the Hermetic Order of the Golden Dawn, A. E. Waite (see p. 195).[69] Doinel returned to the Église Gnostique as a bishop in 1900.

The Église Gnostique had a number of schisms. In 1906 two bishops, the occultist and writer on Tarot Gérard Encausse, better known as Papus (1865–1916), and Jean Bricaud (1881–1934), split from the Church, naming their faction the Gnostic Catholic Church. (Papus was briefly a member of the Theosophical Society in the mid-1890s; he joined the Hermetic Order of the Golden Dawn in 1895; and he co-founded the Kabbalistic Order of the Rose-Croix in 1898.)

Although Papus was never a regular Freemason, in 1908 he organised the International Masonic and Spiritualist Conference in Paris. There Theodor Reuss, founder of the OTO, conferred an irregular masonic charter and degrees on him, and gave him a high grade in the OTO. In return Papus made Reuss a patriarch of the Gnostic Catholic Church, and Reuss set up his own branch of the Church, which he integrated into the OTO.

Up to this point it seems that the bishops did not have a genuine line of Apostolic Succession – Doinel had apparently been consecrated directly by Jesus Christ – but in 1913 Bricaud received legitimate consecration from a Wandering Bishop whose Apostolic Succession went back to the Syrian Orthodox Jacobite Church. In 1919 Bricaud reconsecrated Reuss, ensuring that he had legitimate Apostolic Succession that he could then pass on to others.

Although Reuss gave Aleister Crowley a charter to head the OTO in Britain in 1912 there is no record of Crowley's consecration as a bishop with Apostolic Succession. Nevertheless

Crowley, as a national head of the OTO, became a patriarch of the Gnostic Catholic Church, and his successors as leaders of the various versions of the OTO are also bishops or patriarchs of a variety of versions of the Gnostic Catholic Church. Rather than variants of the Catholic or Orthodox Mass, they use a Gnostic Mass written by Crowley in 1913.

A Church or denomination might have only a handful of churches, but it is still an organisation with an Episcopal structure; a bishop is, by definition, a spiritual and organisational overseer of priests within his diocese. But in addition to bishops in such Churches there are large numbers of individuals with a valid but illicit apostolic succession, but with no denomination at all; these are often known as Wandering Bishops. They may come from any of the many apostolic lineages in existence, or indeed from several, because one hallmark of such bishops is that they often collect as many lineages as they can to strengthen their Episcopal legitimacy – at least in their own eyes. These bishops may ordain priests to assist them in the celebration of the Eucharist, but often it seems their 'Churches' have more clergy than members – and, as with esoteric organisations, the size of a movement's website is absolutely no indicator of its actual size or significance.

Some Wandering Bishops are colourful, even controversial figures. For example, two in Britain, past and present, have been renowned for their belief in real vampires: Montague Summers (1880–1948), whose translation of the fifteenth-century *Malleus Maleficarum* (The Hammer of the Witches) is still widely available, and Seán Manchester, founder of the Vampire Research Society. Both trace their apostolic succession, one way or another, back to the Old Catholic Church. Manchester's Ordo Sancti Graal (Order of the Holy Grail) has no connection with the Liberal Catholic Church Grail Community.

I AM MOVEMENT

The overall I AM movement, with its various offshoots, has its roots in large part in Theosophy (see p. 23); it was founded in the early 1930s by Guy and Edna Ballard, whose own organisation was called the I AM Religious Activity.

In 1930 Guy Warren Ballard (1878–1939), who had read widely in Theosophy and other esoteric religions, was on a walking holiday on Mount Shasta in California, looking for a supposed esoteric Brotherhood of Mount Shasta, when he claims to have met the Ascended Master the Comte de Saint-Germain, an historical eighteenth-century alchemist who features in a number of esoteric movements. For example, Richard Lawrence of the Aetherius Society writes:

> For a period in European history – especially the eighteenth and early nineteenth centuries – he lived, worked, travelled and openly demonstrated some of the powers he had attained, using them in the interests of peace, humanitarianism and the advancement of culture. As a refined, knowledgeable and spiritual giant of a man, who lived for hundreds of years in the same physical body, he is well worthy of further study, if only to show what supernormal abilities can be gained by someone from this Earth, never mind a space traveller from beyond it.[70]

Saint-Germain had apparently been scouring Europe for centuries looking for someone to whom he could give the Great Laws of Life; finding no one worthy he had turned his attentions to the United States. He appointed Guy Ballard the Messenger of the Great White Brotherhood for the Seventh Golden Age; this would be the coming millennium of spiritual realisation.

The Ballards began to make regular contact with Saint-Germain and other Masters. They set up the Saint Germain Press to publish their books on I AM, including *Unveiled Mysteries* (1934) and *The Magic Presence* (1935) under the pseudonym Godfre Ray King, and *I AM Adorations and Affirmations* (1935) and *I AM Discourses* (1936).

They also began teaching classes, initially under Guy Ballard's pseudonym, with Edna as 'Lotus', and training other teachers of their message across the United States. Many of their initial students had been followers of William Dudley Pelley, author of the Soulcraft metaphysical teachings later published by Fellowship Press;[71] they seem to have left Pelley after he founded the ultra right-wing anti-Semitic Silver Shirts in 1933.[72] Pelley later wrote about his UFO beliefs; his book *Star Guests* (1950) was one of the first UFO contactee books.[73]

By 1938 it was claimed that the Ballards had up to a million students. After experiencing problems with hecklers at their open meetings, they started to hold membership-only classes.

As with the later Aetherius Society (see p. 119) Guy Ballard apparently had visitations from extraterrestrial entities: 'Presently, twelve Guests from Venus stood in our midst, robed in white scintillating garments, surpassing all power of description. There were seven gentlemen and five ladies, all extremely handsome.'[74] Ballard met with criticism, mainly from a former member, Gerald B. Bryan, who wrote in *Psychic Dictatorship in America* that Ballard's accounts of his experiences were full of contradictions[75] and that some of them borrowed freely from a number of occult novels.[76]

After Guy Ballard's unexpected death following a stroke in 1939, the movement, now led by Edna Ballard (1886–1971), ran into a series of difficulties. Guy Ballard had taught mastery over death, and many members felt cheated. As with many religious leaders, the Ballards had become wealthy through their movement; some ex-members accused them of using the US postal service for fraudulent purposes – obtaining money for a false religion. Effectively the charge was that 'the beliefs of the group were so unbelievable that the Ballards and other leaders could not possibly believe them. Therefore they must be insincere and the movement a fraud.'[77]

Unusually, the validity of the teachings of a religion were tested in court, all the way up to the Supreme Court, which in 1944 ruled in a far-reaching majority opinion:

> The Fathers of the Constitution were not unaware of the varied and extreme views of religious sects, of the violence of disagreement among them, and of the lack of any one religious creed on which all men would agree. They fashioned a charter of government which envisaged the widest possible toleration of conflicting views. Man's relation to his God was made no concern of the state. He was granted the right to worship as he pleased and to answer to no man for the verity of his religious views. The religious views espoused by respondents might seem incredible, if not preposterous, to most people. But if those doctrines are subject to trial before a jury charged with finding their truth or falsity, then the same can be done with the religious beliefs of any sect. When the triers of fact undertake that task, they enter a forbidden domain. The First Amendment does not select any one group or any one type of religion for preferred treatment. It puts them all in that position.[78]

Despite this landmark ruling the case went backwards and forwards in the courts for some years. From 1942 to 1954 the movement was unable to use the normal mail, and had to distribute its books and magazines by rail; it was not granted tax-exempt status as a religion until 1957. Edna Ballard died in 1971, leaving the leadership in the hands of a board of directors.

The I AM Religious Activity teaches that the omnipotent, omniscient and omnipresent creator God (I AM – Exodus 3:14) is in all of us as a spark from the Divine Flame, and that we can experience this presence, love, power and light – the power of the Violet Consuming Flame of Divine Love – through quiet contemplation and by repeating 'affirmations' and 'decrees'. By 'affirming' something one desires, one can cause it to happen; the I AM movement overlaps with the personal development or human potential movements, because of this 'positive thinking' aspect of its teachings (see p. 147). All believers may experience the Christ Self within them. It is the duty of believers to use the divine power wisely, for harmony and purity; its misuse has been the cause of discord and death throughout the centuries. The emphasis on the power of the will echoes in some ways the reasoning behind Aleister Crowley's dictum 'Do as thou wilt shall be the whole of the law' (see p. 213–4).

The Ascended Masters are religious adepts who have (like Buddhist *bodhisattvas*) stepped off the wheel of reincarnation and now devote themselves to the guidance of mankind; they are the same as the Great White Brotherhood. Because Jesus is one of the Ascended Masters the movement calls itself Christian. The Ballards and their son Donald (who left the movement in 1957) were the only Accredited Messengers of the Ascended Masters; they received over 3,000 messages between them. Guy Ballard, whose previous incarnations included Richard the Lionheart and George Washington, is now the Ascended Master Godfre; Edna Ballard, whose previous incarnations included Joan of Arc, Elizabeth I and Benjamin Franklin, is the Ascended Master Lotus.

Although the teaching on Ascended Masters came from Theosophy, the I AM affirmations and decrees came from New Thought, a religious movement founded in the 1880s by Emma Curtis Hopkins (1853–1925), who split from Mary Baker Eddy, founder of Christian Science, in 1885. New Thought encompasses a number of different religions and schools, including the Unity School of Christianity (founded by Charles and Myrtle Fillmore), Divine Science (Melinda Cramer) and Religious Science (Ernest Holmes) amongst others. All of them, in different ways, are religious expressions of the power of positive thinking through affirmative prayer.[79]

As with most new religious movements or 'alternative spiritualities' the teachings of the Ballards were not new, but the publicity they gave to them encouraged their spread through the developing New Age movements, many of which have taken up the idea of the Masters.

CHURCH UNIVERSAL
AND TRIUMPHANT

The Church Universal and Triumphant (CUT) and its publishing arm, the Summit Lighthouse, have much in common with the I AM movement (see p. 65) – they recognise Guy Ballard as an Ascended Master – though they are quite independent. In the 1990s they received a great deal of attention and criticism from anti-cult organisations in the United States.

In the 1950s Mark L. Prophet (1918–73) had been involved in an I AM offshoot, the Bridge to Freedom (later the New Age Church of the Christ and now the Bridge to Spiritual Freedom – not to be confused with the Church of Scientology's 'Bridge to Total Freedom'). Founded by Geraldine Innocente, who began receiving messages from the Masters in 1951, this group differed from the Ballards' I AM Religious Activity in two ways: it believed that messages from the Messengers should continue (although she was a Messenger, Edna Ballard was inactive after her husband's death), and it believed that messages should be translated into other languages such as Spanish, which the Ballards' organisation had always forbidden. The Bridge to Freedom published the messages received through Innocente and her successor Lucy Littlejohn, though without naming them as the Messengers.

One leader in the Bridge to Freedom, Frances Ekey, split to form the Lighthouse of Freedom, and began publishing a new set of messages received through Mark Prophet, also anonymously. Prophet also published his messages as *Pearls of*

Wisdom, still published today by CUT. In 1958 Ekey and Prophet founded the Summit Lighthouse with Prophet as Messenger, though Ekey left the following year to return to the Lighthouse of Freedom.[80]

In 1961 Mark Prophet met Elizabeth Clare Wulf (1939–2009), who had been raised a Lutheran, had joined Christian Science in her early teens and had started reading I AM literature when she was eighteen.[81] She was trained by Mark Prophet and by the Ascended Master who had appointed him a Messenger, El Morya, who had been King Arthur, Thomas Becket and Sir Thomas More in three of his incarnations. She married Mark in 1963, and a year later she too became a Messenger. The Ascended Master Saint-Germain instructed them to form the Keepers of the Flame Fraternity to teach others about the Masters.

The Summit Lighthouse grew slowly through the 1960s. In 1970 it set up a Montessori International School to give children both secular and spiritual education from nursery age through to high school. In 1971 it launched Ascended Master University (now Summit University).

In 1973 Mark Prophet, like Guy Ballard, died suddenly following a stroke, leaving the running of his organisation to his wife; but unlike Edna Ballard, Elizabeth Clare Prophet made something new from what she had been left. In 1974 she set up the Church Universal and Triumphant, and Summit Lighthouse became its publishing house; CUT was incorporated in 1975. She grew in importance as the Church grew; within the movement she was known formally as Guru Ma and usually as Mother, though not as Ma Prophet, her popular name in the US press.[82]

Over the years CUT has been based in several areas, outgrowing each one and moving on to the next. Mark Prophet was living in Washington, DC when he founded Summit Lighthouse. In 1962 they moved to Fairfax, Virginia, and in 1965 to Vienna, Virginia. In 1966 they moved to a mansion in Colorado Springs, which became the world headquarters of

Summit Lighthouse. During these years the two Messengers travelled around the United States and Europe spreading their teachings. They also set up 'the Motherhouse' in Santa Barbara, California, which housed Summit University for a few years; other centres were set up around the United States. CUT leased a Church of the Nazarene college campus in Pasadena, California, in 1976, then moved yet again the following year, buying from the Claretian Fathers an estate in the Santa Monica Mountains near Malibu; this they renamed Camelot.

In 1981 the Church bought its present home, the 24,000-acre (10,000-hectare) Royal Teton Ranch in Paradise Valley, near Livingston, Montana; it is next to the famous Yellowstone National Park. Along with many other organisations it bought up everything from caravans to kitchen equipment from the Bhagwan Shree Rajneesh community in nearby Oregon when that broke up in 1985. CUT moved its headquarters to the Royal Teton Ranch in 1986.

The Church was at the centre of controversy for some years. Misunderstandings had first developed because the Church bought up large areas of land, which local people found worrying in light of the political takeover attempt by Rajneesh's followers at Rajneeshpuram in the early 1980s, which had also begun with the buying up of land;[83] then because it built fallout shelters against the threat of imminent nuclear disaster; and then in 1989 when two members, including Prophet's then husband, Edward Francis, illegally attempted to buy weapons under false names. Francis was jailed for a short time for his involvement – which the authorities determined was not linked to the Church – and the Church suffered for a while from negative public perception. Relations with neighbours, and with both state and federal government, were to improve markedly in later years. (Francis was Prophet's fourth husband, whom she married in 1981; her first, before Mark Prophet, didn't join in her belief in the Ascended Masters; she also had a brief third marriage after Mark's death. In 1994, at the age of 54, Prophet had a fifth child, Seth. She was divorced from

Francis in 1996, but he continued as executive vice-president of the Church until 1998.)

Prophet continued to receive messages from the Ascended Masters, particularly Saint-Germain, 'the Knight Commander of the Keepers of the Flame Fraternity',[84] and Lanello, the Ascended Master name of her late husband; the weekly *Pearls of Wisdom* publishes these messages. Her many books, incorporating these teachings (and the teachings given earlier to Mark Prophet), have gained a much wider circulation than the Church itself, becoming influential in more general New Age circles.

Elizabeth Clare Prophet led the Church for twenty-five years, but in the late 1990s she was diagnosed with Alzheimer's disease and revealed a lifelong condition of petit mal epilepsy. She retired as both Messenger and Vicar of Christ – 'the representative of Christ to all of the Church's members'[85] – in 1999, and died in 2009. The Church believes that she is now an Ascended Master.

The Church Universal and Triumphant is run by its board of directors. In 1996 management consultant Gilbert Cleirbaut was elected Church president, with the remit to make major changes in the Church's management structure and culture. In the ten years after the announcement of Prophet's illness the Church prepared carefully for its stable continuation once she was no longer with them. It reduced its focus on her, and aimed to become less authoritarian and more decentralised. In sociological terms, it consciously changed from charismatic leadership to rational/legal leadership.[86]

Elizabeth Clare Prophet was trained by Mark Prophet and by El Morya, and had been a Messenger for ten years when Mark died. After that she was the only Messenger. She did not appoint a successor or future Messenger; since her retirement the Church has been in a post-prophetic stage, though there are means by which the Council of Elders can 'recognise ongoing revelation through a new Messenger or Vicar of Christ, should the Ascended Masters choose to anoint an individual to one of these offices in the future'. A year after her death the Church's Council of Elders was 'currently working to fulfil their responsibility of appointing a spiritual leader or spiritual director'.[87]

Leadership will not stay 'in the family'; all of her four children by Mark Prophet have now left the Church. Eldest son Sean, a minister at twenty-three and vice-president of the Church by twenty-five, left in 1993 and now has a website repudiating not just CUT but all organised religion.[88] Second daughter Moira spoke out against CUT on *The Oprah Winfrey Show* in 1989. Their eldest daughter Erin trained as a Messenger in the 1990s before she too left the Church, though she was her mother's legal guardian, with senior member and long-time friend Murray Steinman, in her last years, and co-edited, with her sister Tatiana, their mother's memoirs. Prophet's ex-husband Edward Francis has also left the Church, taking their son Seth with him.[89]

As with the I AM Religious Activity a number of members have left CUT and set up new movements with themselves as Messengers: Caroline and Monroe Shearer started the Temple of the Presence in 1995, Kim Michaels started Shangra-la in 2002, Marsha Covington started New Wisdom University in 2003 and David C. Lewis started The Hearts Centre in 2005. The Church says, 'Over the years, both before and after the messenger's retirement, the organisation has heard from numerous individuals claiming to carry one of these offices, but none has been recognised . . . While we are not closed to the possibility of a new Messenger or Vicar of Christ, the Elders are not actively seeking applicants for these offices.'[90]

The Church Universal and Triumphant teaches that people are born with an innate spark of divinity (see p. 12) and can realise their full potential of oneness with God – the same mystical message which they say is embedded at the heart of all the world's major religions: 'Each individual soul has a divine plan – a mission to fulfil and lessons to learn. Earth is a schoolroom and souls may require more than one life to fulfil their debts to life (balance their karma) and fulfil their spiritual destiny. The ascension (reunion with God) is the goal of life.'[91] It teaches that many people have mastered life, realised their full potential and ascended back to God; these enlightened spiritual beings, or Ascended Masters, now assist humanity from spiritual realms.

Some of its teachings, such as on Ascended Masters, derive from the I AM movement, and ultimately from Theosophy (see p. 23), though 'Theosophy has a far more intellectual approach,' says Murray Steinman, formerly the Church's director of media relations.[92] But CUT has developed its own distinctive theology, which in recent years has embraced large elements of Gnostic Christianity. It identifies itself as a Church firmly based in the Judaeo-Christian tradition.

> Jesus Christ and Saint-Germain – together with all of the heavenly hosts: Ascended Masters, Elohim, archangels, angels and servant-sons of God, who comprise the Spirit of the Great White Brotherhood (the multitude of saints robed in white witnessed by Saint John) – have come forth from the inner Mystery School at the end of Pisces and the beginning of Aquarius to teach us how to call upon this name of the Lord, alchemical formulas whereby we may put on our individual Christhood even while we overcome personified evil and the *energy veil* of our negative karma, the so-called sins of our past lives.[93]

In common with the I AM movement, CUT teaches that there is an element of the Christ, a divine spark of the God flame, within each of us:

> The fundamental principle of the teachings of the Ascended Masters is that all sons and daughters of God have a divine spark which is their potential to become, or realise, the Christ within and ascend to God as Jesus did. This concept is at the heart of the major religions, East and West. And it was part of Jesus' original teachings to his disciples which were either destroyed or obscured by Church Fathers.[94]

His teachings were also corrupted by the New Testament writers. Jesus studied in India and Tibet between the ages of twelve and thirty; two of CUT's publications are *The Lost Years of Jesus* and the four-volume *The Lost Teachings of Jesus*. The first is based on old Buddhist stories of Saint Issa, who travelled to the East and studied under Masters there before returning to Palestine to take up his ministry: 'Then it was that Issa left the parental house in secret, departed from Jerusalem, and with the merchants set out towards Sind, with the object of perfecting himself in the Divine Word and of studying the laws of the great Buddhas.'[95] Jesus is here given the same sort of 'early-life mythology' as Madame Blavatsky (see p. 23), G. I. Gurdjieff (see p. 44–5), L. Ron Hubbard (see p. 362–3) and other founders of modern religions.

The Lost Teachings incorporates some of the ideas of such non-canonical works as the Secret Book of James and the Gnostic Gospels of Philip, Thomas and Mary Magdalene, but is actually 'a reconstitution of Jesus' basic message through the Messengership of Mark and Elizabeth Prophet, which they have written down,' says Steinman. CUT emphasises particularly the Book of Enoch, another of the many books which never made it into the Bible.

The Church does not accept all the Gnostic teachings but, Steinman says:

> a lot of the things we totally agree with, like where Jesus is saying in the Gospel of Thomas, 'If you drink from the same stream that I have, you will be just like me, we'll be twins'; that's essentially our core teaching, that you can become like Jesus. If you miss that point, then you're missing the point of his message.[96]

While the Church believes that Jesus was God the Son, its beliefs differ from traditional Christianity; Jesus was a man in complete touch with the Christ-consciousness within him, and said that we are all Sons and Daughters of God who can do the same. He ascended to God immediately after leaving his human

body, and is now one of the Ascended Masters. Mary
Magdalene, who was Jesus' twin flame, is now the Ascended
Master Magda. The Virgin Mary is venerated as the perfect
expression of the Mother aspect of God. In this Aquarian Age
the Church places equal emphasis on the masculine and
feminine aspects of both God and individual people, whether
they are female or male. The Statue of Liberty is symbolic of
the Goddess of Liberty.

Saint-Germain is a very significant figure in the Church's
teachings. He is an Ascended Master who sponsors projects
that promote soul freedom, including the founding of the
United States where he inspired the American Constitution
and the Declaration of Independence. Before becoming an
Ascended Master he lived on Earth as the prophet Samuel,
Mary's husband Joseph, Merlin, Roger Bacon, Christopher
Columbus and Francis Bacon. The nineteenth-century writer
Voltaire mentioned him as 'the Wonderman of Europe'.
According to former CUT spokesman Christopher Kelley,
'Saint-Germain also introduced at large a high-frequency spir-
itual energy long-known to mystics as the violet flame, which
can be invoked through spoken prayer and visualisation for
healing of body, mind and spirit.'[97]

Central to the Church's teachings – and its art – is 'the violet
flame': 'When invoked and visualised in the giving of dynamic
decrees, this seventh-ray aspect of the sacred fire transmutes the
cause, effect, record and memory of negative karma and
misqualified energy that result in discord, disease and death.
Those who correctly call forth the violet flame daily, experience
transformation, soul liberation, and spiritual upliftment.'[98]

The Church teaches that we can step off the wheel of
reincarnation – in ascension – by becoming united with our
Christ-consciousness through study and prayer and, as in
I AM, through affirmations and decrees. Affirmations affirm
the person's relationship with God; decrees use the name of
God (I AM) to make statements of power such as 'I AM the
light of the heart, shining in the darkness of being, changing all

into the infinite mind of Christ', or 'I AM a being of violet fire, I AM the purity God desires'. Ascension is not physical, but 'a spiritual acceleration of consciousness which takes place at the natural conclusion of one's lifetime when the soul returns to the Father and is freed from the round of karma and rebirth'.[99]

But CUT does not claim to be an easy shortcut to God: 'The path to the summit of being is steep. With fellow seekers and with the Ascended Masters who have gone before us we can make our way through these hitherto uncharted paths, and reach the summit of being.'[100] CUT does not believe that it is the only path to heaven. Neither is the Church dogmatic in its teachings: members are not required to believe every aspect. It also believes that it is more important to look for the similarities between religions than to emphasise the differences. In keeping with this philosophy it explores the mystical paths of all the world's religions, including Hinduism, Buddhism and Christianity, and has published a book on its interpretation of Kabbalah.

'The Ascended Masters present a path and a teaching whereby every individual on earth can find his way back to God,' said Prophet:

> I do not claim to be a Master but only their instrument. Nor do I claim to be perfect in my human self. I am the servant of the Light in all students of the Ascended Masters and in all people. My books and writings are intended to give people the opportunity to know the Truth that can make them free – so they can find God without me. My goal is to take true seekers, in the tradition of the Masters of the Far East, as far as they can go and need to go to meet their true Teachers face to face.[101]

Elizabeth Clare Prophet, like her husband, was a Messenger of the Ascended Masters. The Church sees this as similar to the prophets of the Old Testament, who delivered messages from God. While she was still the active Messenger CUT explained:

> She is fully conscious and in possession of her faculties, yet in an exalted state, while delivering the words of the heavenly host as

'dictations'. Her work is not a form of psychism or spiritualism in which a discarnate entity from the spirit world takes over the body of a channeller. Rather it is a conveyance by the Holy Spirit of the sacred fire and the teaching of immortal beings who with Jesus have returned to the heart of the Father.[102]

There have been many criticisms of the Church, by some of their neighbours in Montana, by some ex-members and by anti-cultists.

Like the I AM Religious Activity, CUT is morally conservative and intensely patriotic, and has been accused of being right-wing; but Steinman suggests that middle-class Americans in general tend to be more patriotic and more conservative than their British counterparts. The Church makes the point that they follow what the Ascended Masters teach on various issues, so their stance is more spiritual than political.

It is often said that Prophet forecast the end of the world – or at least a cataclysmic disaster – for April 1990. This, says former spokesman Christopher Kelley, is an exaggeration of her prediction of twelve years of increased negative karma as the age of Pisces ends and the Age of Aquarius begins. Saint-Germain had apparently requested they have the underground shelters ready – not just for sheltering members of the Church, but also for protecting all the world's spiritual teachings in the event of a major attack. Church membership dropped dramatically after what became known as the 'shelter phase', when no nuclear attack occurred.

On the firearms story, which brought the Church a lot of bad publicity, the facts – as established in court – are that the Church itself owns no weapons; individual members may own whatever weapons they want for sporting purposes or for self-defence. Edward Francis, Prophet's then husband, with another Church member, tried to buy guns to defend the Church's fallout shelter if necessary against local right-wing extremists. The weapons would have been quite legal if Francis had not tried to buy them under a false name – ironically to avoid publicity. 'Obviously we screwed up. It was a huge mistake and it was ill-conceived,' says Francis,[103] who was at the time vice-president and business manager of the Church. The Church says that Prophet did not know of the firearms purchase in advance, though her daughter Erin disagrees.[104]

Prophet was also criticised for wearing expensive clothes and jewellery; her response was that the clothes were a gift, and the jewellery was a focus of spiritual energy, and belonged to the Church, not to her.

Like many other alternative religious movements, the Church has in the past been accused of brainwashing its members, a charge that it calls absurd. An independent scholarly study of the Church in 1993, sponsored by the Association of World Academics for Religious Education (AWARE), concluded that there was no evidence of anything approaching brainwashing. It found that the members were predominantly white middle-class adults; three-quarters were aged between thirty and sixty; a quarter had an advanced degree. They were generally of above-average intelligence. Politically they did tend to be right of centre; a half described themselves as conservative, and a further 8 per cent as very conservative; a quarter said they were moderate, and only 4 per cent said they were liberal. But as for CUT being another Waco-in-the-making, as some anti-cultists have asserted, the study found that adult members 'scored lower than the normed population on the Aggression subscale'. Using a number of different indicators the study concluded that CUT had the characteristics of a denomination rather than those of a cult; for example, as with mainstream denominations it is quite possible to be a 'nominal' member. Part of the study concentrated on the children in the Royal Teton Ranch; 'contrary to the claims of critics, they found the children bright, well taken care of, loved, and well educated'.[105]

Like many other religious movements the Church will not give membership figures. There are practical reasons for this. It has a core membership of communicants, who have committed themselves completely to the Church, pledging acceptance of the Tenets and tithing their income to the Church; Keepers of the Flame are 'signed-up members', not necessarily deeply committed; and in addition there are thousands of people around the world who, having read Prophet's books, may accept some of the teaching, but are not actually members of the Church.

CUT has members in 31 countries, with around 200 centres. The number of staff living at the headquarters at the Royal Teton Ranch in 2010 'are much reduced' from what they once were. Over 40 per cent of members 'are not affiliated with any local group but study and apply the ascended masters' teachings in their homes and daily lives'.[106]

EMISSARIES/EMISSARIES
OF DIVINE LIGHT

The Emissaries, or Emissaries of Divine Light, could be called one of the earliest 'New Age' movements. They were founded in Tennessee in 1932 by Lloyd Arthur Meeker (1907–54), the son of a farmer and minister. He had searched through philosophies and religions for a purpose to his life, and had found nothing to satisfy him: 'He finally looked to himself and came to the profound realisation that he was completely responsible for the state of his world and the quality of his experience in it. He knew he could not continue like the mass of humanity, victim or victor in the world of circumstance. He saw and experienced a life of peace and value.'[107]

Meeker wrote widely under the name Uranda; his ideas began to spread. In 1940 he met former Royal Navy officer Martin Cecil (1909–88), who on his brother's death in 1981 inherited the title of the Marquess of Exeter, though not the family seat of Burghley House, a huge Elizabethan mansion and estate in Lincolnshire, England. Cecil took Meeker's mass of ideas and developed them into a more systematic and comprehensible system – in a similar way to Ouspensky clarifying Gurdjieff's teachings (see p. 45–6). Their writings and the transcripts of their talks are now collected in a set of volumes called *The Third Sacred School*.

When Meeker and his wife died in a plane crash in 1954 Cecil took over the organisation, which became known as the Emissaries of Divine Light, particularly in the United States.

In Britain the movement has been known since 1993 simply as the Emissaries, which is how they are referred to here for brevity. Other early names for the movement included the Foundation of Universal Unity, the Ontological Society and the Integrity Society.

The international headquarters, established by Meeker in 1945, is Sunrise Ranch in Colorado. By 1948 the Canadian headquarters of the movement was at a property connected to Bridge Creek estate, Martin Cecil's cattle ranch at 100 Mile House, British Columbia, which eventually became a thriving Emissary community. A British community at Mickleton House in Gloucestershire, England, was opened in 1980. There were several others, mainly in the United States. This was all to change around the turn of the century (see below).

It is difficult to pin down the Emissaries on exactly what they believe; one scholar wrote in evident frustration: 'Trying to describe Emissary spirituality with any kind of precision is like trying to nail Jello to the wall'.[108] The quotations on Emissary belief in this entry come from a variety of sources, old and new.[109]

Emissary teachings perhaps could be described as a combination of Gurdjieffian self-awareness and the Christian ideal of loving one another, with a Gnostic sense of the immanence of the Divine. According to Tessa Maskell, a former UK director of the Emissaries, 'the philosophy was – and is – sometime in the past, before memory, we human beings forgot that we are divine and that is the truth of us. We began to create a complex and confusing world. The opportunity is now available to experience the reality of ourselves and create another world as we remember these simple truths.'[110]

Meeker had expressed it in more esoteric terms: 'You are the means by which the invisible becomes visible'.[111] But the purpose of the Emissaries, again in his words, is more straightforward: 'to assist in the spiritual regeneration of the human race'.[112] It all comes down to the individual's relationship with the Divine: 'Divine Action, as it appears through the actions and interactions of the individual, is anything that springs from the desire to bring unity rather than separation, to participate rather than isolate, to create rather than destroy, to understand with the heart rather than attack with the mind.'[113]

It is the very individuality of each human being that displays the power and diversity of God; and in a community of such people the whole is greater than the sum of its parts:

> When a group of conscious people each agree to commit them-
> selves to surrendering to the inner impulse, the intensity of the
> group energy is magnified . . . This means that Divine energy has
> a bigger area available, which means that more of it can be made
> manifest than if the same number of people were surrendering
> in separate places, unknown to each other.[114]

By 'group energy' or 'Divine energy' the Emissaries mean something almost tangible; at one time they called it 'Pneumaplasm' (Spirit Substance), but now it is simply known as Substance.

Community is important to the Emissaries. William Duffield, head of the Emissaries in the UK, speaks of their members in Britain and Europe who are more dispersed today than in the past:

> Primarily, as always, this community is composed of those who
> see themselves as unified through awareness of themselves as
> essentially spiritual or Divine beings who find themselves
> moving together in oneness of purpose and trusting in the
> Divine Design to guide them. There is therefore no separation at
> that level between the Emissary Body here and that anywhere
> else in the world. However every spiritual being needs
> equipment in order to act creatively at the different levels of
> manifestation, including at the level of form. At that level each
> individual needs a material body to relate to the rest of the
> material world.
>
> For collectives it is no different, so each Emissary Community
> has a legal entity or organisational aspect to enable it to relate to
> and operate in the world of matter. Hence Emissaries of Divine

Light in North America and The Emissaries Limited here in
Europe. This is the way of Life. United and focused in oneness
at the levels of energy/Spirit/Divine being but infinitely diverse
in its manifest forms. These are not contradictory but integral
aspects of the whole, wondrously woven together.[115]

The Emissaries teach a practice called attunement: 'a sacred
healing art which uses a refined non-touch technique to access
the subtle vibrational energies of the body, mind and heart'.[116]
Kate Hall, events manager and visitor contact at Mickleton
House in the mid-1990s, describes attunement as 'a gentle,
meditative technique for aligning subtle body energy with
universal energy for increasing divine awareness within'.[117]
    The heart of the beliefs, in Meeker's words, is that:

> God is not just one Being, but God is one Being. The Body of
> God is made up of many God Beings. But we do not have a
> multiplicity of gods, just one God. All the parts of God are
> perfectly co-ordinated, perfectly cohesive, and every part of
> the Body of God is an individualised God Being. That indi-
> vidualised aspect of God is in you, in your body. So it is with
> every man, woman and child on the face of the earth, good,
> bad or indifferent.[118]

Hall explains further:

> To Emissaries, this is known as Divine Identity, or True
> Identity. Most people are not in touch with their own True
> Identity, but most Emissaries believe that we can begin to
> become more conscious of our True Identity by choosing to act
> with greater awareness of the effect of all our actions, great and
> small, and by consciously taking full responsibility for our
> behaviour and how it affects everyone around us.

To put it another way, if we were created in God's image then
we can each manifest the divine nature on Earth. If hate, fear,
anger or other negative emotions or influences get in the way,
the divine nature is distorted; we have the choice, however, of

accepting divine control, of letting the divine nature and the divine design re-manifest through us in a process known simply as healing. This is what Emissaries aim for, to experience reality (God) and to manifest divine truth and love in a distorted world.

Hall lists the main spiritual principles that Emissaries recognise:

Love: To the degree that individuals fail to let love permeate themselves and all their thoughts, words and deeds, they function outside the realm of the Divine.

Trust: Trust in the Divine process – that no matter how it looks, everything is happening for a reason.

Thankfulness: Be truly thankful for all your blessings, whatever they are.

Acceptance: Accept that everything is just as it is meant to be, without judgement, condemnation or resignation.

Forgiveness: Letting go of our negative feelings towards others and allowing healing to happen. As we each heal our own lives, so the whole world may become healed.

It could perhaps be said that Meeker was a hippie, at least in his ideals, thirty years before anyone else. Hall comments, 'Scratch a middle-aged Emissary and you may well find a Sixties hippie, still full of those peace and love ideals, underneath' – but makes it clear that she is referring to the values of the idealistic youth of the 1960s, not to their supposedly common lifestyle of sex 'n' drugs 'n' rock 'n' roll.

At their height the Emissaries had around 4,000 members, many living in their (then) 12 communities in 6 countries. Many of their members come from the professions, the arts, media and small businesses.

As with many alternative religious movements, especially those living and working in communities, the Emissaries have been the target of anti-cult organisations. The main criticisms levelled by former members, before the changes described below, were that the organisation was strongly hierarchical and could be authoritarian or even abusive; that members were allowed very little free time outside their assigned work in the community; they also had to spend hours each week listening to tapes or reading transcripts of sermons by Meeker or Martin Cecil, both alone and in services and classes; it has also been alleged that many of the male leaders would have both a wife and a 'concubine' who took the public role of secretary.[119]

For thirty years the Emissaries were guided firmly by Martin Cecil. Every community, at its Sunday morning service, would read a transcript of a talk he had delivered the week before to the main community in Colorado; it was a link between all the groups. Martin Cecil died in 1988 aged seventy-nine, and his son Michael (b.1935), now the eighth Marquess of Exeter, took over. He had married Lloyd Arthur Meeker's daughter Nancy Rose Meeker in 1967, in what has been called an arranged 'royal marriage' between the offspring of the two founders;[120] they divorced in 1993 and Nancy Meeker left the Emissaries to join another movement.

After his father's death Michael Cecil decentralised the leadership, putting it into the hands of a governing board of eight trustees and locally selected representatives. He also brought in other speakers at services, a major innovation.

Few movements make an easy transition from a one-person focus, effectively a guru, to a functional collective body.[121] For the Emissaries the transition was difficult; many members missed the strong, charismatic, centralised leadership of the patriarchal Martin Cecil and disliked the new regime where they had to take on much more personal responsibility. Membership fell by over two-thirds, but eventually each community became used to being self-governing. Tessa Maskell, Director of the UK Emissaries at the time, comments on the change: 'Having had one external point of focus, in Uranda [Meeker] and Martin [Cecil], each one now takes responsibility themselves for their spiritual expression and all come together in increased spiritual maturity to bring the Divine expression, Heaven, into the earth now – not in some afterlife!'

What I Believe . . .
Gods and Spirits – Objective or Subjective?

They are both objective and subjective; they're out there, and they're in here. They are composed of energy, certainly with the deities, I would see them as energy shaped by human attention over many, many thousands of years. They have a very powerful independent existence of their own.

Jack Gale, Magician
Retired school teacher

If you say divinities aren't real but are only subjective then it's reduction by psychology, which is something that is anathema to an outlook of enchantment and engagement with the unknown and mystery. So I reject that. To say that gods are objective reality, in a simple straightforward factual way, the way that a chair or a table is, is reduction by materialism, which I equally reject.

Dr Christina Oakley Harrington, Wiccan priestess
Owner of Treadwells esoteric bookshop, London; former
university lecturer in History and Religious History

How much are the gods of Paganism or occultism projections from ourselves? Well, they wouldn't be human-shaped if they weren't. Or we wouldn't try and picture them. You very rarely see a goddess of love as a really ugly old woman or a really ugly old man for that matter. They *are* projections from ourselves, but we're part of the universe too, and so are they.

I think that the idea that there are lesser and greater, and that there are bits or aspects, has to be accepted: a kind of henotheism, a-god-for-a-job approach, is very much one that is used in contemporary Paganism and occultism.

Steve Wilson, Thelemite
Civil Servant

There is no god, there is no goddess; I work with the Earth.
Terry Dobney, Keeper of the Stones at Avebury
Retired motorcycle restorer

All these things belong to multidimensional reality
which for me is ultimately all a mystery; but within
this mystery there are many beings and realms
considered fantastical by those with no spiritual or
poetic imagination. I both believe in and experience
these realms.
Dr William Bloom
Author and educator in a holistic and modern
approach to spirituality

We automatically anthropomorphise things and give them
faces. Maybe they have got faces, but maybe they know that
that's how they have to communicate themselves to us. They
have to be understandable within our reference. I firmly
believe that they do exist and I firmly believe that they are
subjective as well.
Geraldine Beskin, third-generation esoteric witch and
eclectic occultist
Co-owner of the Atlantis Bookshop, London

I see them essentially as metaphors, and through shamanism that
metaphorical realm takes on an ontological reality in its own right; so
it's not something empirical, but you can through trance and other
techniques make that metaphorical world or encounter it as a bona
fide reality. That's where I basically encounter the gods.
Dr Michael York, Shaman
Retired Professor of Cultural Astronomy and Astrology,
Bath Spa University

In 2003 the British community sold the headquarters it had used since 1980 at Mickleton House in Gloucestershire. 'Mickleton House was sold in 2003 primarily because there were insufficient numbers of Emissary Associates who felt called to live and work there and also because of a decline in Emissary Educational activities. The Community therefore became decentralised but sustained their sense of unified function through increasing use of modern communications technology and teleconferencing,' says Duffield.[122] The Emissary community near the Cecils' ranch at 100 Mile House in Canada, which had been one of the two earliest and largest communities, closed, as did Green Pastures in the eastern United States and La Vigne in France.

In the United States and Canada the Emissaries appear to have remade themselves after the disruption of the 1990s. Most Emissaries today live in eight main communities of from twenty to 150 people, the largest being Sunrise Ranch in Colorado. They also have centres in Southern California, Oregon, Indiana and New York, and a retreat and conference centre in British Columbia.

In Britain the remaining members of the Emissaries seem well integrated into the wider New Age scene. Former director Tessa Maskell is still a leader in the Emissaries and is also a trustee of the Wrekin Trust (see p. 96), while the current chair of the Emissaries in the UK, William Duffield, also runs the Mangreen Trust near Norwich, 'a place where people can come for soul nurturing, without being directed to a particular pathway'.[123] It also practices attunement, 'a non-touch form of energy healing'. Emissaries in the UK and Europe, says Duffield, are:

> willing to collaborate with other organisations who share complementary aims and objectives whilst in no way denying or diluting their own heritage or essences. There is so much that we can do together that we cannot do alone, so why not explore that and realise the potential? . . .

That which is universal never threatens the diversity of culture or form but rather enables and empowers us to transcend those apparent differences without in any way being disrespectful to them or those who helped build our histories. One result of this is that Emissaries in Europe sit easily within the holistic spirituality scene but without considering themselves a religion.[124]

It is rare for the leader of a movement to leave his own movement, but in 1996 Michael Cecil left the Emissaries. 'I feel the organisation had become quite introverted. Some people who join such groups are just looking for a safe place to be,' he told the *Vancouver Sun* in 2003:

I didn't want to be part of an enclave separate from the world, which had the view we had the answer to life and nobody else did. But a number of Emissary stalwarts found that very difficult to tolerate. They wanted to stay in a cocoon, close to the way things were in the past. As a result, I felt I needed to move out into the larger sphere myself.[125]

In 2000 he co-founded a new group, the Ashland Institute, in Ashland, Oregon; it runs a variety of personal development courses with a focus on spiritual-based transformation. It too practises attunement, which it describes as 'an approach to healing based on the premise that the body is a dynamic, self-healing expression of a deeper spiritual self'. Michael Cecil stresses that the Ashland Institute has no connection with the Emissaries.[126] His father and Meeker are mentioned on the history page of the Emissaries website, but Michael Cecil is conspicuous by his absence. With his son Anthony John Cecil, Lord Burghley, he is still co-director of the family cattle ranch at 100 Mile House in British Columbia.

FINDHORN

Findhorn is one of the largest and longest established New Age communities in Europe, and one of the most respected internationally.

It dates back to 1962 when Peter and Eileen Caddy and their Canadian friend Dorothy Maclean were sacked as managers of the Cluny Hill Hotel in the small town of Forres, near Inverness in north-east Scotland, which they had run since 1957. They moved into a large caravan in the nearby Findhorn Bay Caravan Park with the young Caddy children, and having little money they began an organic garden on poor soil on an overgrown patch of land, with remarkable results. From that garden developed what is today the Findhorn Foundation. The success of the garden, which produced nutritious and exceptionally large vegetables, according to one source including 42lb broccoli and 60lb cabbages,[127] came to the attention of the BBC, which broadcast a radio programme about Findhorn in 1965 and a TV documentary in 1969.

The three founders, individually and together, had been involved in alternative spirituality for many years before setting up Findhorn. Peter Caddy (1917–94) had links with the Rosicrucian Order Crotona Fellowship on the south coast of England, which ran a Rosicrucian Theatre (see p. 32), and with UFO groups. Eileen Caddy (1917–2006) had been receiving guidance from an inner, divine voice since the 1940s. Both also had a background in Moral Re-armament, an Evangelical

Christian movement which practises receiving divine guidance through 'quiet times'. Dorothy Maclean (b.1920) worked with *devas*, nature spirits or intelligences overseeing the natural world, who guided her on how to get the best out of the garden. All three were strongly influenced in the 1940s and 1950s by a Scottish-born but London-based spiritual teacher, Sheena Govan (1912–67), who became Peter Caddy's second wife (Eileen was his third; he was eventually to be married five times).

In the late 1950s and early 1960s the future Findhorn leaders believed that they were in telepathic contact with extraterrestrials, and even built a landing strip on the mound behind the hotel for their flying saucers, leading to a front-page headline in the *Sunday Pictorial* (20 September 1960), 'The Martians Are Coming'.[128] In the 1950s Peter Caddy had written an 8,000-word report, 'An Introduction to the Nature and Purpose of Unidentified Flying Objects', copies of which were given to, amongst others, the former prime minister Clement Atlee and Prince Philip.[129] But these beliefs, common to the alternative culture of the time (see p. 66, p. 113 etc.), slipped into the background, replaced by guidance from God.

By the end of the 1960s, through the BBC programmes, a small book by Eileen Caddy, *God Spoke to Me*[130] and word of mouth in the wider New Age community – including 'the Father of the New Age', Sir George Trevelyan (see p. 96) – the still-small Findhorn had been discovered by hippies, bringing a great increase in numbers, an influx of younger blood (the founders were by now in their late forties and early fifties) and a broadening of New Age ideas, including self-realisation and healing.

In 1970 a young American, David Spangler (b.1945), visited Findhorn; apparently the three founders, without knowing who he was, had been expecting him by name. He was made joint director with Peter Caddy, and in the next three years he helped transform Findhorn from a settlement of like-minded New Age enthusiasts into a residential centre for alternative spiritual education. In 1972 the Findhorn community was

formally registered as a Scottish charity under the name the
Findhorn Foundation. In 1973 Spangler, with one of the
Findhorn founders, Dorothy Maclean, returned to the United
States where they set up the Lorian Association, a spiritual
educational organisation. Maclean later returned to Findhorn,
where she still lives.

Peter Caddy left both Eileen and Findhorn in 1979 and set
up a new community in California; he died in a car crash in
Germany in 1994. Eileen Caddy received the MBE in 2004 for
services to spiritual enquiry. She died at Findhorn in 2006.
Under the title 'Eileen Caddy's Daily Guidance' her teachings
are still prominent on the Findhorn website.[131]

Over the years the Findhorn community pursued a number
of fashionable New Age beliefs, practices and therapies, at
times raising some negative responses. But in general Findhorn
seems well respected, drawing a variety of well-known New
Age speakers and teachers including William Bloom and
Eckhart Tolle.

Today the Findhorn Foundation Community describes
itself as 'an experiment in conscious living, an education centre
and an ecovillage'. It supplies its own power through wind-
mills and solar heating. It has over 300 full-time residents living
in a variety of eco-homes, including yurts and straw-bale
housing, in The Park, a 30-acre (12-hectare) site that was
formerly the caravan park. Carin Bolles, of Findhorn's communications department, comments on the effects of the community's growth:

> Over the past 45 years the community has grown so much that
> not everyone in it gathers together on a regular basis any longer.
> Smaller groupings of people, with specialised interests or areas
> of work, have formed smaller communities within the larger
> community. Each of these smaller groupings organises itself in
> its own unique way, while at the same time being part of the
> wider Findhorn Foundation community. They are all linked by
> their shared positive vision for humanity and the planet and to
> the non-doctrinal spirituality that characterises Findhorn.[132]

The 'experiment in conscious living' applies to decision making at various levels, which includes 'meditating to open a space for intuitive information to be included in the decision-making process', she says.

The original Cluny Hill Hotel, which fired Peter and Eileen Caddy in 1962, is now Cluny Hill College, which also houses staff and the thousands of people who visit Findhorn every year for courses and workshops. The five-sided Universal Hall, built in the 1970s, hosts workshops, conferences, concerts and communal activities such as sacred dance. The New Findhorn Association comprises over 350 individual members and 30 organisations including publishing, crafts and ecological businesses. There is also a retreat house on the sacred island of Iona, and a smaller satellite community in the Inner Hebrides on the west coast of Scotland. Since 1997 Findhorn has been a non-governmental organisation associated with the United Nations – a far cry from its beginning as a penniless family planting a few vegetables outside their caravan.

SIR GEORGE TREVELYAN
AND THE WREKIN TRUST

Not many New Age leaders get full-length obituaries in the national press when they die, but Sir George Trevelyan, Bart., built up a wide respect during his ninety years. Sometimes known as 'the Father of the New Age', Trevelyan (1906–96) began his 'exploration into God' in 1942 when he went to a lecture given by a student of Rudolf Steiner (see p. 34). 'I have no doubt that this event in my life was staged by higher destiny, and that the time was ripe for a leap in consciousness,' he said.[133]

Sir George Trevelyan came from a British liberal aristocratic family; his father Sir Charles was a Labour cabinet minister under Ramsay MacDonald and his uncle G. M. Trevelyan was a well-known Cambridge historian, author of the classic *Illustrated English Social History*.[134]

After reading history at Cambridge he was apprenticed for two years as a furniture-maker in the tradition of William Morris. In the early 1930s he learned the Alexander technique (a system for relieving stress in the mind and body through movement, balance and posture) from its creator. Before the Second World War he taught at Gordonstoun School (later attended by Prince Charles), and in 1947 was appointed principal of Attingham Park, an adult education college in Shropshire. There he raised eyebrows by inviting Anthroposophical speakers and by teaching courses on 'Finding the Inner Teacher', 'Holistic Vision' and 'Death and Becoming'. He became a baronet in 1958 on the death of his father, who effectively disinherited him by leaving the family seat, Wallington Hall in Northumberland, to the National Trust.

Sir George Trevelyan explored a wide range of alternative ideas including organic farming (long before it became fashionable), communal living, the power of ley lines and the use of crystals. He was closely involved with a number of diverse organisations, not all of them New Age, including the Soil Association, the Findhorn Foundation (see p. 92), the Chalice Well in Glastonbury, the Teilhard de Chardin Society and the Lamplighter Movement, set up by his friend Wellesley Tudor Pole. He wrote numerous books, most of them now available online.

In 1982 he received the Right Livelihood award, known as the 'Alternative Nobel Prize', honouring those 'offering practical and exemplary answers to the most urgent challenges facing us today',[135] for 'educating the adult spirit to a new non-materialistic vision of human nature'.[136]

When Trevelyan retired in 1971 he set up the Wrekin Trust (named after a well-known hill near Attingham) as an educational trust, not promoting any particular doctrine but 'a holistic and spiritual world view which is based on the twin approaches of both science and mysticism'.[137] For twenty years, from 1971 to 1990, the Trust put on conferences and programmes so that thousands of people a year could 'explore leading edge topics in a non-sectarian way'. It believes:

> It is for each new generation, each new group, to work with the knowledge and the principles of spirituality in ways that are fresh, vibrant, bursting with life and relevant to their time. Our time is one of rapid change, great opportunity and great challenge too. It is also a time when the impulse for consciousness to awaken is very actively present.[138]

In 2000 the Wrekin Trust, with a number of other organisations, took the first steps to setting up what they call a 'University for Spirit', taking the root of the word 'university' to mean learning that is 'turned to the One'. Initially they have created the Wrekin Forum for Contemporary Spirituality, 'to bring together visionary individuals and organisations and to support their diverse work in seeking to deepen spiritual connection across society. By exchanging ideas and perceptions in a supportive environment and by combining resources and skills, a greater synergy can be created and projects of local, regional and even national significance can be initiated.'[139]

The Wrekin Forum, run largely by volunteers, is basically a network of like-minded people and organisations working on developing spiritual learning initiatives. One aspect of this is 'the raising of consciousness from one of separation to one of oneness and love as underpinning all life. This incorporates a holistic world view and the transformational journey we all need to make to shift from an egoic to a soul based level and thus play our part in the unfolding whole.'[140]

It has set up a number of regional and local forums for contemporary spirituality, which have their own events and workshops, sometimes in conjunction with other groups such as the Foundation of Holistic Spirituality (see p. 143). It has a particular focus on the needs of young people, and ran the Stoneleigh Project, 'taking marginalised young people on one week camps in remote places to help them find deeper connection within themselves, with nature, with each other and with "something other"'.[141]

The Wrekin Trust is deeply rooted in the ideals and aspirations of Sir George Trevelyan, whom it quotes: 'Out of the confusion of a crumbling society will emerge individuals who are touched by higher guidance. These will inevitably flow together with others of like inspiration, and a new quality of society will begin to form. This is the true adventure of our time.'[142]

TEMPLATE NETWORK
(FORMERLY EMIN)

The Template Foundation or Template Network developed from an organisation called the Emin, which began in 1972. According to senior British member Nick Woodeson:

> The Template Network is an international network of independent groups, with interests including personal development, spiritual development, personal religion, psychology, meditation, music, dance, ecology, healing, sustainable development, evolution and well-being ...
>
> There is no organisation called the Emin today. The name Emin has come to represent the philosophy and inspiration behind these groups which share the same philosophical foundations.[143]

The change from Emin to Template Network occurred gradually from 1996 onwards; there are websites under both names.

Like many other spiritual movements they say that they are not a religion as such: they are a group of people pursuing 'a natural philosophy and way of life'.[144] They were stung by an article in the *Observer Magazine* in 1995, 'A to Z of Cults', which described the Emin as 'a highly secretive British cult' that held 'clandestine meetings'.[145] In response, they pointed out at the time that they had been holding public meetings for over twenty years; they had also published an introductory booklet and had a website.

The usual media story about the origins of the Emin has its founder Leo, then known as Raymond Armin (1924–2002), sitting under a tree on Hampstead Heath in London receiving enlightenment. Emin spokesmen said that as a boy, like many others, he had a favourite place to go and think about life, but that this story is 'really a simplistic misinterpretation of what, for any human, is a complex process'; in any case, this had nothing to do with the start of the movement per se. The Emin began some thirty years later when 'a group of people searching for the meaning and purpose of life, most of whom were widely travelled, academically qualified, and had spent years investigating numerous philosophies and religions' without finding satisfactory answers, happened to meet Armin 'through a chance encounter' in 1972.

The chance encounter was when Armin's son John, then an ambulance driver, picked up a young woman who was carrying a book of Sufi tales. John mentioned that his father read similar books, the two met, a few of the woman's friends joined them, and the Emin began. Emin (pronounced E-min rather than Em-in) is apparently an Arabic word for 'Faithful One'.

Raymond Armin, born Raymond Schertenlieb, was the son of a Swiss immigrant to Britain. The family surname was changed to Armin; it was quite common to change Germanic surnames between the wars. As related by Emin members his early years appear to have had much in common with other founders of esoteric religious movements, from Madame Blavatsky (see p. 23) to G. I. Gurdjieff (see p. 44–5) to L. Ron Hubbard (see p. 362–3):

> His quest to discover the truth about living began as a young boy . . . During his young adult life he extensively researched and studied world history, science, world religions, philosophy and a whole range of other subjects. National Service took him to the Far East, where he explored Indian and other Eastern religions and traditions. These explorations were not just academic . . . The paramount quest in his life was to be true and aligned to whatever causes each human to be.[146]

How factual this is, or how much it is an idealised foundation myth, cannot really be said.

The Emin/Template Network say that Leo never looked for followers, and they do not see him as their founder or leader as such, 'but certainly the prime inspiration of those who formed the Emin endeavour'. When the early members of the Emin met him, 'they were staggered to find the great tangible results of his own researches and studies into many of the fundamental questions in living, which they found to be of uttermost use, not only in their own quest, but also in their everyday lives'. They persuaded him to provide them with writings and tapes of his researches, and began to pay him consultancy fees to enable him 'to pursue his research full time for the benefit of the growing number of Emin companions'.

Within two years of the first meeting there were about seventy members; by 2010 there were 360 in Britain, out of a total of around 1,700 worldwide. These numbers have been roughly stable for over a decade, as new members balance those who leave. Around 200 of the British members have been in the Emin for over fifteen years; Nick Woodeson and David Pearce, leading members in Britain, between them have 'nearly sixty years of experience in the Emin and the Template Network'.[147]

Leo himself retired from direct involvement in the Emin in 1985, but from his home in Florida continued 'to carry out commissioned work and assistance to different groups right up until the time of his death,' says Woodeson.[148] He died in 2002, aged seventy-eight.

In the early 1980s seven Emin families established a new settlement, known as the village of Maalé Tzvia, in Northern Israel:

> It is important to bear in mind that the Village is, firstly, a domestic Israeli settlement supported by the Jewish Settlement Agency and the government and, secondly, an Emin village, in the sense that the adults are Emin members who have sought to build a way of life for themselves which recognizes both local custom and Emin principles, tenets and understandings.

The Emin Village has now grown to over 130 families; because of its success 'it is now often used as a showcase example by the

Israeli authorities', say Woodeson and Pearce. But it has also faced considerable local opposition, accused by some of being a cult.[149]

There are Template Network groups in England and Wales, Canada, the United States, Australia, New Zealand, Israel, Brazil and seven European countries.

The movement has had a number of names over the years, which has led to some confusion. They now see their first ten years as experimental, trying out various paths and researching different areas. In 1977 they began 'a more advanced exploration' called the Eminent Way, which 'marked the transition of the Emin from external researches to internal processes, from learning to living'. That name is no longer widely used, though some individual members still pursue this area of work, which involves meditation. Although they still use the name Emin on one website,[150] from 1996 the Emin changed their name to the Template Network.[151]

The movement accept that they have made mistakes in the past. 'The whole evolution of the Emin endeavour has been trial and error because it is a real human endeavour,' say Woodeson and Pearce. Even Leo, who is clearly regarded simply as a wise man rather than any sort of spokesman for the divine, made mistakes in the way he guided the movement. In 1978, for instance, he established a Church in the United States, and wrote a book called *The Poem of the Church of Emin Coils*. 'This was an attempt to establish a foundation upon which a religion could develop. This attempt was abandoned, and the book has long since been withdrawn,' say Woodeson and Pearce.

In 1978 the satirical magazine *Private Eye* alleged that Leo was a fraud; the Emin began the process of suing for libel, but dropped the case because of the expense. There was further controversy in 1983 and 1984 when Conservative MP David Mellor tried to prevent the Emin from continuing to use a hall in Putney, south London, which they had been using since 1976; a public inquiry ruled that they should be allowed to continue using it. Around the same time there were several articles and interviews with Leo and members of the Emin in local papers, none of which did the movement's credibility much good, though the Emin deny that Leo actually uttered the more sensational quotations attributed to him.

The movement is still developing. Leo's teachings, and the discoveries and researches of members, are gathered in the Emin Archives, 'one of the most extensive and original bodies of philosophical writings in the world'.[152] In 1993, 'an effort was made to place all of the research that had taken place up to that time into a cohesive framework. Out from this came the "Emin Loom of Research Starters"' (see below); this remains part of the basis for the first few years of a person's engagement with the Template Network. When asked about the beliefs of the movement Woodeson and Pearce say, 'The dictionary definition and the popular use of the word "belief" implies the acceptance *without proof* of things or statements. No one in the Emin is required to believe anything. People are encouraged to undertake their own research upon which they may prove, or disprove, the content of Emin teaching.'

The teachings are open to constant revision and development, as members explore subjects more deeply. All their publications bear the statement: 'This publication is sold on the condition that the reader understands that the content herein is entirely philosophical until such time as it may be proven as fact.' As well as allowing for 'continuous revelation', this presumably covers them against any possible errors of fact, and also against the possibility of disgruntled ex-members claiming they have been required to believe any particular principles.

The movement has had several versions of its Philosophical Tenets over the years. The Emin website shows twenty-one,[153] but Woodeson says that an earlier version of just seven is still valid:

1. That the creation is ordered by natural law and that it grows towards completion and that human life is a high point of this growth.

2. That the human also grows and is pressing toward its own evolution and completion.
3. That the human is spiritual and has a duty to the universe, to itself and to the rest of humanity.
4. That the endeavour of human life is to learn and develop and upgrade the ways and contents of the mental faculty and the whole human potential according to natural law.
5. That the human race is meant to be in unison and agreement concerning the conduct of life on earth.
6. That there is life after death and that this must be planned for and worked for individually.
7. That to be constructive and opportunity engendering is the true way to be properly participant in life.

From these Tenets come material responses, such as:

1. To uphold the rightful elected law of the land . . .
2. To seek to develop one's own potential to the uttermost and to use one's natural gifts to the full.
3. To be resistant to the lowering of standards . . .
4. To be constructive in the keeping of good order and stability . . .
5. To strive to be useful by one's own work . . . and to be supportive of natural freedoms . . .
6. To be pathfinder in various ways that unlock situations in learning which otherwise prevent further progress, and to try to expand boundaries of understanding as a duty to the future.
7. To seek to be constantly well informed and increasing so as not to offer hypocrisy or deception to others or to self from the standpoint of ignorance.[154]

Generally there is a somewhat old-fashioned courtesy about the Emin/Template Network; for example, like some conservative religious movements, both Christian and Eastern, they tend to refer to women as 'ladies'.

Some members take new names, a practice common to many religious movements both new (the Hare Krishna movement ISKCON) and old (in the New Testament, Simon becoming Peter, Saul becoming Paul, and in the Roman Catholic Church, priests and nuns taking on different names to symbolise leaving their old lives behind). The Emin's names are often colours or precious stones (Emerald, Opal), or qualities on which the member wants to concentrate (Patience, Hope).

The emphasis in the movement is on individual and group study and discovery; Leo's writings in the Emin Archives are seen more as guidelines than as gospel. The Emin Stream – the first few years of members' work – is 'a live discovery into an array of subjects from theatre, the arts, barding, oratory, dance, to science, architecture, world history, the natural laws and the whole realm of personal development, behavioural sciences and becoming true to one's natural self'.

The 'Emin Loom of Research Starters' is a complex seven by seven chart on a 21 by 14 inch (53 by 36 cm) sheet. Down the left are two Connection Domains – 'Mentality Imagery' and 'Brain Perception'; two Alignment Domains – 'Emotions (Higher and Lower)/Feelings' and 'Process Reasonings/Instinct, Thinking, Moving Centres'; and three Reference Domains – 'Functions, Soul Related/White-Red-Blue, White-Pale Yellow-Pale Blue', 'Groundwork, Headwork, Heartwork, Practice, Meditation' and, finally, 'Learning, Understanding, Mixing, Matching'. Along the top are 1. Governing Views – 'Genius'; 2. Governing Reason – 'Genetic'; 3. Governing Intentions – 'Generation'; and four further unlabelled columns.

Woodeson makes the point that this is a summary chart, and that 'the concepts within it are explored, explained and referenced in many other archives', but the contents of the chart, or Loom, are an excellent example of the specialist use of language within a religious movement (Scientology is another prime example). Language is used in such a way as to make sense of the movement to a member, who has been introduced to the concepts and terminology gradually and systematically, while being utterly baffling to the outsider. This accounts in part for the accusations of secrecy often made against some alternative religious movements, especially those with a progressive path of learning and development.

(Pointing out the use of complex language is not necessarily a criticism of such movements. Most academic disciplines have their own terminology which can be quite opaque to outsiders, while someone with no familiarity with standard Christian terminology would be equally baffled by such 'technical terms' as salvation, atonement and Trinity, let alone Paraclete, predestination or transubstantiation. When the New Testament was put into Basic English, which has a vocabulary of only 850 words, it was found necessary to use 150 additional words because of the specialist nature of the text.)[155]

Quoting just two examples taken at random from the forty-nine boxes of the Emin Loom will illustrate the point:

2–5 That the human complex, carnal and electromagnetic, is plasmagenic theatre allowing, in which the cosmic relation and government is 1/3 expendable, 1/3 maintenance, 1/3 custodial.
3–6 That human in planetary domicile is evolutary, individually and/or collectively, in the presence of transference, which is the persuasions of human semi-conscious and superior conscious alignment by design and attribute and acumen.[156]

Leo's books also use language in unusual ways. One of the primary Emin texts, Leo's first book *Dear Dragon*, begins:

Hello, another person, whatever is your way and style. My name, self-chosen – for this, in truth, must it be – is POEM. Welcome to my purpose, that is not a story. Within this, you will learn and flavour much, that somehow, in some mysterious way, will move you, touch often something deep and powerful in your person.

   Description of normal kind will not suffice; for the Blue Roses of Forgetfulness and that very fast something, seen from the corner of the eye, instantly gone, seen, but not understood, are only the path that leads to the first gate of passing through to the Way of the Dear Dragon . . .

   Pemero sends you this gift . . . And although, you not remembering it in its entirety, I tell you, there are parts of you that will retain its essence eagerly.[157]

Dear Dragon is a mystical, poetical book, and its style of writing reflects this, but the language is strange, at times unwieldy and often syntactically convoluted. A critic might ask – particularly as members of the movement (like those of many other alternative religions) tend to be intelligent, well-educated, cultured middle-class people – why they do not at least tidy up Leo's grammar.

Perhaps because the teachings of the Template Network are constantly developing, there has been confusion over some matters. In the (now withdrawn) *Poem of the Church of Emin Coils*, for example, Leo asserted: 'At no time will homosexuality, lesbianism, transvestism, nymphonic or any other unnatural condition or freak practice . . . be permitted'.[158] Now, according to Woodeson and Pearce, the movement 'does not refuse entry to homosexuals'. However, like many of the esoteric schools, it does refuse to take on drug addicts or people with mental illness.

Like several other quasi-religious philosophical movements the Template Network is clearly involved in developing human potential, using different terminology and techniques but perhaps reaching towards similar ends to such personal development movements as Insight, Landmark Forum and the former est (Erhard Seminars Training).[159] Much of its terminology also reveals an esoteric element analogous to, for example, Builders of the Adytum (see p. 220) – for example, 'birth on earth is the beginning of a universal organic immortality', and 'human life is designed to be "living spirit of God" in unquickened universal expansions'.[160] They do not consider that they are the only ones with the truth: 'Personal spiritual development has always been possible for any human life . . . Emin companions hold their own religious beliefs. Many are Christians, Jews, Muslims etc. We uphold the right of all individuals to pursue their own faith,' say Woodeson and Pearce.[161]

Among the many areas of study for members are astrology and Tarot. Their own Gemrod Tarot pack (Major Arcana only) is substantially different from traditional designs; some of the card titles have been changed, including the Lover to Life, the Hermit to the Searcher, Temperance to 'The Communication (the Searcher reaches Land's End)', the Devil to the Green Man, and the World to the Nymph of Ability; the unnumbered Fool card has been dropped altogether. A later Major Arcana, marketed as the Frown Strong pack, also shows many differences from traditional packs, though this one does have a Fool equivalent, called 'The Card of Negation'. The attitude towards Tarot has modified over the years. In 1995 Woodeson and Pearce said:

> It is widely recognized that the Tarot has been significantly misrepresented and misused throughout the course of history. Early Emin research included the construction of a pictorial mosaic of understanding, based on the study of the laws and the influences that affect human development. This was an attempt to rediscover the original nature of the Tarot, which constituted a comprehensive encyclopedia of human development ... definitely not a fortune-telling tool.

But in 2010 Woodeson said: 'Whilst the Taro [*sic*] packs still form part of the archives, they are not very often used today within the Template Network.'

Accounts of the Emin/Template Network often include a number of 'laws' based on numbers:

> The law of two [concerns] opposites/adjacencies, the male/female principles, energy and matter etc. The law of four concerns cyclic phenomena, i.e. the seasons, the phases of the moon, biorhythms, the four elements. The law of seven concerns the major planets and the spectrum colours, and the law of five concerns the five centres of the human, which are thinking, moving, instinctive, emotional and sexual.[162]

Although one writer on new religious movements asserts dismissively that 'Leo's laws seem to be a bizarre mix of psycho-babble and New Age interests',[163] it is clear that members of the Template Network, like many other alternative religious, philosophical and personal development movements, take an eclectic approach to their study and their teachings; if they find something useful, they use it (compare the similarly eclectic approach of many esoteric groups, particularly 'Chaos Magic', p. 244). For example, both in their teaching of laws of number and in their emphasis on dance and music as means of approaching inner truths, there are strong echoes of Gurdjieffian philosophy (see p. 48).

One area which might be called 'New Age' is Aura Cleaning. They teach that: 'the electro-magnetic radiation of the human constitutes a field known as the aura. As the physical body needs regular cleansing, so does the aura. Headaches and irritability are often caused by imbalances in the aura. There are specific yet simple movements that we have developed to clear the pathways and balance the energy levels in the aura.'[164] This is known as Electrobics. Former members mention groups of people flexing their fingers and flapping their arms rhythmically; members simply say that it works.

One of the most visible expressions of their work, for outsiders, is their use of music, dance, theatre and art as means to unlock human potential; the Template Network may be first encountered in its music or theatre work, in addition to philosophical workshops. Members who are musicians have produced a number of music CDs which seek 'to capture and clothe in sound, rhythm and harmony the fine essence qualities and values that can balance, refresh and realign a person to cause much well-being'.[165] The use of colour is also important to the Emin: 'green promotes vigour, yellow promotes value, blue promotes regulation',[166] and so on. Such attributions could be compared to magical correspondences (see p. 202–3). The Emin website has, in addition to the more usual Home, Background and Contact links, unlabelled green, yellow, blue, red and white buttons leading to pages on different concepts.[167]

What I Believe . . .
Secrecy

Yes, there is a need for it. The secrecy about the art of magic is necessary. First of all – things that are very intimate are always best kept secret, you don't share that with everybody. Magic is a secret between yourself and the gods.

This intimacy is also built on a mutual trust between you and the community with whom you work, so there is a privacy, you don't throw that trust on the street.

Then there is the discretion that is necessary when people have intensive experiences.
**Ina Cüsters-van Bergen, Magister,
Hermetic Order of the Temple of Starlight**

Not in my world. It's open to argument, to conjecture, because that's how I learn. I do public rituals; I don't do anything private, nothing secret.
**Terry Dobney, Keeper of the Stones at Avebury
Retired motorcycle restorer**

I would bring back the D word, discretion. I really do think that that's important . . .

You go into something because you want the benefits of that group, and one of the benefits of that group is a gentle exclusivity. And you should respect that group. There are no secrets other than the experience of working in the group with people who know what they're doing, whatever it happens to be.
**Geraldine Beskin, third-generation esoteric witch
and eclectic occultist
Co-owner of the Atlantis Bookshop, London**

Secrecy in religion: every one of them has it to some extent, and I do feel that most of them have it for fashion reasons; there aren't many secrets, and of those some probably aren't worth knowing.

Dr Dave Evans, Chaos magician
Social Sciences researcher

With certain kinds of ceremonies such as initiation what is unknown to you is not in fact the content of the ritual which you might well have read beforehand but something much more subtle which couldn't be put into words – an unspeakable secret not in the sense that you're not supposed to speak it, but something can happen which you couldn't explain in words to somebody who hadn't experienced it. That can happen with rituals and initiations. I think those things are the real secrets. The actual words and actions in a ritual generally speaking are not secret in any sense – though some people try and pretend they are.

Gareth J. Medway, Priest Hierophant of the
Fellowship of Isis
Writer and assistant psychic

What I think is the real issue or the more important issue is *privacy* in religion . . .

We have lost the ability to trust and no longer can tolerate the idea that people and groups might prefer to do some things in private.

Dr Michael York, Shaman
Retired Professor of Cultural Astronomy and Astrology,
Bath Spa University

The Emin Centre in north London, 'the primary meeting place for members and their research and project activities', offers a variety of activities including 'talks and workshops, concerts, research teams, art groups and personal religion to healing workshops, theatre experiments, musical cafés and a weekly parent and toddler group'.[168] Unlike some movements the website makes it clear that 'The majority of events at The Centre are based on, or derived from, the Emin philosophy'.

Nick Woodeson stresses that the Template Network is a continuously evolving movement:

> The Template Network today is very different from the Emin of years ago. The Emin had more of an emphasis on teaching and learning, where many of the larger meetings were lectures. The Template Network has much more emphasis on individual initiative, practical application, independent research and project groups. The Template Network is also more fluid in its organisation than the Emin of the past. Different groups in each country manage their own affairs independently, although there is constant communication between different groups and many international gatherings, workshops and projects.[169]

The terminology of the Template Network might frequently be unusual if not incomprehensible to outsiders, but its aims, and the various paths of study that the members follow, appear to be an eclectic mixture of ideas common to many esoteric, New Age and personal development movements; the main difference from most other religious and quasi-religious movements is that, under whatever name, it started from scratch rather than being based on an already existing tradition.

UFO GROUPS AND
MILLENNIAL EXPECTATIONS

Idaho businessman Kenneth Arnold has a lot to answer for; to be more accurate, the blame should attach to the newspaper reporter who misquoted him in 1947 as saying he had seen 'flying saucers'. He had actually told the reporter that the objects he saw 'flew erratic, like a saucer if you skip it across the water';[170] the word 'saucer' applied to their movement, not to their shape. But within a year or so, flying saucers (or unidentified flying objects) were everywhere.

It was inevitable that people would interpret certain passages in the Bible in the science fictional light of UFOs – for example, Ezekiel's vision:

> The appearance of the wheels and their work was like unto the colour of a beryl; and they four had one likeness; and their appearance and their work was as it were a wheel in the middle of a wheel ...
> I heard also the noise of the wings of the living creatures that touched one another, and the noise of the wheels over against them, and a noise of great rushing. (Ezekiel 1:16, 3:13)

Erich von Däniken also has a lot to answer for, with a host of popular books such as *Chariots of the Gods* and *In Search of Ancient Gods*, which sparked off a legion of imitators. But to adapt the title of a similar book, he was not the first.[171]

For many, the subject of alien visitations, let alone alien abductions, raises only an amused reaction.[172] But there are many religious movements linked to UFOs and extraterrestrial beings, some more serious than others, and some very serious indeed. The group which became known as Heaven's Gate after the name of their website committed mass suicide in 1997 in order to free the divine spirits trapped within physical shells, their human bodies, and go off to the next level of existence in a spaceship. When Earth was approached by Comet Hale-Bopp in March 1997 one photograph appeared to show a small dot behind the comet. Someone claimed on the Art Bell radio show that this was a UFO; when a well-known practitioner of so-called Scientific Remote Viewing said this was an alien space-craft, Heaven's Gate leader Marshall Herff Applewhite had the sign he had been waiting for, that they should 'disconnect . . . from the human physical container'. The group, apparently perfectly happily, went to join their brothers in space.[173]

Some UFO groups spring up, flourish for a year or two, and fade away; others are longer-lasting. One, British in origin, has been around since 1955 and shows no sign of vanishing into the deep blue sky (see p. 119).

One of the earliest flying saucer groups, in the American Midwest, predicted that a UFO would come to collect them before a destructive flood on 21 December 1954. How the group coped with this not happening became the basis of the sociological classic *When Prophecy Fails* (1956) by Leon Festinger et al., and lay behind the development of Festinger's famous theory of cognitive dissonance, when beliefs or expec-tations are out of step with reality. Two of the group, including its leader, 'Mrs Keech', 'had been involved in Dianetics and Scientology prior to their commitment to this esoteric movement' (see p. 361).[174] The event (or non-event) and the controversial infiltration of the UFO group by social scientists also inspired the novel *Imaginary Friends* (1967) by Alison Lurie, who taught literature at Cornell University.

Festinger's theory and his methodology have been chal-lenged, most notably by one of the leading American scholars of new religions, J. Gordon Melton, who points out flaws in the co-authors' suppositions and reasoning, and their lack of understanding of millennial religions.[175]

The thwarted millennial expectation of Festinger's UFO group was nothing new. There is a long tradition of Christian groups being disappointed by the non-arrival of Jesus on the date they foretold. William Miller's 'Great Disappointment' of 1843 and 1844, the Jehovah's Witnesses in 1874, 1914, 1925 and 1975, and the Worldwide Church of God in 1975[176] are the best known examples in recent years.

Despite the expectations of popular writers, few religious groups forecast Jesus's return in 2000. Just as few, if any, had done so in 1000: the idea that thousands of believers in sackcloth and ashes awaited Jesus's second coming exactly a thousand years after his first is 'a romantic invention, dating back no further than the sixteenth century'.[177] At the time of publication of this book in 2011, many individuals and groups are still foretelling something supernaturally or galactically spectacular, if not the end of the world, for 2012 (see p. 141). Time will soon tell if they are right, or not.

Belief in Jesus's imminent return goes right back to the New Testament writers,[178] and has been a feature of millennialist groups in almost every century since then.[179] How do they cope with the fact that he has not (at least yet) kept to the schedule others keep setting for him?

Sometimes the failure of their expectations leads to loss of membership; both the Jehovah's Witnesses and the Worldwide Church of God lost some members, who were both disappointed by Jesus's non-arrival and disillusioned by the failed prophecies of their Churches' leaders – seen as either their fallibility or, worse, their falsehoods. But in fact comparatively few left either religion because, as Melton argues, 'within religious groups, prophecy seldom fails'.[180] Over the centuries religious groups have developed a number of coping techniques to deal with the disconfirmation of their deeply held beliefs. These include: 'We miscalculated; come back next year', which is broadly what the Adventist William Miller said in 1843;[181] 'It occurred, but on an invisible plane', which adds another layer of belief but has the twin advantages that the religion can still claim they were right, and that they can't be proven wrong; or 'The Lord was merciful and stayed his hand', which emphasises God's love and restraint; or 'Our faith wasn't strong enough', shifting the blame to the Church members; or a flat denial, 'We never actually claimed that anyway' (millennial religions have a long history of rewriting history); or, very occasionally, an honest 'We were wrong' or 'Our enthusiasm got the better of us'.

A beautiful late-Victorian description of cognitive dissonance, decades before Festinger's coining of the term, comes in a description of the English nineteenth-century millennial group, the Catholic Apostolic Church, who when Jesus didn't return on schedule were: 'forced by the stern logic of life to turn their backs upon their past history, and to make their doctrines square with facts when facts absolutely refuse to square with doctrines'.[182]

The coping strategies of disappointed millennialist Christians are much the same as those of other prophets of near-future events. Benjamin Creme's explanation for the Maitreya not turning up in the East End of London when he said he would was the insincerity and lack of belief of the journalists assembled to greet him (or not) (see p. 42). The Raelians (see p. 127) want to build an embassy for when the Elohim visit the Earth, and expect this to happen before 2030 – but they have already said that the space visitors will not come if they feel they are not welcome by the majority of mankind, which seems a safe advance get-out clause.

Uriel (Ruth Norman, 1900–93), one of the founders of Unarius, a UFO movement based near San Diego, California, told her followers that aliens would come openly to Earth in 1974, then 1975, then 1976 and then 2001 – by which time she could no longer be embarrassed by her failed prophecy. The movement's justification of the non-event is that the Space

Brothers have now decided not to appear visibly 'until people stop their warlike attitudes and practices'.[183] It may be waiting some time.

Several religious movements have UFO or other science-fictional elements, including Scientology (see p. 360–1), Guy Ballard's I AM Religious Activity (see p. 66) and the early Findhorn Foundation (see p. 93); but shortly we shall look in detail at just two flying saucer groups – the Aetherius Society (see p. 119) and the Raelian Movement (see p. 127).

Many outsiders who are quite prepared to accept the sincerity of Moonies and Mormons throw up their hands at the thought of people seriously believing that alien beings have come in flying saucers to bring mankind a message from the gods. But is this really any more unbelievable than the basis of many other religions, including Christianity? To quote one sociologist of religion: 'After all, suspension of disbelief is *de rigueur* in religious groups, if not all groups for that matter.'[184] As the White Queen says to Alice, 'Why, sometimes I've believed as many as six impossible things before breakfast.'[185] Most people, if they are prepared to be honest, do so – at least by lunch.

It is important to accept that the members of these movements believe in the extraterrestrial origin of the messages given to them, just as Mormons believe in Joseph Smith's golden plates, and Christians believe that the Creator of the Universe became a man for thirty-three years; they should not be dismissed as 'UFO nuts'. They are normal, intelligent people; their belief is genuine, and their religions are worth as much attention as all the others in this book.

For those who question either the rationality or the truthfulness of these movements and their founders, it should be pointed out that there are now many thousands of people who say they have talked with aliens, or have been abducted by them. They don't just claim this; they believe it. For them it is as much a fact as the colour of their car or the name of their home town. So far as other people are concerned they might well be deluding themselves, but if so they are not doing it deliberately. Psychologists and sociologists have a number of theories – including False Memory Syndrome (see p. 257–8), well-studied sleep phenomena such as sleep paralysis, and hypnagogic and hypnopompic hallucinations,[186] or the combined effect on our collective world view of Cold War fears, science fiction films, 'future shock' and sexual insecurity – but most agree that such 'abductees' are sincere in their beliefs. So are those whose religions originated in messages from extraterrestrials.

It is not only the flying saucer groups which have some belief in UFOs. Like a number of other Christian groups, the Family (formerly the Children of God) see UFOs as a clear sign that we are in the End Times. Some see them as the way that Satan's forces will wreak havoc upon the Earth. But others see their occupants as angels, and their purpose as more benign: to carry true believers away to the glorious next life after death.[187] The Norse myths tell of the Valkyries, shining beings who carried away fallen warriors to their reward in Odin's hall; UFOs are, perhaps, amongst many other things, today's version of that myth.

An alternative perspective considers that people have been having profound religious experiences and visions (or visual and auditory hallucinations), whether of the Fair Folk or of the Blessed Virgin Mary, for millennia; receiving messages from aliens could be seen as simply a modern rendering of the same thing.[188] The initial personal experience is important, but it is the later narrative explanation placed upon it that determines the interpretation, the ultimate meaning, of the event – and turns subjective personal history into religious myth. The same process that creates religious myth also creates narratives of alien abduction, past lives as Marie Antoinette and 'recovered memories' of abuse (see p. 258).

It could, of course, be possible that extraterrestrials have spoken to the founders of these movements; in any case, no one can prove otherwise.

AETHERIUS SOCIETY

His Eminence Sir George King (1919–97), born in Shropshire, England, founded one of the first and certainly the longest lasting of the flying saucer groups in 1955. His titles included, amongst others, Metropolitan Archbishop of the Aetherius Churches, Grand Master of the Mystical Order of St Peter, Count de Florina, His Serene Highness Prince George King de Santorini and Knight Grand Cross of Justice with Grand Collar in the Sovereign Military Orthodox Dynastic Imperial Constantinian Order of Saint Georges, as well as the rather more mundane Doctor of Science, Theology, Literature, Sacred Humanities and Philosophy – though according to Richard Lawrence, Executive Secretary of the Aetherius Society,[189] he did not usually make use of most of his titles and degrees.

Neither the chivalric titles nor the 'doctorates' were recognised by any mainstream bodies; the 'doctorates' were awarded by, amongst others, the International Theological Seminary of California, a degree mill with no accreditation and a tiny faculty.[190] (Both Gerald Gardner, founder of Wicca, and L. Ron Hubbard, founder of Scientology, also claimed dubious doctorates; see p. 291 and p. 363)

King's consecration as a bishop was from the Theosophy-related Liberal Catholic Church (see p. 56). His 'knighthood' was from the Byzantine Royal House in exile, and was not recognised by the College of Arms in England.[191] According to Mark Bennett of the Aetherius Society, King was given these titles and 'doctorates' as 'a token offer of gratitude' for his work.[192]

Lawrence admits that King did not have either a British knighthood or a baronetcy, as the title 'Sir' might imply, and that he did not hold any academic doctorates.[193] Despite this the Aetherius Society continues to give him one title or the other in their books, leaflets and website.

King began practising yoga in 1944 and 'developed his latent powers to such an extent that he attained the much sought-after deep trance state of Samadhi in which many of the hidden secrets of the Cosmos were revealed to him.'[194]

According to his own testimony, King was in his London flat in May 1954 when he clearly heard a voice saying 'Prepare yourself! You are to become the voice of Interplanetary Parliament.' A week later 'an Indian Swami of world renown' stepped through the locked door of his flat and instructed him to 'form a group of willing helpers'; he should also extend his training in yoga, and 'Pray, be still, meditate and open the doors of your heart and mind to the precious waters of Truth.' Before long, King was receiving telepathic messages: 'A message from Venus was recorded on our tape recorder for the first time.'[195]

King hired a room in Caxton Hall, London, and began to deliver messages from the Cosmic Masters based on other planets. The first Cosmic Master to speak to him, from the planet Venus, used the pseudonym Aetherius. King founded the Aetherius Society in 1955.

Cosmic Masters are highly advanced beings from other planets, and are not the same as Ascended Masters, who are humans who have stepped off the wheel of reincarnation and have now returned to live extremely long lives on Earth. The Ascended Masters or the Great White Brotherhood in the Aetherius Society are a variant of beliefs shared with many other esoteric religious movements, including Eckankar,[196] Theosophy (see p. 23), Benjamin Creme's Share International (see p. 41), the I AM movement (see p. 65) and the Church

Universal and Triumphant (see p. 70): a living spiritual hierarchy of Masters, who included Jesus, Buddha, Krishna and
other great religious teachers.

Over the next forty years King received over 600 'Cosmic
transmissions', and wrote over thirty-five books based on
them, including *The Twelve Blessings*, *The Nine Freedoms*,
The Five Temples of God, *The Day the Gods Came*, *Flying
Saucers*, *My Contact with the Great White Brotherhood* and
others; his last book, co-written with Richard Lawrence, was
*Contacts with the Gods from Space: Pathway to the New
Millennium* (1996); another, *Realise Your Inner Potential*, was
completed after King's death.

King received most of the messages when he was on his own
or with a few members of the society. When receiving a Cosmic
Transmission in public, King would sit on stage wearing dark
glasses and go into a trance state. Sometimes a voice known as
Mars Sector 6 would speak through him, perhaps giving
warnings of impending troubles on Earth. Then Aetherius, or
one of the other Cosmic Masters, would speak through him,
delivering spiritual and moral teaching, and messages of hope
and encouragement.

George King died in July 1997. The movement, more so
than many, had made plans for how they would continue after
his death, making sure that there was a clear administrative and
ecclesiastical structure in place. According to Lawrence, 'We
looked at other groups when their leader died, and learnt from
it.' The organisational structure was set up by King; Lawrence
says: 'He had a prerogative; we deferred to him by choice, to
his authority. It's probably more democratic since he died, but
this was set up before he died.' The beliefs and practices of the
Aetherius Society have not changed since King's death, but
Lawrence is clear that there will be no more Cosmic
Transmissions. They were specific to King's lifetime, and the
movement is now in a post-prophetic phase.

Although George King never made this claim during his life,
his followers now believe that 'his full being was a Cosmic

Master native to another planet'[197] – whose number include the Buddha, Jesus, and many other prophets and god-figures of other religions. Lawrence says that King is revered as an avatar, but not worshipped.[198]

The Church hierarchy currently comprises three active bishops, of whom Lawrence is one, half a dozen priests and perhaps twenty-five ministers. There are also ten senior engineering officers (five in Britain, five in the United States) with technical responsibility for the Church's missions. King's widow, also a bishop, is on the board of directors at the American headquarters in Los Angeles. The Church's spokesman is clear that neither she nor Lawrence is the leader of the Aetherius Society.

> We do not have a leader. That is to say, Dr King will always be regarded as our Spiritual leader, despite not being physically incarnate among us, but no one else has ever assumed or will ever assume this position in any respect. The organisation is run by three international bodies which run different aspects of the Society's work. The members of these bodies all have equal votes within the body to which they belong.[199]

Current worldwide membership of the Aetherius Society, according to Lawrence, is 'in the thousands, but not tens of thousands'. The largest numbers of members are in the UK, USA, New Zealand and Africa. In Britain there are maybe 600, with about 6,000 on their mailing list. Many of the members have been with the movement for three decades or more. There are a dozen groups around Britain and four in North America, with others in Africa and Australasia. There is an outside impression that the membership is middle-aged and elderly, but Lawrence says that there has been an increasing number of young people in the last few years. The only rule for full members, says Lawrence, is that 'they must attend a certain number of activities'.

The beliefs of the Aetherius Society are Theosophical and New Age, and also include aspects of Christianity and Buddhism, amongst others; their religious services use both Christian prayers – including a new version of the Lord's Prayer – and Buddhist mantras. They believe in reincarnation based on the Law of Karma – or, in Paul's words, 'whatsoever a man soweth, that shall he also reap' (Galatians 6:7). We progress, life by life, towards perfection: 'Man came forth from God and all things are a part of God. There is nothing but God in the Cosmos, in varying stages of evolution. Everyone will eventually become a Master and will continue evolving from there.'[200] Masters can be male or female.

Although George King often wrote of his journeys in space-craft to other planets, he made it clear that this was a form of astral travel; in these journeys his body never left his London flat. The beings whom he met and conversed with on other planets were in some cases the inhabitants of those planets, spiritual beings with physical bodies, though not in the same way that humans are physical. Even in the 1950s it was thought unlikely that physical Martians or Venusians could exist; these beings live on these planets in another dimension, on another plane. Although they are higher than us in their spiritual development, like us they are progressing through their spiritual evolution. But the beings who gave King his teachings are way beyond this; they are Cosmic Masters.

Specific to the Aetherius Society is the belief that each planet in our solar system is akin to a classroom, where we learn certain life-lessons before progressing to the next planet: 'A person may have to live on a Planet for thousands of lives before he has learned the required lessons and can pass the "examination" so that he can graduate to the next higher Planet – the length of time spent in "school" varying with each individual lifestream, depending on how much effort he puts into living by God's Laws.'

The solar system is governed by a Cosmic Hierarchy, or Interplanetary Parliament: 'This is made up of very highly elevated Masters and is based on the Planet Saturn. This Hierarchy, in turn, is responsible to the Lords of the Sun for the evolution of every lifestream in the Solar System.'

Of the great Cosmic Masters who have come to Earth, Jesus and Buddha came from Venus, and Krishna came from Saturn:

> They all taught the same principles or Laws of God. Therefore, man's great major religions sprang from the same source (Masters from other Planets) and the principles were identical.
>
> Some of these Cosmic Masters spoke through King; in 1958, for example, the Master Jesus gave some new teachings entitled the Twelve Blessings, which he urged mankind to accept as their Bible.

The Aetherius Society see Jesus in a very different way from mainstream Christianity: 'The Master Jesus was an exceptionally elevated being from the planet Venus ('the bright and morning star' referred to in Revelations [sic], chapter 22, verse 16) who came to Earth in an extraterrestrial spacecraft in order to live among us. His main mission here was to die in order to bear karma on behalf of the human race.'[201]

A few Masters live on Earth; before long another great one will come, whose 'magic will be greater than any upon the Earth – greater than the combined materialistic might of all the armies. And they who heed not His words shall be removed from the Earth'[202] – not to be destroyed, says Lawrence, but to go to another planet to continue their evolutionary process elsewhere. The coming Master will appear openly, as with Benjamin Creme's Maitreya, but unlike him he will appear in a flying saucer.

They believe that 'a great millennium of peace will come to Earth as prophesied throughout the ages, but there will be much turmoil and suffering before this occurs'. The millennium depends largely on man's own efforts, rather than being imposed from above.

The Aetherius Society's belief in cooperation with people from other planets is quite sincere – and they do not claim exclusivity. 'We're not out to change existing religions so much as to add a cosmic dimension to them,' says Lawrence.

The Aetherius Society is happy to call itself New Age. It teaches and practises spiritual healing, alternative medicine, yoga and dowsing, amongst others. Healing is 'the transfer of Prana, the Universal Life Force, from the Healer to the patient. This energy, which flows freely throughout space, when channelled into a person suffering from disease can bring about a state of balance within that person.'[203] Anyone can heal; it is not a special gift, but the birthright of every person on Earth.

The basis of all the Society's teachings is 'service to others'. The most unusual aspect of this work is known as Operation Prayer Power. A group of members invoke spiritual energy by chanting mantras and prayers. This energy is focused and transferred to trained prayer team members, who then pour it into 'a specially designed radionic apparatus' known as a Spiritual Energy Battery. These batteries can store vast amounts of spiritual energy indefinitely; the energy can later be released, specifically to help in times of crisis, such as a war or earthquake.

The Aetherius Society regularly engages in 'Spiritual Pushes' in which, by praying and meditating, they are able to draw Prana (a concept borrowed from the Vedas) down to Earth from a huge spaceship, Satellite Number Three, in close orbit around the Earth; the spaceship is shielded so that it does not show up through telescopes or radar.

In addition to charging Spiritual Energy Batteries, between 1958 and 1961 members of the Aetherius Society took part in Operation Starlight, climbing eighteen mountains around the world so that the Cosmic Masters could charge them with spiritual power. Members now make regular pilgrimages to the peaks of these mountains, where the movement's symbol is painted.

The Society's literature quotes various prophecies made by the Cosmic Masters through George King, which they claim have since come true. In 1958, for example, their magazine *Cosmic Voice* gave details of an atomic accident in Russia that was not known about in the West until 1976; reporting on this in 1978, *New Scientist* magazine apparently said it had 'been scooped by a UFO'. Also in the 1950s, King was receiving messages warning of the long-term genetic effects of radiation.

Among the evils that the Aetherius Society campaigns against are pollution and nuclear power; they argue they were several years ahead of today's green movement. However, such issues are symptoms of a greater problem.

'The Aetherius Society believes that the only major crisis on Earth is the spiritual energy crisis. If that is solved, all other crises will also be solved,' says Lawrence.

RAELIAN MOVEMENT

On 13 December 1973, in Clermont-Ferrand, France, a twenty-seven-year-old sports journalist and would-be racing driver, Claude Vorilhon (now known as Raël), was contacted by a being from another planet and given a message for mankind; he related this in his first book, *Le Livre qui Dit la Verité* (1974). The basic message is that mankind was created by an extraterrestrial race, referred to as the Elohim in the Book of Genesis in the Bible. They are not God or gods, but humans just like us – though physically a little smaller, with pale green skin, and thousands of years more advanced.

On 7 October 1975 Raël was contacted again, and this time he was invited into a spacecraft and taken to the Elohim's own planet; this is not in our solar system, but is in our galaxy. Raël wrote about this experience in his second book, *Les Extra-Terrestres M'ont Emmené sur Leur Planete* (1975).

These books have been reissued under a bewildering number of titles in French, English and other languages. The first two books, in one volume, have been translated into English several times, first as *Space Aliens Took Me to Their Planet* (1978); then as *The Message Given to Me by Extra-terrestrials: They Took Me to Their Planet* (1986); then in 1998 as *The Final Message*, a new translation by former Reuters foreign correspondent Anthony Grey, at the time head of the British Raelian Movement; and then in 2005 as *Intelligent Design: Message from the Designers*, which also included a new translation by

Grey of Raël's third book, *Accueiller les Extra-Terrestres* (1979), originally published as *Let's Welcome Our Fathers From Space* (1986). Further teachings can be found in *Geniocracy* (1978) about a proposed new political system; *La Méditation Sensuelle* (1980) – *Sensual Meditation* (1986); *Yes to Human Cloning* (2000); and *The Maitreya* (2004), extracts from Raël's teachings at his seminars. The first two books were also published in one volume as *Le Vrai Visage de Dieu* (The True Face of God) in 1999.

The world entered 'the Age of Apocalypse' with the first nuclear bomb in 1945;[204] Raël was born in 1946. A Frenchman was chosen for the Elohim's message because France is 'a country where new ideas are welcomed and where it is possible to talk about such ideas openly'. Raël himself was chosen because his father was Jewish and his mother Catholic; 'we considered you an ideal link between two very important peoples in the history of the world'. However, Raël's *biological* father was one of the Elohim, named Yahweh. While on their planet he was told:

> The person whom you looked upon as your father was not your real father. After the explosion at Hiroshima, we decided that the time had come for us to send a new messenger on Earth. He would be the last prophet, but the first one to address Mankind asking them to understand and not to believe. We then selected a woman, as we had done in the time of Jesus. This woman was taken aboard one of our ships and inseminated as we had done with the mother of Jesus. Then she was freed after we had totally erased from her memory all traces of what had happened.[205]

Raël is thus Jesus's half-brother.

This account of Raël's visit to the Elohim planet and what he learned there is the basis, the foundation myth, of the Raelian Movement.

In his speeches Raël frequently identifies himself as the Messiah. His followers also refer to him as the Maitreya, or 'Maitreya from the West', which seems to link the Raelian

Movement with Theosophical ideas, the Great White Brotherhood, Krishnamurti (see p. 31) and Benjamin Creme (see p. 41–3); this title appears strangely at odds with the movement's claim to be an atheist religion.[206]

Their appropriation of the term Maitreya, with its very specific associations with a number of other religions, could lead to some confusion. However, Glenn Carter, a British actor and singer-songwriter who has been UK leader of the Raelians since 2002, says that 'Maitreya' is simply how Japanese Raelians, with their cultural background in Buddhism, refer to Raël as a term of respect, and 'that's caught on in the movement'.[207] He dismisses any other religion's usage of the term as irrelevant: 'That's nothing to do with us; that's for other people. We're not linking it to any other historical reference or anything else.'

The Raelian Movement also sells statues of Raël in the typical pose of the Buddha.[208] Carter emphasises that while Raël is 'special and respected and revered' in the movement 'he is in no way worshipped'.

Raël teaches that mankind is now sufficiently developed to understand that we were deliberately created by a race called the Elohim who are some 25,000 years more advanced than we are. In Genesis the word Elohim is translated as 'God', but in Hebrew it is actually a plural noun; according to Raël it means 'those who come from the sky'. (Raël means 'the messenger of those who come from the sky'.) Mankind was created, by manipulation of DNA, in the image of the Elohim.

> Leaving our humanity to progress by itself, the Elohim nevertheless maintained contact with us via prophets, including Buddha, Moses, Jesus and Muhammad, all specially chosen and educated by them in order to progressively educate humanity by delivering this message, adapted to the level of culture and understanding at the time. They were also to leave written references to the Elohim so that we would be able to recognise them as our creators and fellow human beings when we had advanced enough scientifically to understand them.[209]

We are now, apparently, at that point. The Elohim have appeared to Raël as the prophet for our age, have explained themselves in late twentieth-century scientific terminology and will shortly be returning physically to Earth to greet all of us. However, knowing that Earth has many different nations, and not wishing to be identified politically, morally or culturally with any particular one of them, they instructed Raël to build an embassy in internationally recognised neutral territory, where they can meet representatives of governments: 'When they land, the only philosophy they wish to endorse is their own, so therefore they will only arrive at an embassy built by the movement they created.'

Once the embassy is built the Raelians expect the Elohim to return to Earth some time before 2030. Raelians believe that it is the mission of Israel to welcome the messenger of the Elohim; the Elohim apparently requested that the embassy should be built on a piece of land given to the Raelian Movement by the State of Israel. This is because the message of the Elohim was first brought to the Jews; also, the Jewish race is descended from when the sons of Elohim (the Nephilim) mated with the daughters of men (Genesis 6:2), creating 'a race of people with superior intelligence'.[210]

If Israel is not willing to offer land the movement allowed that the embassy could be built in a neighbouring country – Jordan, Syria, Lebanon or Egypt. But as there has been no indication that any Middle Eastern country will offer the land for the embassy, it may now be built in any country. According to Eric Bolou, the UK leader in the late 1990s,[211] it is the responsibility of each country's Raelian leader to approach the government of their country to ask for land on which to build the embassy.

'Any country that offers extra-territoriality would be able to have the embassy,' says Carter. 'There's enough money to build the embassy, so it's not a financial issue. We could in fact buy land and build the embassy ourselves, but that would be against the whole ethos for building it – the criteria have always been the same: extraterritoriality must be granted by the country in which the embassy is to be located.'[212]

But the Elohim will not come unless very large numbers of people want them to; they respect us as their creations, and will not impose their will on us. (Those familiar with prophecies of returning spacecraft – or of the second coming of Christ – will recognise this as one of several explanations, on this occasion in advance, for 'when prophecy fails'; see p. 144–7.)

Critics of the Raelian Movement have claimed that Raël's account of aliens creating mankind plagiarised other writers, particularly Jean Sendy's *La Lune, Cle de la Bible* (The Moon, Key of the Bible) (1968) and *Ces Dieux qui Firent le Ciel et la Terre: le Roman de la Bible* (Those Gods who made Heaven and Earth: the Novel of the Bible) (1969). Sendy apparently gave a lecture in Clermont-Ferrand, Raël's hometown, in March 1974, some months before the self-publication of Raël's first book.[213] Raël has responded forthrightly to these allegations:

> Some writers may have had similar theories long before I met the Elohim, but these were just theories. Jean Sendy is not the only one, there is also Robert Charroux, Erich von Däniken, Le Poer Trench and many more. The difference between them and I is that the messages are not the fruit of fiction writing nor the fruit of imagination, but were given to me by the Elohim themselves. That some writers may have had similar theories doesn't change anything. They really just had an intelligent read of the Bible and other ancient texts that already contained the truth. But they never were contacted nor did they receive any messages! Their fiction writing doesn't contain any spirituality, meditation teaching, nor philosophical keys to our future. There are so many things that the books of those writers don't hold that you can find in the messages.[214]

Carter states that all accusations of plagiarism are unfounded and unsubstantiated.

From its formation in 1973 the Raelian Movement spread initially into French-speaking countries in Europe, Africa and

North America (i.e. Québec); it has since spread into over fifty countries. By 2002 it was claiming around 55,000 members – though in Britain the movement was tiny, with only about forty full members and a further 200 sympathisers.[215] By 2010 it says it has around 75,000 members worldwide, with 1,100 to 1,200 members in the UK.

Carter claims that 'almost nobody has ever apostised from the Raelian Movement', but he also says that 95 per cent of members have been with the movement for over ten years which, if true, would necessarily imply very low growth of the movement.

The Raelian Movement is organised hierarchically, from level 0 members (trainees) through level 1 members (assistant organisers), level 2 members (organisers), level 3 members (assistant Guides), Guides level 4 (priests and trainee guides), Guides level 5 (bishops) to the Guide of Guides level 6 (one person, currently Raël, who in 2010 was coming to the end of his fifth seven-year term as Guide of Guides).[216] Altogether there are forty-sex level 5s and one hundred and sixty-four level 4s, plus thirty-four trainee level 4s. No one, at any level, receives a salary.

The minimum annual membership fee is £60, but as in many other religious movements, members are encouraged to tithe a tenth of their net income; in Britain 30 per cent of this tithe goes to the British Raelian Movement and the remainder to the International movement.

Raël's writings have been translated into over twenty languages. Raël himself now lives in Québec, though the international headquarters is in Switzerland.

Born in 1946 Raël is still relatively young, but the movement has indicated that on his eventual death someone else will be elected Guide of Guides, and the movement will continue unchanged. This would be helped by the fact that Raël has had no further extraterrestrial experiences since 1975; effectively, and unusually, they are already operating in a post-prophetic phase while their founder is alive.[217] On the other hand, because their mythology, teachings and practices stem wholly from the reported experiences of one man, when that man and his charismatic authority are gone there may not be sufficient glue to hold the movement together, as several other 'flying saucer movements' have found in recent decades.[218] However, the experience of the Aetherius Society after their founder's death (see p. 121) shows that if the organisation, beliefs and activities of the movement are sufficiently well established it may be able to continue without the founder's presence.[219]

Raelians say they are not ufologists; they find evidence on our own planet to confirm the messages given to Raël by the Elohim. They don't demand blind faith; 'the Elohim invite us to verify their work of creation referred to in our ancient texts, by our own scientific development, and by our opportunity to rationally understand the universe'.

Raelians do not believe in gods, but say that the God of the Bible and the gods of all other religions were mankind's misinterpretation of the Elohim. From time to time the Elohim send messengers to Earth, each one of them born of a human woman with an Elohim father; these include the Buddha, Moses, Jesus, Muhammad and, most recently before Raël, Joseph Smith, founder and prophet of the Mormons. Raël is the final messenger. (Many religions, including Christianity and Islam, claim that their founder/prophet is the final messenger.)

The Raelian Movement states adamantly that we are not spiritual beings; we do not possess a spirit or soul which continues in any way after our death. We are purely physical beings who have a certain period of time alive; and after death, nothing. However, there is an equivalent of heaven or hell, at least for some. Each human being since the creation of our race by the Elohim has a unique DNA pattern and a unique electromagnetic frequency pattern, and the Elohim have a cell from each person's body. 'There are remote computers in orbit which sample people's DNA at birth and at death,' says Carter, though he does not explain how this is done.

On the Elohim's home planet there are vast computers which monitor our lives: 'We observe everyone. Huge computers ensure a constant surveillance of all people living on Earth. A mark is attributed to everyone depending on their actions during their life whether they walked towards love and truth or towards hate and obscurantism.' If our good deeds outbalance our bad deeds, we may be recreated at some time in the future, in new bodies grown from our DNA pattern, on the Elohim's planet, and 'will have the right to eternity on this heavenly planet'. Those who were neither particularly good not evil will simply not be recreated, but, 'for those whose actions were particularly negative, a cell from their body will have been preserved, which will allow us to recreate them when the time comes, so that they can be judged and suffer the punishment they deserve'.[220]

A ritual specific to the Raelian Movement is transmitting the cellular code, seen as the Raelian equivalent of baptism. This takes place on the four annual Raelian holidays, 6 August, 7 October, 13 December and the first Sunday of April. A Raelian Guide (level 4 to 6), who is already known to the Elohim, places his or her hands on a person's head, receives their unique code and transmits it to the Elohim. The Raelians say that this does not give their members any advantage when people are recreated scientifically on the Elohim planet; in fact, those who have transmitted their code will be judged more strictly than those who have not, because it is a sign that they have received and understood the truth of the Raelian message.

The Raelians now claim to be following in their creators' footsteps. In 1997 some members started a company called Valiant Venture, and a research programme called Clonaid, with the aim of offering cloned children to infertile and homosexual couples, created from their DNA. In December 2002 its director Dr Brigitte Boisellier, a Raelian bishop, announced that they had successfully cloned an American woman, with the birth of a baby called Eve. The movement gained great publicity from this announcement, but despite assurances at the time that there soon would be evidence, none was ever offered, and the claim has not been followed up. UK leader

Glenn Carter is unable to give any further information, pointing out that Clonaid as an organisation is independent of the Raelian Movement: 'It was separated years before any claims were made. The truth is I don't know anything about the internal workings of Clonaid, or anything about Clonaid at all.'

In 2006 Raël launched a new organisation, Cliteraid, with the intention of restoring the clitorises of African women who have suffered genital mutilation. In 2010 it was about to open a 'pleasure hospital' in Burkina Faso.[221] This new enterprise has met with opposition from other medical professionals and from feminist groups who say its campaign urging supporters to 'adopt African women's clitorises' denigrates African women.

Apart from spreading the Elohim's message and raising funds (so far over $7 million) to build the embassy, Raelians aim:

> to build a society adapted to the future, not the past. This is done through courses of Sensual Meditation held all over the world, enabling individuals to regain control over their lives by questioning all their habits, beliefs and attitudes and implementing choice to retain only what is useful to their development. As each individual becomes more happy and fulfilled, so humanity as a whole becomes more happy and fulfilled and the society of the future begins to develop.

In some ways this last sentence echoes the ideas of, for example, the Transcendental Meditation movement, which believes that a small number of people meditating together can affect the wider world.[222] It is also similar to the ideals expressed in the Rosicrucian manifestos (see p. 179–80), that through improving oneself one can improve the world. For Raelians this philosophy applies to all areas of life, including education, love, sexuality, work, leisure and self-development.

The Raelian Movement, says sociologist Susan Palmer, is 'a rare example' of a new religion 'which promotes in its members a tolerance for sexual ambiguity and encourages homosexual expression'.[223] Sensual Meditation helps members to learn how to gain the fullest enjoyment from every aspect of their lives, including sex. The ultimate experience is a Cosmic Orgasm, though it is not clear how this differs from any other especially good sexual experience.

Sensual meditation is a set of techniques to help us 'link with the infinity that we are a part of'. It enables people to 'understand how our minds and bodies function; question the Judaeo-Christian inhibitions of guilt and the mysticism of Eastern traditions; develop our minds and discover our bodies; and reprogramme ourselves by ourselves into what we really wish to be. Sensual Meditation enables us to love ourselves better and to better love others, to discover our individuality and our common humanity.'

Some of the meditation techniques are intended to be used with a partner of the opposite sex. Members are encouraged to experiment sexually if they wish, and to develop their sensuality. This is a key part of Raelian teaching: 'Sex is an important source of pleasure, which along with "choice" and "infinity" (correctly identified) is a very important element of Raelian philosophy. The messages state "Pleasure is the fertiliser which opens the mind. A life without pleasure is like an uncultivated garden."' This emphasis on sexual pleasure goes back to Raël's visit to the Elohim's planet, where he 'spent the most extravagant night of my life' with a selection of beautiful genetically created robot women.[224]

The movement has a completely free attitude towards sexual relationships; it depends entirely on individual choice. They have monogamous heterosexual couples, others 'who prefer to have different partners', homosexuals, transsexuals . . . 'In sexuality, as in all other things, the promotion of choice is all-important; and furthermore, that sexually as in every other way (race, appearance, etc.), we more than tolerate, we love the differences . . . A varied community is essential for the equilibrium of the whole,' says a former Raelian official.[225]

The Raelian Movement holds major 'Courses of Awakening' in France, Canada, Japan, Korea and Australia, and smaller courses in Britain, the United States and other countries. The aim is 'to create a world of leisure, love and fulfilment where we have rid ourselves of the moralistic social inhibitions which paralyse our joy for life, so that everyone has the courage to act as they so wish, as long as this action does not harm others'. This last sentiment is the same as one of the main principles of Wicca: 'An [If] it harm none, do as thou wilt shall be the whole of the law' (see p. 293).

Infinity is an important concept in the Raelian Movement; they believe that sub-atomic particles are themselves galaxies, containing stars, planets and people; and that our own galaxy is a tiny particle of an atom of a living being on a planet revolving around a sun in a galaxy. This is a concept which has been covered in science fiction, but is not generally accepted in human science, though the Raelians say that the Elohim have proved it to be true.

The symbol of the Raelians, worn as a pendant by members, is a six-pointed Star of David made up of two triangles, the one pointing upwards representing the infinitely large, and the one pointing down representing the infinitely small. Integrated within the star is a swastika, an ancient symbol of peace. From 1990 to 2005 the swastika – apparently the symbol of the Elohim – was replaced by a swirling design inside the star representing infinity in time: 'This was done out of respect for the victims of the Nazi holocaust and to facilitate the building of the embassy in Israel, despite the fact that the Elohim's symbol is the oldest on Earth and that traces of it still remain in Israel today.'[226] But in 2005 Raël decided to reinstate the swastika within the Star of David as the only official symbol of the Raelian Movement worldwide.[227] He explained why:

However this courteous gesture [replacing the swastika with the swirl] didn't help educate people so that they know this symbol is the symbol of the Scientists who created us, symbol that has been given to every one of their Messengers, which explains why we find it on every continent, usually associated to spiritual and peaceful groups.

The swastika has been a symbol of peace for millions of
Hindus and Buddhists and for the Raelians as well as it is their
symbol of infinity in time, their symbol of eternity.[228]

The reinstatement of the swastika, together with Raël's
teachings on 'geniocracy', have caused some critics of the
Raelian Movement to brand it as racist or supremacist.
Geniocracy is a proposed political system to be run by the most
intelligent for the benefit of all, or as the splash on the front
cover of Raël's book *Geniocracy* says: 'Government of the
People, for the People, by the Geniuses.' In essence this would
restrict the electorate to those with an IQ of 110 or higher, thus
ruling out more than half of the population from being able to
vote, while candidates must have an IQ of 150 or higher.

Geniocracy can perhaps be compared with the nineteenth-
and early twentieth-century ultra right-wing French concept
of Synarchy, government by a secret elite, or even with the
fictional idea of awarding extra votes for intelligence and
achievement, proposed in Nevil Shute's novel *In the Wet*
(1953). Many religions try for political influence, from the
powerful Christian Right in the United States to the
Transcendental Meditation organisation's failed attempt to get
into politics in Britain and other countries through its Natural
Law Party in the 1990s. The openly elitist political stance of the
Raelian Movement stands in awkward contrast to its liberal
views on sexual morality.

However, if both of these, along with the movement's incur-
sions into medical science, are seen as ways intended to improve
society, then the aims of the Raelian Movement are not
dissimilar to those of many other esoteric religions; the
difference is that their revelation came from extraterrestrials
rather than from Ascended Masters or God.

ALTERNATIVE HISTORY

The success of Dan Brown's 2003 novel *The Da Vinci Code* (DVC) puzzled many commentators. The novel, a carefully marketed publishing phenomenon,[229] followed in the wake of a large number of 'alternative history' or 'speculative history' books over the past few decades. Some focused on Rennes-le-Château and the Priory of Sion; others on the Knights Templar and the origins of Freemasonry; others on a supposed relationship between Jesus and Mary Magdalene. Another stream of books followed a different path, sometimes called 'cult archaeology/cosmology', in the tradition of Zecharia Sitchin and Erich von Däniken. Taking pseudo-history and pseudo-science together Jesus was anything from a Freemason to an astronaut, but rarely a first-century Jewish preacher.

These books, even Baigent, Leigh and Lincoln's *The Holy Blood and the Holy Grail* upon which much of the 'historical' background of DVC was based,[230] had a devoted but relatively small following, but with *The Da Vinci Code* such ideas were put before multiple millions of readers and presented, albeit within a novel, as if fact. Since its publication many books and TV documentaries have pointed out the vast number of very basic historical errors in the novel,[231] but for a lot of the novel's readers factual reality seems to be irrelevant. Post-DVC, many books, both fiction and non-fiction, websites and online forums now take it for granted that Jesus and Mary Magdalene were married, and that she or they moved to France after the crucifixion, their children establishing a spiritual royal line there.

As with some New Age, occult and Neo-Pagan movements, the lack of any historical evidence is no barrier to belief. But unlike, for example, most Wiccans today who have the sophistication to accept the theories of J. G. Frazer, Margaret Murray and Robert Graves as foundation myths rather than as fact (see p. 285–9), these new mythologists tend to have an uncritical acceptance of such historically unsound ideas.

In 591 CE Pope Gregory I conflated three women in the gospels into one, so launching the idea that Mary Magdalene was a repentant prostitute; this teaching was quietly dropped by the Roman Catholic Church in 1969. Now this belief, accepted for centuries, has for many people been replaced by the equally dubious belief, based on a number of popular books since the 1990s,[232] that Mary Magdalene was not only without any doubt Jesus's wife and the mother of his children, but also of royal blood herself. Especially in the United States, for some readers, largely women, Mary Magdalene has effectively taken the place of the Virgin Mary as a focus of veneration, with a sacred bloodline or lineage of her own today.[233]

Online forums and websites show some overlap between believers in the Magdalene lineage and believers in so-called Indigo Children – children with behavioural problems who are supposedly a new stage in human evolution, though this has absolutely no scientific validity:

> Mary Magdalene and the Children of the Grail
> Mary Magdalene herself is considered by many to be the Grail, the womb through which a sacred bloodline, or bloodlines ensued. Are these bloodlines here today as the Indigo Children? The coming of the Indigos is intimately connected to the return of the Sacred Divine Feminine; they are here to help us awaken the 'sleeping beauty' within all of us![234]

The wholesale imposition of the very largely modern concept of the Divine Feminine on historical religious cultures which almost certainly would not have recognised it can be compared to the unquestioning acceptance by late twentieth-century feminists and Wiccans of the myth that nine million women died as witches in 'the Burning Times' (see p. 288). The power of a myth bears no relation to its historical reality (see p. 13).

A different set of mythology comes from 'cult archaeology/ cosmology' books based on Mayan prophecies, the Centuries of Nostradamus, angel visitations or even messages from Mary Magdalene,[235] prophesying that the world will come to an end, or a new world will begin, in 2012. As with the many prophesies of the return of Christ or of aliens, the normal progress of time will reveal the accuracy or otherwise of this widely-pronounced belief (see p. 114–7).

The pseudo-historical and pseudo-scientific ideas of the Magdalene lineage, Indigo Children and the 2012 mythos, amongst many others, have become popular in some New Age circles, though far less so in Britain than in the United States. In some ways they have become a socially acceptable equivalent of the conspiracy theories about the Illuminati, the New World Order and the 'Jewish-masonic conspiracy', equally empty of factual evidence and full of weak arguments, which find their greatest acceptance amongst the extreme right-wing, in both Christian and New Age circles.

OTHER NEW AGE
AND HOLISTIC GROUPS

There are many other New Age organisations, international, national and local; it would be impossible to attempt to list them all. As with the Findhorn Foundation (see p. 92) and the Wrekin Trust (see p. 96), many work with each other, sharing common spiritual goals but also celebrating their diversity. They can be found under a variety of 'umbrella' labels such as Mind, Body, Spirit (MBS), alternative spiritualities, holistic spirituality, well-being, complementary healing and others. Books on New Age beliefs and practices are often found in the MBS section of bookshops. There are dedicated MBS publishers, and several mainstream publishers have MBS imprints.

In Britain many groups and individual speakers, healers, therapists and other practitioners come together at the annual Mind, Body, Spirit festivals in London and Manchester; their founder, Graham Wilson, set up similar festivals in New York, Los Angeles, San Francisco, Sydney and Melbourne.[236] In addition smaller MBS fairs can be found in cities and towns across most Western countries.[237]

MBS festivals attract a diversity of speakers; the 2010 festivals held in London and Manchester included Richard Lawrence, UK leader of the Aetherius Society (see p. 119), Tao expert the Barefoot Doctor, Timothy Freke, who writes on Gnostic religion, Scottish shaman Barbara Meiklejohn-Free, assorted psychics, and practitioners of yoga, feng shui, astrology, hypnotherapy and neuro-linguistic programming (NLP), amongst many more. As well as talks the festivals include practical workshops, music, dancing, drumming, chanting and meditation sessions. (It is notable that many NLP practitioners use the technique of Affirmations – psychological rather than spiritual, but broadly equivalent to the Affirmations of the Church Universal and Triumphant, the I AM Movement and, before them, New Thought; see p. 68.)

The word holistic is increasingly used to draw together the wide range of alternative spiritualities, teachings, meditation, therapy and healing. Dr William Bloom, formerly a lecturer in Psychological Problems in International Politics at the London School of Economics, is founder of the Foundation of Holistic Spirituality. He has worked with adults and adolescents with special needs, teaches workshops on leadership in both the corporate world and the public sector, including the National Health Service, and is a meditation master. He set up and for ten years ran the Alternatives Programme at St James's Church, Piccadilly, London – an Anglican church that since 1982 has hosted weekly talks and weekend workshops in 'spirituality, creativity, wellbeing and personal development'.[238]

The Foundation of Holistic Spirituality is establishing what it calls Spiritual Companions, a network of holistic support and pastoral care from people who follow a number of guidelines including:

> Regularly connect with, experience and explore the wonder of existence.
> Appreciate that all life is in a continual process of emergence and are comfortable with unknowing.
> Are grounded and centred in our bodies.
> Provide a non-intrusive, welcoming, healing and holding presence.
> Celebrate diversity and welcome the many different paths of spiritual development.[239]

It is in the process of creating the Holistic Map UK, or a Holistic Yellow Pages or directory: 'It maps and lists all UK centres, projects and people who are involved in a holistic approach to contemporary life and spirituality. It also shows all sacred sites, places of worship and public bodies that welcome all visitors regardless of their belief and background.'[240]

It has set up the Holistic Spiritual Alliance, which seeks to ensure that people who take an holistic approach to spirituality are represented on public consultative bodies including Interfaith, local education committees and hospital boards. This is a similar aim to the work done by both the Pagan Federation in gaining official recognition for prison visitors and hospital chaplains from the Pagan faiths, and Pebble, the Public Bodies Liaison Committee for British Paganism (see p. 341).

In the same way that Wiccans, Druids, Heathens and others encouraged their followers to write in 'Pagan' in answer to the question on religion on the 2011 Census form (see p. 343),[241] the Foundation of Holistic Spirituality encouraged people who share their beliefs to write in 'Holistic',[242] in each case to avoid a multiplicity of small groups being named.

The Isle of Avalon Foundation is a study centre for New Age teaching, based in Glastonbury. It was originally set up as the University of Avalon in 1991, 'with the vision of creating a recognised University of the Spirit in Avalon within the temenos of Glastonbury, known for centuries as the Isle of Avalon. We are a University in the original sense of the word – meaning an educational establishment concerned with exploring the whole of creation, encompassing spiritual as well as material values and systems.'[243]

The British government did not see it quite the same way; they were told that as they were not an officially recognised university offering academic degrees they could not use the name. In April 1995 they changed to their current name, and reassessed their aims and ideals: 'Isle of Avalon Foundation is a spiritual education centre whose main purpose is to make available to visitors and residents the transformative energies of Avalon and the experience of people who live in Glastonbury and elsewhere on the planet.'[244] Over the years the Foundation offered talks and courses on personal development, music and magic, healing and other areas. In 2010 its website showed a focus on shamanism (see p. 277) and counselling.[245]

There are other organisations which aim to draw together practitioners in various areas of alternative healing, both teaching and practice.

The Healer Foundation is a network of around 140 complementary therapists working with reiki, hypnotherapy, NLP, acupuncture, homeopathy, reflexology and many other areas. It offers a course of workshops over two years leading to its own Diploma in Healing.[246]

The School of Intuition and Healing, based in London, aims 'to provide high quality education in healing, spirit release, psychic development and spiritual awareness'.[247] It offers a Healing Course held on eighteen Sundays spread over two years, and costing £1,600. The School says the course will be accredited with the British Alliance of Healing Associations and therefore also with UK Healers (see below); director Sue Allen explains further:

> At the moment things are changing and the Complementary & Natural Healthcare Council is to be the new body that will register all healers, provide one National Code of Conduct, disciplinary procedures and continue to develop regulatory standards etc. This aims to meet Government standards and so healers etc. registered with the CNHC will be recognised by Local Authorities and the NHS etc.
>
> Our membership and accreditation with BAHA means that our healers will be registered with the CNHC once this is available.[248]

Many of the tutors on the Healing Course have the letters MCPS or MNFSH after their names: Member of the College of Psychic Studies (founded in 1884)[249] or Member of the National Federation of Spiritual Healers (now known as the Healing Trust, founded in 1954). It should be noted that these are not formal qualifications but paid-for annual memberships, though the NFSH requires evidence of a minimum of two years experience and competence in spiritual healing.[250]

Two further umbrella groups are the Confederation of Healing Organisations (founded in 1984) – its dozen members include amongst others the NFSH, the College of Healing, the Spiritualist Association of Great Britain and the School of Energy Healing[251] – and UK Healers, a self-regulatory body founded in 1999.[252]

Although sceptics and many medical doctors would dismiss all of these complementary healing practitioners, it is clear that these organisations aim to bring professional standards to their members' practice. The Confederation of Healing Organisations developed a Code of Conduct for healers in consultation with the General Medical Council, the British Medical Association and the Royal Colleges. It has instituted complaints and disciplinary procedures, and has encouraged malpractice and liability insurance for healers. It also funds university and NHS research into spiritual healing.

PERSONAL DEVELOPMENT
MOVEMENTS

There is some overlap between New Age movements and personal development or self-help movements; there can be quite a thin line between spiritual development and emotional and psychological development.

For example, for years advertisements in magazines offered 'The Realisation System: Private Lessons in Practical Psychology'. The promotional letter promised that a correspondence course 'will start to build the structure of a new and dominant YOU, a serene and successful YOU, a more courageous and capable YOU, a happier, healthier, more wonderful YOU ... A triumphant YOU born of Greater Self-Knowledge which THE REALISATION SYSTEM will bring you, just as it has done for countless others in all walks of life.' Although it said that it was not in any way a religion, later in the course the student would be introduced to the concept of 'the Universal Creative Mind' of which we are all a part.

In 2010 the Realisation System has its own website, which now openly proclaims:

Religion and Science United
To Redeem the World from Poverty, Sickness, Failure,
Sin, Disappointment and Unhappiness
The Redeeming Truth is Free[253]

The cover of its introductory Realisation audiobook/e-book says: 'Discover the simple, scientific way of fulfilling every

What I Believe . . .
Magic

I still adhere to the Crowleyan principle of science and art causing change to occur in conformity with will: that's magic. There are many different ways of experiencing it. Spontaneous laughter is a form of magic: what makes that happen? It's much more than the sum of the people there and what was said; it's everything about the moment – and it's that moment of divine combustion that is magic, I think.

Geraldine Beskin, third-generation esoteric witch and eclectic occultist
Co-owner of the Atlantis Bookshop, London

I believe in a magical world; I believe that magic comes from the fact that the world is animate, it's animated by something, and I do believe that that something is not understood by our current consensus culture. So magic is the art of getting yourself in conformity with that unknown in order to perceive something which you had not perceived previously.

Dr Paul Newman, Wiccan with interest in Eastern spirituality
Sessional Lecturer in Mathematics, University of London

Magic is trying to effect a change in the material world by some non-causal, non-material means.

Gareth J. Medway, Priest Hierophant of the Fellowship of Isis
Writer and assistant psychic

The changing of existing circumstances in accordance with the magician's will.

Jack Gale, Magician
Retired school teacher

The art of causing changes by methods that don't
bear scientific analysis. The corollary to that is that
magic is the last thing that you should normally do;
all normal methods of achieving something should
have been exhausted.
Steve Wilson, Thelemite
Civil Servant

Magic is the ability of the human mind, emotions and imagination
to move energy and create vibrational effects.
Dr William Bloom
Author and educator in a holistic and modern approach
to spirituality

Magic is about changing reality with the powers of the mind.
I see it as a black-box process with a start and an end state, but
with the process itself being unexplainable. If we can explain it,
it becomes Science. Like cycling and balance, magic cannot be
taught but has to be learnt by experiences.
Mani Navasothy, Wiccan High Priest and founder of
Hern's Tribe
Physicist

Coincidence control through probability enhancement.
Oberon Zell-Ravenheart,
Co-founder, Church of All Worlds

Magic is the science of changing your consciousness, exalting
your mind, and using it in such a way that you start to develop
your talents from your true essence. You develop as a person,
astrally, emotionally, mentally and spiritually.
Ina Cüsters-van Bergen, Magister, Hermetic Order of
the Temple of Starlight

lawful desire of your heart.' 'The Redeeming Truth' itself may be free, but various versions of the course teaching it cost between US$97 and US$197; or for US$2004 over twelve months you can be trained to become a certified Realisation System teacher yourself and earn money by doing so.

Personal development is nothing new. Samuel Smiles wrote his famous *Self-Help* in 1859, with the aphorisms 'he who never made a mistake never made a discovery' and 'the shortest way to do many things is to do only one thing at once'. Dale Carnegie's *How to Win Friends and Influence People*, published in 1936, was a result of courses in which he taught business and professional people 'to think on their feet and express their ideas with more clarity, more effectiveness and more poise'; it had sold nearly five million copies by his death in 1955. L. Ron Hubbard's system of Dianetics, first launched on the world in 1950, promised 'a condition of ability and rationality for Man well in advance of the current norm' and 'a complete insight into the full potentialities of the mind' (see p. 360–1). Norman Vincent Peale's *The Power of Positive Thinking* was first published in 1952; its chapter headings include 'Expect the best and get it' and 'I don't believe in defeat'.

Such books are still being written, but the later decades of the twentieth century saw an explosion in the number of techniques, courses and seminars available, all offering ways to help you improve yourself. In the 1970s est (Erhard Seminars Training) was popular; others include the Landmark Forum, Insight, which is linked to the Sant Mat offshoot the Movement of Spiritual Inner Awareness, and neuro-linguistic programming.[254] New Age speakers at Mind, Body, Spirit festivals offer teachings on self-motivational techniques that have much the same ends in view, and often give courses in 'inner potential'.

Self-improvement seminars often seek to improve a person's awareness of and confidence in himself or herself by awakening and experiencing, in one phrase or another, 'the heartfelt energies' – which is a similar goal to that of many esoteric religions, without necessarily involving any form of divinity.

NOTES TO PART ONE

1   Melton et al. 1991: 3.
2   Campbell and Brennan 1990: 7.
3   Heelas 1996: 1.
4   Bloom 1991: xvi.
5   Heelas 1996: 2.
6   Melton and Baumann 2002: 938.
7   Bloom 1991: 1.
8   Leaflet: *Theosophy and the Theosophical Society*, The Theosophical Society in England, 1995.
9   Flier: 'Some Facts about Theosophy', The Theosophical Society in England, n.d.
10 Lachman 2008: 121.
11 Blavatsky 1977: 200.
12 Rawlinson 1997: 195–6.
13 T. Polyphilus, 'The Moon under Her Feet', http://hermetic.com/dionysos/abk.htm.
14 http://www.hogd.co.uk/gd_history_ciceros.htm.
15 http://marygreer.wordpress.com/2009/10/08/source-of-the-kybalion-in-anna-kingsford%E2%80%99s-hermetic-system/.
16 http://www.katinkahesselink.net/blavatsky/articles/v10/y1888_082.htm.
17 Gilbert 1987a: 6.
18 http://www.katinkahesselink.net//esinstr.htm.
19 Gilbert 1987a: 8–9.
20 See http://www.templeofthepeople.org/.
21 See http://www.ult.org/.
22 See http://www.theosophycanada.com/fohat_annie2.htm for example.
23 Pedro Oliveira of the Theosophical Society in correspondence with the author, 9 October 2010; the Theosophical Society (Pasadena) declined to give membership figures when asked.
24 Gerald Suster, *Crowley's Apprentice* (London: Rider, 1989), 2; cited in Evans 2007: 220.
25 See Barrett 2001: 312–21.
26 http://www.astara.org.
27 See http://user.cyberlink.ch/~koenig/steiner.htm.
28 http://www.lucistrust.org/en/meetings_and_events/three_major_spiritual_festivals/about.

29 Bailey 1951: 1.

30 http://www.lucistrust.org/en/arcane_school/introduction/about_the_arcane_school.

31 Sarah McKechnie, president and chairman of the Lucis Trust, in correspondence with the author, 23 July 2010.

32 Bailey 1957: 16.

33 http://www.lucistrust.org/en/service_activities/the_great_invocation_1/a_statement_on_the_adaptation_of_the_great_invocation.

34 Information leaflet: *The Reappearance of the Christ and the Masters of Wisdom*, 1994: 2.

35 *Share International Special Information Issue*, n.d.: 10–11.

36 *The Reappearance of the Christ and the Masters of Wisdom*, 1994: 2.

37 Creme 1996: 44.

38 *The Emergence Newsletter*, 1994, 3: 3.

39 http://www.share-international.org/av/v_maitreya_emergence.htm.

40 Author of *Stuffed and Starved: Markets, Power and the Hidden Battle for the World Food System* (2008) and *The Value of Nothing: How to Reclaim Market Society and Redefine Democracy* (2010). As I wrote at the time: 'But there's a bit of a difference between being a currently fashionable left-leaning developmental guru, and a spiritual guru who will unite and save the world.' Barrett 2010a: 8.

41 http://rajpatel.org/2010/01/25/call-me-brian/.

42 http://www.nytimes.com/2010/02/05/us/05sfmetro.html?_r=1&emc=eta1.

43 Unless otherwise stated, quotations are from Professor Tilo L.V. Ulbricht on behalf of the Gurdjieff Society, in correspondence with the author, 11 November 1999.

44 Moore 1999: 319.

45 Rawlinson 1997: 282.

46 See Barrett 2000.

47 Routledge & Kegan Paul, London: 1950.

48 Moore 1999: 205; Rawlinson 1997: 293.

49 Rawlinson 1997: 284.

50 Tilo L. V. Ulbricht, 'Gurdjieff's Teaching': undated article sent to the author by Ulbricht.

51 Moore 1999: 57.

52 Unless otherwise stated all quotations are taken from an untitled Subud information leaflet.

53 See Barrett 2000.

54 Frequently Asked Questions on http://www.xploreheartlinks. com/subud.html; originally seen at http://www.subud.org.

55 http://www.subud.org.uk/about/what_is_latihan.html.

56 http://www.subud.com/spiritual.html.

57 http://www.subud.com/english/english.contacts.html.

58 Subuh, quoted in Lyle 1983: 91–2.

59 http://www.subud.org/start.php?mcat=1&scat=45.

60 Taylor 1987: 5.

61 Elizabeth Stuart in correspondence with the author, 14 November 2010.

62 Pickering 1989: 198; see also George Pitcher, 'Sex is a stumbling block for Anglicans on the road to Rome', *Daily Telegraph* (26 October 2009); Andrew Brown, 'The clergymen came out two by two', *Independent* (18 March 1995).

63 Jonathan Blake in correspondence with the author, 21 July 2010.

64 http://www.openepiscopalchurch.org.uk/organisation/videos. html.

65 Jonathan Blake in correspondence with the author, 21 and 30 July 2010.

66 http://www.crossdenominationalmission.org.uk/liberalcatholic. html. This site has a brief and very readable history of Liberal Catholic Church schisms over the years.

67 http://ecumenism.net/denom/independent.htm.

68 The medieval Cathar religion, mainly in what is now southern France, is outside the scope of this book. See O'Shea 2000; Weiss 2000; Barrett 2001: 137–8; and Barrett 2007a: 43–50.

69 Waite 2003; Barrett 2007a: 152–4.

70 Lawrence 2010: 125.

71 http://www.soulcraftteachings.com.

72 Beekman 2005: 110.

73 Weston 2009: 203–4.

74 Ballard, *Unveiled Mysteries*: 247, cited in Medway 2007.

75 See Barkun 2003: 114.

76 Medway 2007.

77 J. Gordon Melton, 'The Church Universal and Triumphant: Its Heritage and Thoughtworld', in Lewis and Melton 1994: 12–13.

78   http://caselaw.lp.findlaw.com/cgi-bin/getcase.pl?court=us&vol=
     322&invol=78.
79   J. Gordon Melton, 'The Church Universal and Triumphant: Its
     Heritage and Thoughtworld' in Lewis and Melton 1994: 4–7.
80   http://www.alpheus.org/html/articles/esoteric_history/messengers_
     organizations.html.
81   Note the link with Christian Science, which was related to New
     Thought, one of the sources of I AM Religious Activity.
82   From this point on in this entry 'Prophet' refers to Elizabeth
     Clare Prophet.
83   Barrett 2001: 290–96.
84   Booklet: Church Universal and Triumphant 1986: 24.
85   Statement from CUT to the author, 5 November 2010.
86   See 'After the Prophet Dies: How Movements Change' in Barrett
     2001: 58–69.
87   Statement from CUT to the author, 5 November 2010.
88   http://www.blacksunjournal.com.
89   Olp 2008.
90   Statement from CUT to the author, 5 November 2010.
91   Ibid.
92   Murray Steinman in telephone conversation with the author, 7
     September 1995.
93   Prophet 1985: 255–6.
94   Booklet: Church Universal and Triumphant 1992: 7.
95   'The Life of Saint Issa', 4: 12–13, in Prophet 1987: 218.
96   This is Steinman's paraphrase; the actual verse reads, 'Jesus said,
     "He who will drink from my mouth will become like me; I
     myself shall become he, and the things that are hidden will be
     revealed to him."' The Gospel of Thomas, verse 108, in
     Barnstone 1984: 307.
97   Christopher Kelley, spokesman, Church Universal and
     Triumphant, in correspondence with the author, 17 March 2000.
98   Church Universal and Triumphant 1992: 9–10.
99   Church Universal and Triumphant 1992: 8.
100 Video: Church Universal and Triumphant 1994.
101 Church Universal and Triumphant 1992: 16.
102 Church Universal and Triumphant 1992: 10.
103 *Royal Teton Ranch News*, 7: 2 (February/March 1995), 8.
104 Olp 2008.

105 Lewis and Melton 1994: 62, xii, passim.

106 Statement from CUT to the author, 5 November 2010.

107 Booklet: *The Emissaries*, 1992.

108 Michael S. Cummings in Christensen and Levinson 2003, vol. 1: 445.

109 Because the teachings of the Emissaries are broadly the same as in the past, quotations from Tessa Maskell in 2000 and from Kate Hall in 1995, which are particularly clear, are being retained though neither person is in the position she was when these quotations were made.

110 Tessa Maskell, then Director of the UK Emissary Charity, in correspondence with the author, 19 March 2000.

111 Emissary document: *Mickleton House: Guidelines for Residents*, June 1995.

112 Leaflet: *Lloyd Arthur Meeker; William Martin Alleyne Cecil*.

113 Emissary document: *Mickleton House: Guidelines for Residents*, June 1995.

114 Ibid.

115 William Duffield, head of the Emissaries Ltd in the UK, in correspondence with the author, 22 October 2010.

116 Course leaflet: *An Introduction to the Attunement Process*, n.d.

117 Kate Hall, former events manager at Mickleton House, in correspondence with the author, 24 January, 3 July, 9 August and 9 September 1995.

118 Lloyd Arthur Meeker, *The Divine Design*, vol. 1, 1952.

119 http://www.factnet.org/cults/Emissaries_Divine_Light/Barbara_Clearbridge.html.

120 *Vancouver Sun* (29 September 2003), cited at http://www.religionnewsblog.com/4651/leader-left-divine-light-behind-him.

121 See 'After the Prophet Dies: How Movements Change' in Barrett 2001: 58–69.

122 William Duffield in correspondence with the author.

123 http://www.mangreen.co.uk/spiritual_companions/.

124 William Duffield in correspondence with the author.

125 *Vancouver Sun* (29 September 2003), cited at http://www.religionnewsblog.com/4651/leader-left-divine-light-behind-him.

126 Michael Cecil in correspondence with the author, 23 April 2009.

127 Storm 1991: 203.

128 Andy Roberts, 'Peter Caddy, Contactees and the Findhorn Community', *Magonia*, 89 (August 2005).

129 Andy Roberts, 'Saucers Over Findhorn', *Fortean Times*, 217 (December 2006).

130 Forres: Findhorn Press 1967.

131 http://www.findhorn.org/online/?tz=-60.

132 Carin Bolles, Communications Department, Findhorn Foundation, in correspondence with the author, 3 August 2010.

133 http://www.sirgeorgetrevelyan.org.uk/obit-times.html; http://www.sirgeorgetrevelyan.org.uk/obit-telegraph.html.

134 4 vols, London: Pelican, 1949–52.

135 http://www.rightlivelihood.org/award.html?&no_cache=1.

136 http://www.rightlivelihood.org/trevelyan.html.

137 http://www.wrekintrust.org/history.shtml.

138 http://www.wrekintrust.org/ourvision.shtml.

139 http://www.wrekintrust.org/forum.shtml.

140 Janice Dolley, development director of the Wrekin Trust, in correspondence with the author, 28 October 2010.

141 Ibid.

142 Ibid.

143 Nick Woodeson in correspondence with the author, 3 September 2010.

144 Unless otherwise stated, all quotations are from Nick Woodeson and David Pearce, in correspondence with the author, 17 August, 17, 25 September and 12 November 1995, and 13 March 2000, and from Nick Woodeson, 3 September and 24 October 2010. Woodeson and Pearce are senior British members of the Emin/Template Network, but stress that 'the Emin has no spokespeople; the people speak for themselves'.

145 *Observer Magazine* (14 May 1995).

146 Woodeson and Pearce, August 1995.

147 Nick Woodeson in correspondence with the author, 24 October 2010.

148 Ibid.

149 Beit-Hallahmi 1992: 24ff.

150 http://www.emin.org.

151 http://www.templatenetwork.org/en/. This website archives articles from the movement's magazine, *Topaz*.

152 Emin leaflet, *Saturday Amber Workshops*, November 1999–February 2000.

153 http://www.emin.org/Blue.shtml.

154 Woodeson and Pearce, August 1995.
155 *The New Testament in Basic English* (Cambridge: Cambridge University Press, 1944), v–vi.
156 Chart: 'Emin Loom of Research Starters' (Gemstone Press 1995).
157 Leo 1992: 15.
158 Cited in Beit-Hallahmi 1998: 93.
159 See Barrett 2001: 427–31, 434–7.
160 Chart: 'Emin Loom of Research Starters': boxes 2–1 and 3–7.
161 Woodeson and Pearce, August 1995.
162 Ibid.
163 Ritchie 1991: 216.
164 Woodeson and Pearce, August 1995.
165 *Essence Music Catalogue*, 1993: 1.
166 Ibid.
167 http://www.emin.org.
168 http://www.thecentrelondon.org.
169 Woodeson, October 2010.
170 http://www.csicop.org/si/show/truth_is_they_never_were_saucers/.
171 Andrew Tomas, *We Are Not the First* (London: Sphere, 1971).
172 In one of Terry Pratchett's Discworld footnotes, he says: 'It's amazing how good governments are, given their track record in almost every other field, at hushing up things like alien encounters. One reason may be that the aliens themselves are too embarrassed to talk about it. It's not known why most of the space-going races of the universe want to undertake rummaging in Earthling underwear as a prelude to formal contact' (Terry Pratchett, *Hogfather*, London: Gollancz, 1996: 154).
173 Barrett 2001: 91–2; Bromley and Melton 2002: 38–40; Zeller 2010: 142–62.
174 Andreas Grünschloß, 'Scientology: A "New Age" Religion', in Lewis 2009: 240.
175 Melton 1985.
176 Founder Herbert W. Armstrong's booklet, *1975 in Prophecy*, first published in 1956, ceased to be available from the mid-1970s.
177 Thompson 1996: 37.
178 I Peter 4:7, I John 2:18, etc.
179 See Chapter 7, 'It's the End of the World as We Know It', in Barrett 2001: 70–81; also Thompson 1996, Weber 1999, etc.
180 Melton 1985: 20.

181   Miller had not taken account of the fact that there is no Year Zero between 1 BCE and 1 CE.

182   Edward Miller, 'Irvingism: or the Catholic Apostolic Church', in *Religious Systems of the World* (London, 1908), 598.

183   Diana Tumminia, 'When the Archangel Died', in Partridge 2003: 78.

184   Diana Tumminia, 'How Prophecy Never Fails: Interpretive reason in a flying saucer group', in Lewis 2003: 175–6.

185   Lewis Carroll, *Through the Looking Glass*, chapter 5.

186   See articles by Professor Chris French at http://www.guardian. co.uk/science/2009/oct/02/sleep-paralysis and http://www. guardian.co.uk/science/2009/nov/09/the-fourth-kind-sleep-paralysis.

187   See Mikael Rothstein, 'The Family, UFOs and God: A Modern Extension of Christian Mythology', *Journal of Contemporary Religion*, 12: 3 (1997), 353–62.

188   Patrick Harpur's *Daemonic Reality: A Field Guide to the Otherworld* (London: Viking, 1994) explores this idea in depth.

189   Quotations from Richard Lawrence are from conversations with the author in 1995, 1998, 1999 and 2010.

190   http://www.angelfire.com/fl3/freenunreal/Degree.txt.

191   King was in company with the 'speculative historians' (see p. 139) Laurence Gardner and 'HRH Prince Michael of Albany' in his use of spurious chivalric titles.

192   Mark Bennett, Media Relations, the Aetherius Society, in conversation with the author, 12 October 2010.

193   Richard Lawrence in conversation with the author, 14 October 2010; he also acknowledged that his own title of 'Dr', used on his books and in publicity for his talks, is not an academic doctorate but also came from the International Theological Seminary of California. He is not the only British religious leader to make use of an unaccredited doctorate; the Rev Ian Paisley gained his from the American Pioneer Theological Seminary in 1954.

194   Aetherius Society information booklet, n.d.

195   Quotations in this paragraph are taken from King 1961: 19–23.

196   See Barrett 2001: 312–21.

197   Mark Bennett, conversation, 12 October 2010.

198   When asked by the author, Richard Lawrence said that he himself is not an avatar.

199 Mark Bennett, in correspondence with the author, 12 October 2010.

200 Unless otherwise stated, all quotations in this entry from here on are taken from the leaflet *The Aetherius Society: Some basic principles included in its teachings*, 1988.

201 Lawrence 2010: 88.

202 This teaching, deeply profound for the Aetherius Society, is quoted in *The Aetherius Society: Some basic principles included in its teachings*, 1988.

203 Aetherius Society information booklet.

204 Raelians date their calendar from 6 August 1945, the date of the first atomic bomb, so 6 August 2010 was year 65 of the Age of Apocalypse, written as year 65aH (after Hiroshima).

205 Raël 2005: 290.

206 L. Ron Hubbard, founder of Dianetics and Scientology, also referred to himself as the Maitreya: Andreas Grünschloß, 'Scientology: A "New Age" Religion', in Lewis 2009: 233.

207 All quotations from Glenn Carter, UK leader of the Raelians, are from a conversation with the author, 19 July 2010.

208 Raël, 2004: 190. Large statues (30 cm) cost 140 Swiss francs (£85, US$126) and small ones cost 65 Swiss francs (£40, US$59), plus p&p.

209 Unless otherwise stated, all quotations are from the leaflet *The Raelian Movement: Information*, n.d.

210 George D. Chryssides in Partridge 2004: 405.

211 Eric Bolou, then UK Raelian leader, in conversation with the author, 2 December 1998.

212 Glenn Carter, conversation, 20 July 2010.

213 http://raelian.com/en/, http://raelian.com/en/jean_sendy.php, http://www.facebook.com/note.php?note_id=154051564798.

214 http://www.facebook.com/notes/raelians/clarification-from-rael-about-slanders-related-to-the-book-of-jean-sendy/182192344798, http://forum.raelian.com/viewtopic.php?f=21&t=61.

215 George D. Chryssides, 'Scientific Creationism: A Study of the Raelian Church' in Partridge 2003: 45.

216 Assistant to Glenn Carter, in correspondence with the author, 9 November 2010.

217 This was also the case with the Church Universal and Triumphant in the last years of Elizabeth Clare Prophet's life after her retirement through ill-health in 1999 (see p. 73).

218 Lewis 1995; Lewis 2003; Partridge 2003.

219 See Chapter 6, 'After the Prophet Dies: How movements change', in Barrett 2001: 58–69.

220 This and the previous two quotations are from Raël 1998: 153–4; the middle quotation in Raël 1986: 210 reads 'paradisiac planet'.

221 http://www.clitoraid.org.

222 Barrett 2001: 280–81.

223 Susan J. Palmer, 'Women in the Raelian Movement: New Religious Experiments in Gender and Authority', in Lewis 1995: 105.

224 Raël 1998: 151–3.

225 Giles Dexter, then Secretary of the British Raelian Movement, in correspondence with the author, 17 July 1995.

226 Booklet: *An Embassy for Extra-Terrestrials*: 7.

227 http://www.raelpress.org/news.php?item.47.1.

228 http://raelianews.org/news.php?item.206.

229 'It is impossible to ignore the fact that *The Da Vinci Code* launch was one of the best orchestrated in history . . . There were more Advance Reader Copies given away for free of *The Da Vinci Code* than the whole print run for *Angels & Demons*.' Dan Brown witness statement, Royal Courts of Justice, London, February–March 2006.

230 '*HBHG* was the essential tool for the Langdon/Teabing Lectures' in *The Da Vinci Code* and 'I conclude that, in the main, the majority of the Central Themes [in *The Da Vinci Code*] were drawn from *HBHG*,' Mr Justice Peter Smith in his Judgment, 7 April 2006. Despite this the judge ruled that Brown's DVC had not plagiarised Michael Baigent, Richard Leigh and Henry Lincoln, *The Holy Blood and the Holy Grail* (London: Jonathan Cape, 1982).

231 A selection of Brown's errors are listed in David V. Barrett, 'Holy Blood, Holy Code', in Kick 2007: 270–77; available online as 'Holy Code, Bloody Grail', http://www.nthposition.com/holycode.php.

232 For example Margaret Starbird, *The Woman with the Alabaster Jar* (Santa Fe, CA: Bear and Company, 1993), Laurence Gardner, *Bloodline of the Holy Grail* (Shaftesbury: Element, 1996), etc.

233 For example, the popular response to the 'Magdalene Line' novels by Kathleen McGowan.

234 http://www.celticmysticaljourneys.com/conf_tucson.htm.

235 http://www.prlog.org/11040569-mary-magdalene-the-dawning-of-the-golden-age-2012-prepare-yourself.html.

236 http://www.mindbodyspirit.co.uk.

237 See http://www.healerfound.co.uk/mbsevents.htm for a regularly updated list of those in Britain.

238 http://www.alternatives.org.uk/Site/Default.aspx.

239 http://www.f4hs.org/spiritual-companions/guidelines.htm.

240 http://www.f4hs.org/holistic-map.htm.

241 http://www.pagandash.org.

242 http://www.holisticmap.org/about/campaign.htm.

243 *The University of Avalon Prospectus*, September to December 1994.

244 *The Isle of Avalon Foundation: Courses and Workshops*, April 1995.

245 http://isleofavalonfoundation.com.

246 http://www.healerfound.co.uk.

247 http://www.intuitionandhealing.co.uk.

248 Personal correspondence with author, 28 July 2010.

249 http://www.collegeofpsychicstudies.co.uk.

250 http://www.thehealingtrust.org.uk.

251 http://www.confederation-of-healing-organisations.org.

252 http://www.ukhealers.info.

253 http://realizationsystem.com.

254 See Barrett 2001: 427–31, 434–7, 321–4, 431–4.

Part Two:
Hermetic, Occult
or High Magic Groups

As discussed in the Introduction, there are many overlaps between some of the groups in this part of the book and some of the groups in the other two parts. Astrology, Tarot and Kabbalah may be common interests to groups and individuals in all three strands of esoteric religion, and there are many common factors in shared elements of their history and in, for example, ritual and magic, between groups in this part and some Neo-Pagan groups.

Terms such as esoteric, Hermetic and occult were defined in the Introduction. Broadly speaking, each means or implies that the teachings, the beliefs and practices of such movements are, at least in theory, secret or hidden. The teachings of Kabbalah, which this part begins with, were originally passed, one to one, from mouth to ear. When the sixteenth- and seventeenth-century Hermetic Philosophers published their teachings they veiled them in layers of allegory. The original Rosicrucians, in the sense of the writers of the Rosicrucian manifestos, were so secret that they invited people to join them but did not give an address for applications.

The late nineteenth century saw an upsurge in Kabbalistic and Rosicrucian teachings particularly in France and Britain, and also in the United States and Germany, through both individual esoteric writers such as Papus and Eliphas Lévi and a number of esoteric societies. The cross influences between all of these are touched on in this part to demonstrate their inter-relationships – an important point when some groups claim a unique position as the sole inheritor of a tradition, as do several of the present-day American Rosicrucian orders.

Throughout this part the distinction between factual history and 'ritual history' or 'foundation myths' will be made a number of times. Hermetic movements even more than most religious movements seem to need to demonstrate their authority, even if the origin of that authority is fictitious (see p. 197). Some also seek to establish the pre-eminence of their authority in the courts, with varying degrees of success (see p. 186–7 and p. 217–8).

It may be necessary to emphasise once more that 'occult' does not mean 'Satanic'. Apart from a tiny minority, described near the end of this part, there is no connection between any of the movements described here and Satanism. In one way or another these movements trace back to Rosicrucianism, a form of mystical Christianity, and to Kabbalah, mystical Judaism.

KABBALAH

Many people today, hearing of Kabbalah, automatically think of the Los Angeles-based Kabbalah Centre founded by Philip and Karen Berg, which is known for its celebrity members like Madonna, its red string worn on the left wrist and its books, CDs and expensive bottled water.[1] But that is only one fairly recent way of approaching Kabbalah. Many esoteric movements have for centuries studied and in some cases practised Kabbalah in one form or another, and still do today.

In a phrase, Kabbalah is esoteric Judaism, also practised by esoteric Christians historically and today by esotericists in general. Kabbalah is not just a set of texts, but a means of approaching these texts – a process. The meaning of the Hebrew root word *qbl* is variously given as 'receiving' or 'received tradition' or 'mouth to ear'; in other words, its teachings were originally passed by word of mouth, one to one, only to those thought fit to receive them.

Kabbalah is sometimes spelt Cabala or Qabala. One writer differentiates three different meanings for the three spellings: he sees Kabbalah as the original Jewish system, Cabala as the Renaissance Christian version of it and Qabala as the modern occultist use of it.[2] Although there is some truth in this it is something of an *ex post facto* discrimination, and in any case does not always hold true. There have been many varieties and uses of Kabbalah in many lands over the centuries, and different people with different languages at different times have spelt the word in different ways. The spelling 'Kabbalah' is used generally throughout this book, except where a movement might use a different spelling, or in quotations or book titles.

Kabbalah is the root of the word 'cabal', meaning a secret intrigue or a small powerful group, often without any religious connotations. This sense, dating back to the mid-seventeenth century,[3] emphasises three ideas: secrecy, power and perhaps an unease, even a fear, by those on the outside of those on the inside.

The essence of Kabbalah is that most people reading the scriptures see only the outer story or, as it were, a suit of clothes; a few see the person within the clothes; a very few see the soul within the person. One might recognise the beauty of a friend's clothes, and even admire them; but the true value of the friend is much deeper. Kabbalists look for the inner meaning, the secret meaning, the esoteric meaning; they seek to discern the secrets of God and of creation.

There is some truth behind the affectionate stereotype of the Jewish love for telling stories with a moral. Kabbalist writings delight in stories-with-a-message, allegories, parables, myths. (So, of course, does the Bible, a point that tends to be ignored by those who insist on a literal interpretation of it.) The enactment of moral and spiritual stories is at the heart of many rituals in all religions, especially esoteric movements, and societies such as Freemasonry.

In tradition Kabbalah is said to have originated with Moses, who was believed to have written the Pentateuch, the first five books of the Bible; God also gave him secret mystical teachings to be passed on orally rather than in writing.

Others claim it originated some 2,000 years ago. Educated Jews at the time of Christ were split into several factions, of which the rabbinical Pharisees, who followed oral tradition in their interpretation of the scriptures and the law, and the more conservative, aristocratic and literalist Sadducees, who did not believe in angels, demons or resurrection, are mentioned in the

New Testament. There were also the nationalistic Zealots, who had political motivations, and the pious Essenes, about whom speculation outweighs the known facts.[4]

Although these groups all shared the Torah – the law, the Pentateuch, and by extension the whole Old Testament – they had very different ways of approaching it and interpreting it. So did the Jewish mystics, later known as Kabbalists. Based in rabbinical Judaism, in their search for spiritual enlightenment they borrowed over the years both from Jewish Gnosticism and from Jewish Neo-Platonism and Neo-Aristotelianism.

As the Jews were scattered and persecuted throughout Europe over much of the next two millennia, it was important for them to maintain both their scholarship and their spirituality. While medieval Christian priests were often almost completely uneducated, and their bishops often morally and politically corrupt, medieval Jewish rabbis were renowned for their learning and their piety. Rabbis were teachers and judges of their people, interpreters of the law, rather than being priests, though they did conduct ritual ceremonies.

Scholarship and spirituality are a powerful combination. In seeking a greater understanding of and closeness to God, many rabbis delved deeper into their studies of the Torah and the Talmud, the written body of rabbinical tradition and interpretation of the law. (The Babylonian Talmud dates in its written form to around 500 CE, but the Talmud could in one sense be said to be ever-unfinished, as later rabbis have added their interpretations and commentaries on it right up to the present day.)

With a religion so based on law, the interpretation of law is vitally important: hence the importance of, and the deep respect given to, rabbis. In any organisation there is always a conflict between those who insist on obeying the letter of the law and those who believe it more important to follow the spirit of the law; there are traditionalists and legalists (by no means always the same thing), and liberals, and supporters of a variety of different emphases. Legalists should not automatically be condemned for small-mindedness, as liberals are prone to do;

many follow the letter of the law *because of* the importance to them of the spirit of the law, i.e. the underlying reasons behind what might appear to others to be petty legalisms. This can apply to Kabbalists, and certainly includes devoted members of some ritual-based esoteric societies today.

Kabbalists always favoured a more allegorical rather than a literalist approach to the Torah and the Talmud. They also believed that truth could be found deep within the texts themselves, within the words and even the letters. One of the first Kabbalistic works, the *Sefer Yesirah*, or the Book of the Creation, is known from the tenth century, but may date back to the second to fifth centuries. A short work (different versions have from 1,500 to 2,500 words), this first set down the concept of the ten *sephiroth* (singular, *sephira*; see below) and the twenty-two paths between them (see below), showing already the importance that the ten numbers and twenty-two letters of the Hebrew alphabet would have to Kabbalah.

As with Roman numerals, Hebrew letters also represented numbers, and numbers, as Pythagoras taught, are powerfully symbolic of God and man and the relationship between them. In *gematria*, the Kabbalistic study of the spiritual significance of numbers, the numerical values of the letters in a word are added together. If different words or phrases add up to the same sum, it is believed that the words (which themselves are symbols of concepts) are related on a deep level. (Modern-day numerology, finding Personality numbers and Heart numbers from one's date of birth and the numerical equivalent of one's name, is a very much debased version of *gematria*; as practised by most people, it is no more than a trivialised form of fortune-telling, of as much value as tabloid newspaper horoscopes.)

In Genesis 1 God spoke, and through his words the world was created; John's gospel begins 'In the beginning was the Word, and the Word was with God, and the Word was God.' Words, then, have intrinsic power. In Eastern religions words, phrases or invocations may be chanted as mantras. In Kabbalah these words of power include the names of angels and archangels and secret names (or attributes) of God. Through *gematria* the inner meanings of the names of angels and daemons can be determined, revealing magical correspondences (see p. 202–3). Part of the mythology of Freemasonry is the search for the lost word; Pythagoras also taught of the 'music of the spheres', and a related spiritual quest is the search for the lost chord.[5]

Kabbalah became more formalised in the twelfth and thirteenth centuries in southern France and Spain. Although traditionalist Kabbalists claim that the *Sefer ha-Bahir* (Book of Brilliance) dates back to Rabbi Nehuniah ben haKana, a first-century Talmudic sage, it was first published in Provence around 1176. It is often ascribed to Yitzhak Saggi Nehor, better known as Isaac the Blind (*c.*1160–1235), sometimes called the Father of the Kabbalah, but if both his dates and the *Bahir*'s date are correct he would have been far too young; also, Isaac the Blind is known to have criticised some of his students for writing down Kabbalist teachings. Whoever wrote it probably compiled it from existing oral material. The *Sefer ha-Bahir*, which is a commentary on the opening chapters of Genesis in the form of a dialogue between master and students, contains Gnostic symbolism and emphasises the concept of the *Shekhinah* (Hebrew: 'dwelling'), or presence or immanence of God, as a feminine power.

Isaac the Blind is credited with giving the name Kabbalah to Jewish mysticism, and to giving names to the ten *sephiroth*. He also taught the Neo-Platonic concept of metempsychosis, the transmigration of souls after death, against the prevailing Aristotelian ethos of science and philosophy at the time. He was one of the best-known Kabbalist teachers not just of his day but of all time.

Two of his students, Rabbi Azriel and Rabbi Ezra ben Solomon, founded a School of Kabbalah in the small Catalan city of Girona, near to the French Pyrenees; Rabbi Azriel is thought to have written the influential work *Explanation of the Ten Sephiroth*, amongst much else. One of Azriel's students was Moses ben Nachman Girondi, usually known as Nahmanides (1194–1270), who was born in Girona. Nahmanides became the leading Jewish philosopher and teacher of the Talmud in all of Spain; he taught Kabbalah in Barcelona, laying emphasis on its oral transmission and emphasising a mystical interpretation of the Torah through personal enlightenment. Like Isaac the Blind, Nahmanides and his students taught Neo-Platonic mysticism rather than the more rationalist and materialist Aristotelian philosophy that was standard in medieval Europe.

The Girona school of Ezra, Azriel and Nahmanides, following and developing the teachings of Isaac the Blind, was greatly influential in the development of medieval Kabbalah. But following the expulsion of the Jews from Spain in 1492 they were quickly wiped from the collective mind. The huge importance of Girona to mystical Judaism was completely forgotten in the city until the mid-1970s when local poet (and perhaps Kabbalist) Josep Tarrés physically unearthed the remains of the School of Kabbalah near the cathedral.[6]

The next major work of Kabbalah was the publication of the *Sefer ha-Zohar* (Book of Splendour) in Spain around 1285. Although myth attributes its teachings to the second-century Rabbi Simeon bar Yohai it was written (or again, more likely compiled) by Moses de León (1240 or 1250–1305), who lived in Àvila in what is now Castile and León. The *Zohar* is today perhaps the best known Kabbalist text. It discusses divine creation, and teaches that everything in the universe is connected to everything else, and all is an expression of the Oneness of God, who is both transcendent and immanent, and essentially unknowable and indescribable; it uses the term *Ain Sof* (Hebrew: 'without end'). Kabbalah teaches ways towards mystical union with God, the ultimate purpose of mankind.

The expulsion of the Jews from Spain, with their subsequent wanderings through central Europe, had a profound effect on Western esotericism.[7] They took with them their teachings, both exoteric and esoteric. Just two decades after the

Neo-Platonist scholar Marsilio Ficino (1433–99) translated the *Corpus Hermeticum* into Latin for Cosimo de' Medici in Florence, Europe's Hermetic Philosophers became aware of the hidden mystical streak in Judaism. Giovanni Pico della Mirandola (1463–94) and Francesco Giorgi (1466–1540), amongst others, delved into the mysteries of Kabbalah.

Throughout the sixteenth and seventeenth centuries Kabbalah was an essential part of the work, whether study or practice, of esoteric scholars searching for hidden spiritual truths. In the late nineteenth century French occultists such as Eliphas Lévi drew correspondences between the twenty-two paths linking the *sephiroth* and the twenty-two cards of the Major Arcana of Tarot. The Hermetic Order of the Golden Dawn (see p. 195) drew on and developed these concepts, which are now part of the teachings of many present day esoteric orders and schools of occult science (see p. 219ff).[8]

The best-known aspect of Kabbalah is the symbolic diagram of the Tree of Life. According to Dolores Ashcroft-Nowicki, Director of Studies of the Servants of the Light school of occult science (see p. 231), it contains, 'the entire wisdom of the Qabalah . . . Owing to its simplicity . . . the glyph is easily committed to memory; and because of its profundity, from this sparse simplicity can be derived a complete and satisfying philosophy and knowledge of life in both its inner and outer aspects'.[9]

The Tree of Life shows the relationship between God and his creation; it symbolises both God reaching down to man and man reaching up to God. The ten *sephiroth*, meaning 'enumerations', each represents an attribute of God manifest in the physical universe; these can be thought of as names of God. (The sacred name of God, represented by the Hebrew letters for YHWH, or the Tetragrammaton, was believed to be too holy to pronounce.) Together they symbolise the ten rays of light of God's creation of the universe, and thus the secrets of the universe.

What I Believe . . .
Kabbalah

Kabbalah is the mystical and previously esoteric
aspect of Judaism.
**Dr William Bloom, Author and educator in a
holistic and modern approach to spirituality**

A coherent system of elaborate correspondences,
based on Jewish mythology and magickal traditions.
**Oberon Zell-Ravenheart, Co-founder,
Church of All Worlds**

Kabbalah really started with mediaeval Spanish Jews who
were looking for hidden meanings in the Old Testament.
However it could be applied to hidden meanings in all kinds
of other things, for example Robert Graves's book *The White
Goddess* is looking for hidden meanings within Celtic legends
and poetry. In the esoteric world it's changed somewhat
from the mediaeval, because it's generally people who are
not Jewish and who have a very limited knowledge of
Hebrew . . . In today's movements people either put a great
emphasis on the Tree of Life and the correspondences to it
– the correspondences are actually derived more from
Hermeticism than they are from Judaism – or for some
people it's finding secrets in numerology, which can work
various ways.
**Gareth J. Medway, Priest Hierophant
of the Fellowship of Isis
Writer and assistant psychic**

Interesting way to catalogue and link the world but I
feel it is as much a camouflage, something to keep the
mind confused and distracted while other stuff goes
on; a bit like yoga; keep the body contorted and off
somewhere else, while a gap is created in thought to
allow something to coalesce.
**Dr Dave Evans, Chaos magician
Social Sciences researcher**

The ten *sephiroth* are *Kether*, the Crown, *Chokmah*, Wisdom, *Binah*, Understanding, *Chesed*, Mercy, *Geburah*, Power, *Tiphareth*, Beauty or Harmony, *Netzach*, Victory, *Hod*, Splendour, *Yesod*, Foundation, and *Malkuth*, Kingdom.

The *sephiroth* and the twenty-two paths between them correspond to numbers and letters, to colours, planets, angels, parts of the body and much else, including the Tarot; such correspondences are at the heart of ritual magic (see p. 202–3).

The Tree of Life can be used to represent many things, including the nature of God, the way that the universe came into being, and the interrelationship of God and his creation, including mankind. It can be divided in many ways. Different groups of *sephiroth* can represent Root, Trunk, Branch and Fruit, or Will, Intellect, Emotion and Action, and the right and left sides of the Tree can represent active and passive principles respectively. As a symbolic map it can be adapted and extended to symbolise different patterns of teachings. Kabbalah, and the Tree of Life in particular, were fundamental to the Hermetic Order of the Golden Dawn (see p. 195); one scholar writes of their 'use of the Tree of Life as a model of the universe to which every conceivable phenomenon whatsoever could be applied. In a sense, the linear scheme of the Tree of Life became a method whereby it was possible to reach order out of an apparently chaotic mass of phenomena, without necessarily any further knowledge of kabbalistic doctrine.'[10]

The complex symbolism of the Kabbalah, embodying both the theoretical and the practical, exemplifies the link between mysticism and magic, and also the importance of myth as a means of expressing truths. The deep spiritual teachings within it became central to all esoteric religion in the West, and remain so today. Many view Kabbalah as a way for God and man to communicate, interact and work together; for them it is a powerful practical system of mysticism, even magic. And in the sense that it is a way for man to know and *experience* God on an individual, personal basis without priestly mediation, it could be called Gnostic – in common with many other esoteric paths.

Kabbalah is powerful and it is personal. Those who use it believe that through their own spiritual transformation they can also help to transform – and heal – the imperfect world. The Rosicrucian manifestos expressed a similar ideal (see p. 179–80).

TAROT

Many esoteric movements teach and use both the Kabbalah and Tarot, and draw connections between the two. The Kabbalah's Tree of Life (see p. 171ff) is used symbolically to represent the relationship between God and Man; as Tarot authority and science fiction/fantasy author Rachel Pollack has said, 'the Tarot has come into being as a lively pictorial version of the inner knowledge found on the Tree.'[11]

The American group Builders of the Adytum (BOTA, see p. 220) calls Tarot 'one of the foremost aids to spiritual trans-mutation'. The series of cards is:

a record of the inner knowledge of the Western Sages in picture form – the way the Wise regard the Universe and Man in a manner that impresses the consciousness of all who use the Tarot.

As an instrument of mind training, the Tarot is designed in accordance with basic laws of human psychology. It was originally devised as a means of conveying universal principles regarding Man's structure, place and purpose in the Cosmos, through the use of symbols. Symbols are the language of subconsciousness in that they communicate ideas to all individuals, regardless of their native tongue.[12]

In common with most esoteric schools BOTA use Tarot for study, meditation, imagery and ritual, rather than for fortune-telling or divination.

Several esoteric Tarot packs trace back to the teachings of the Hermetic Order of the Golden Dawn (see p. 195). Members were encouraged to hand-draw their own personal packs, copying the one drawn by Mina Mathers, an artist and the wife of one of the founders of the Golden Dawn.

The best-known Golden Dawn-derived pack is the Rider-Waite-Smith Tarot,[13] designed by Pamela Colman Smith to the instructions of A. E. Waite, who wrote of the cards: 'They differ in many important respects from the conventional archaisms of the past . . . For the variations in the symbolism by which the designs have been affected, I alone am responsible.'[14]

Elsewhere Waite writes: 'There is no public canon of authority in the interpretation of Tarot Symbolism';[15] this is somewhat ironic, considering that the popularity of Waite's pack meant that *his* interpretations of the symbolism became set in stone for generations of Tarot users. But Waite does not reveal all the secrets of Tarot; in the book accompanying his pack he mentions the restraints he imposed on his writing: 'There is a Secret Tradition concerning the Tarot, as well as a Secret Doctrine contained therein; I have followed some part of it without exceeding the limits which are drawn about matters of this kind and belong to the laws of honour.'[16]

Rosicrucian societies and schools of occult science each have their own teachings on Tarot, with a variety of detailed symbolism and a host of correspondences. Following Eliphas Lévi (see p. 181), they link the twenty-two cards of the Major Arcana to the twenty-two paths between the *sephiroth* on the Tree of Life; the cards have also been linked to astrological signs, to other systems of divination such as runes and the I Ching, and to a wide range of mythologies.

Other packs influenced in one way or another by the Golden Dawn include Aleister Crowley's Book of Thoth, Robert Wang's Golden Dawn Tarot (based on Israel Regardie's pack, which was based on the pack painted by Mathers's wife to his instructions), Godfrey Dowson's Hermetic Tarot and the Morgan-Greer Tarot, which is based on the interpretations of

Waite and Paul Foster Case. Considering that these all stem from the same root, their images and symbolism are often markedly different from each other, though the BOTA pack, drawn to the instructions of Case, is very similar to the Rider-Waite-Smith pack, and is presumably a copy of Mina Mathers's pack. Crowley's pack in particular is strikingly different from the others.

The Golden Dawn and some of its offshoots were closely linked with Freemasonry and Rosicrucianism; much of the symbolism is similar between all of these groups. Interestingly, the Masonic Tarot, a French pack, is quite different from any of the Hermetic Order of the Golden Dawn-offshoot packs; its images use a lot of geometric symbolism.

What I Believe . . .
Using Tarot, Runes, etc.

All systems of divination are techniques of
extracting meaningful patterns from randomness,
where the presumed sorting template is Spirit or
subconscious awareness.
**Oberon Zell-Ravenheart, Co-founder,
Church of All Worlds**

I use the Tarot as a way to let the language of symbols speak to me, and
I believe that time is a strange and fluid thing, so that the Tarot cards
will speak of the future, and they will speak in this language of symbols
which I'm fortunate to be able to understand a little bit of. I have had
readings where somebody has said to me, 'Somebody wearing a grey
suit, probably next Tuesday, will come with something unexpected and
offer you a large sum of money', and that's exactly what's happened.
And I don't want to live in a world where that's not possible.
**Dr Christina Oakley Harrington, Wiccan priestess
Owner of Treadwells esoteric bookshop, London,
former university lecturer in History and Religious History**

I discovered the runes and it was like coming home.
A wonderful system. Not just for divination, but predominantly
for spell-working, changing existing circumstances in
accordance with the magician's will, using energy channelled via
various runes.
**Jack Gale, Magician
Retired school teacher**

I regularly use Astrology as a predictive tool, when working
out auspicious times for major events in my life, and also to
analyse other people's lives – especially when they are
going through difficult times. I also use Runes, but purely
for magical work and protection, inserting them openly or
subtly in my art, important letters, websites and personal
ritual tools.
**Mani Navasothy, Wiccan High Priest and
founder of Hern's Tribe
Physicist**

ROSICRUCIAN GROUPS

There are many different Rosicrucian organisations in Britain, Europe, the United States and around the world today, with widely differing teachings. Some are quite secretive; others advertise widely. Some reserve their membership to Freemasons of the highest grades; others have a more open membership, but paradoxically are perhaps more difficult to join. Some openly recognise their modern origins; others claim to trace their lineage back to the earliest 'history' of the Rosicrucians.

The 'historic' Rosicrucians have their roots in the Hermetic Philosophers of the sixteenth and seventeenth centuries. In many ways they were the cutting-edge scientists of their day. Some were priests or monks; some physicians; some university teachers. Their interests were eclectic, including amongst others theology, astrology, alchemy, medicine and Kabbalah.

In the early seventeenth century three mysterious works were published in Germany: *Fama Fraternitas* or *The Praiseworthy Order of the Rosy Cross* (1614); *Confessio Fraternitas* or *The Confession of the Rosicrucian Fraternity* (1615); and *Chymische Hocheit* or *The Chymical Marriage of Christian Rosenkreutz* (1616).[17] These told the life story of Christian Rosenkreutz, who was born in 1378, travelled in the Middle East, and died aged 106 in 1484. When his tomb was discovered in 1604 his body had not corrupted. Rosenkreutz had set up a fraternity, the Spiritus Sanctum or House of the Holy Spirit, dedicated to the well-being of mankind, social reform and healing the sick; this reformation of the whole world was to be accomplished by men of secret, magical learning.

Some if not all of the documents are now believed by many to have been written by a Lutheran priest, Johann Valentin Andreae (1586–1654), who created the symbolic myth of Christian Rosenkreutz in an attempt to stimulate others to take up Rosicrucian ideals.

Historian Dame Frances Yates devoted years of study and several books to the Rosicrucian Enlightenment (the title of one of them). She concluded that the three manifestos did not spring out of nowhere, but were part of an ongoing conversation between esoteric scholars of the time, including John Dee. She also drew parallels between *The Chymical Marriage of Christian Rosenkreutz* and the marriage in 1613 of the Winter King, Frederick V, Elector Palatine, to Elizabeth Stuart, daughter of James I of England, and the short-lived progressive Protestant hope for Europe, which was dashed a few years later when Frederick lost the throne of Bohemia. A slightly earlier king of Bohemia, Rudolf II (1552–1612), had been both a patron of the arts and a patron of occult scientists, especially alchemists; he had his own alchemical laboratory, and was host to John Dee and Edward Kelley in Prague Castle in 1584–6.[18]

Within a few years of the manifestos other Rosicrucian writings appeared, including one by the influential physician, alchemist and Hermetic philosopher Robert Fludd (1574–1637), and Rosicrucian societies began to spring up around Europe. One significant German group in the eighteenth century was the Brotherhood of the Golden and Rosy Cross (see p. 198–9).

There was a resurgence of interest in the nineteenth century, particularly in France, Britain and the United States; new societies included the Fraternitas Rosae Crucis (1858), the Societas Rosicruciana in Anglia (1865), the Rosicrucian Fellowship (1907), the Societas Rosicruciana in America (1907), the Ancient and Mystical Order of the Rosy Cross (AMORC, 1915) and Lectorium Rosicrucianum (1924). Significant names in France included Eliphas Lévi (Alphonse Louis Constant, 1810–75), author of *Le Dogme et Rituel de la Haute Magie* (1855–6), Papus (Gérard Encausse, 1865–1916), author of *The Tarot of the Bohemians* (1889), Bernard-Raymond Fabré-Palaprat (1773–1838), the Marquis Stanislaw de Guaita (1861–97) and Joséphin Péladan (1858–1918), the last two of whom founded the influential Kabbalistic Order of the Rosy Cross in 1888, the same year the Hermetic Order of the Golden Dawn was founded. The cross-fertilisation between these people and organisations could in itself fill a book.[19]

Eliphas Lévi deserves particular mention, for good and for bad. Esoteric historian R. A. Gilbert has written of him:

> His three principal works, *Dogme et Rituel de la Haute Magie* (1856), *Histoire de la Magie* (1860) and *La Clef des Grandes Mystères* (1861) were inaccurate, idiosyncratic and utterly enchanting. They also exercised an enormous influence on occultists and ideas that were born out of Lévi's imagination became enshrined as occult dogmas ...
>
> All of these ideas were regurgitated, with embellishments, by his successors – not the least of whom was Madame Blavatsky.[20]

Lévi's ideas were perhaps regurgitated most of all by the Hermetic Order of the Golden Dawn (see p. 195) and its many successors. But before looking in some detail at the Golden Dawn it may be instructive to examine briefly the origins of a few present-day Rosicrucian societies. The few examples that follow show that Rosicrucianism contains a variety of very powerful religious ideas; in the cases of the Church of Light, the Rosicrucian Fellowship and Lectorium Rosicrucianum in particular, it effectively is a religion, and the Fraternitas Rosae Crucis makes a point of distinguishing itself from 'spurious organisations that attempted to usurp the name Rosicrucian for less than spiritual or humanitarian purposes' by emphasising that it is 'a religious organisation and ... a tax-exempt church'.[21] (As noted below – see p. 186–7 – American Rosicrucian orders are not known for their love for each other.)

There are links and cross-influences between Rosicrucianism, the mystical side of Freemasonry, alchemy, astrology, Hermetic Philosophy, the Western Mystery Tradition, Theosophy and esoteric Christianity. And out of all of these was born the Hermetic Order of the Golden Dawn.

FRATERNITAS ROSAE CRUCIS

In its literature and on its website the Fraternitas Rosae Crucis (FRC), based in the United States and also known as the Beverly Hall Corporation, claims to be the sole repository of the original Rosicrucian wisdom; for example, its website states: 'Welcome to the authentic Rosicrucian Fraternity that was first instituted in Germany in 1614.'[22] Many esoteric movements claim an impressive traditional history; the FRC states that Rosicrucian leadership is found in a 'Council of Three', and that in 1774 this was composed of Benjamin Franklin, George Clymer and Thomas Paine. During the Civil War the Council comprised Paschal Beverly Randolph, General Ethan Allen Hitchcock and Abraham Lincoln. It claims that 'The Fraternity has continued in America without interruption since prior to 1773.'[23]

In its own history the FRC claims to have been founded by Paschal Beverly Randolph in 1858, after he had 'received authority from the Grand Dome of France to establish a Grand Lodge'. After two other successors, R. Swinburne Clymer became the 'Supreme Grand Master of the Supreme Grand Lodge' in 1905.

Most esoteric authorities view all of this with some scepticism. Paschal Randolph was, like several other nineteenth-century esotericists, something of a compulsive joiner and founder. He certainly sought out others with esoteric spiritual interests, 'but R.S. Clymer's fantasies of Randolph, Hitchcock,

Alexander Wilder and Abraham Lincoln functioning as the leaders of a Rosicrucian club in the 1860s are just that – fantasy,' writes Randolph's biographer.[24] The various versions of the Council of Three:

> really give room for Clymer to exercise his creativity and are the primary device he uses to cover lapses in his information. Any name associated with Randolph or Western occultism is made a member of one council or another . . .
>
> Clymer's version of events, in other words, despite the evident sincerity of his own belief in the value of his own work in propagating Randolph's practices, is pure fantasy, concocted to satisfy his own followers who approached him as mystagogue, demanding to know his bona fides and the sources of his authority. The mistake is in treating it as history.[25]

Similar sleight of hand in creating an impressive lineage, a fake provenance bestowing the mantle of ancient authority on a brand new movement, can be seen in the founding of the Hermetic Order of the Golden Dawn (see p. 197) and several other esoteric movements.

In fact the FRC was founded in 1922 by R. Swinburne Clymer (1878–1966), though there is an actual link with Randolph. The FRC was originally based on one of the many groups which Paschal Randolph (1825–75) founded, just a year before his death. The Brotherhood of Eulis was a vehicle for promoting Randolph's one significant contribution to esoteric teaching, the concept of sex-magic. Falling out with the other members he dissolved the group a few months later, but some of the members continued it after his death. Clymer joined the Brotherhood, and on the death of its leader in 1922 he became the new leader, and used it as the basis of his own society, the Fraternitas Rosae Crucis, creating a colourful traditional history for his new organisation – but with no mention of sex-magic.

In his book, *One Flesh*, Gerald E. Poesnecker, Supreme Grand Master of Fraternitas Rosae Crucis from 1983 to 2003, does mention Randolph, but he concentrates solely on the spirituality of married sexual love, condemning masturbation as 'destructive . . . injurious . . . harmful', oral sex as an 'ancient perversion' and all forms of homosexuality as 'aberrations'.[26]

Clymer claimed that he and his group were the sole inheritors of the Rosicrucian tradition, now transferred from Europe to the United States: 'Since America is to be the centre of the New Order of the Ages it is obvious that this land will also be the centre from whence all Spiritual wisdom and knowledge will come from as well.'[27] But another Rosicrucian group already existed in the United States, the Ancient and Mystical Order of the Rosy Cross, better known today as AMORC.

AMORC

The Ancient and Mystical Order of the Rosy Cross (AMORC) was founded in 1915 by H. Spencer Lewis (1883–1939). Lewis claimed esoteric legitimacy from his membership of the Ordo Templi Orientis (see p. 212); he was initiated into the International Rosicrucian Council in France in 1909 and authorised to begin a new order in the United States.

AMORC moved to its present headquarters in San Jose, California, in 1927. The following year R. Swinburne Clymer of the Fraternitas Rosae Crucis (FRC, see p. 183) took Lewis to court over the right to call his order Rosicrucian. This is more than likely one reason for Clymer's backdating of the FRC's foundation to before that of AMORC.

The battle went on for several years, with both sides attacking the other viciously. Lewis, possibly aware of the actual rather than the claimed origins of the FRC, accused Clymer of being a fraud; Clymer, who had started the fight, attacked 'the boasting pilfering Imperator with his black-magic, sex-magic connections'.[28] This was a somewhat ironic accusation, because Lewis's AMORC took its authority and some of its early teachings from the Ordo Templi Orientis (see p. 215), which gained its teachings on sex-magic from the Hermetic Brotherhood of Light (see p. 189), which had learned them from Paschal Beverly Randolph, out of whose Brotherhood of Eulis Clymer had forged his own FRC.

The courts eventually decided that no organisation could own the name Rosicrucian – but the FRC's website and literature still warn against 'pretenders' and 'counterfeit organisations'.[29]

H. Spencer Lewis was succeeded as Grand Imperator of AMORC by his son Ralph M. Lewis (d.1987). His successor, Gary L. Stewart, was removed from office in 1990 following a bitter dispute with the directors, and founded his own group called the Order Militia Crucifera Evangelica.

Like several other Rosicrucian orders AMORC runs correspondence courses on its teachings, which it advertises in mainstream newspapers and magazines. It is said to claim around 250,000 members, though it is uncertain whether this figure (as with the claimed membership of the Church of Scientology; see p. 365–6) includes everyone who has ever taken any of its courses.[30]

As a 'mystical fraternity' AMORC claims to teach its students to function 'in accordance with the Cosmic and its laws of nature', to bring about 'a harmonious level of interaction within your body' and to make it possible that, 'through the experiments in the Rosicrucian teachings, your psychic faculties can be one of the greatest powers within you'.[31]

AMORC traces its traditional roots to:

the mystery traditions, philosophy and myths of ancient Egypt from approximately 1500 BC. However, the Rosicrucian movement is eclectic and uniquely draws upon the diverse mystical traditions of ancient Greece, China, India and Persia. The result is a consolidation of mystical principles which focus on a purposeful direction for the future. That being the enlightenment of humanity by way of establishing a mystical study of knowledge.[32]

AMORC is non-sectarian, and members are encouraged to continue in the religion of their choice. It claims to offer 'the world's foremost system of instruction and guidance for exploring the inner self and discovering the universal laws that govern all human endeavour'.

CHURCH OF LIGHT

The Church of Light is also known as the Religion of the Stars, and its members are called Stellarians: 'Its purpose is to help individuals find wholeness and unity in the old and the new by placing reliance on the individual's capacity to read and understand "The Book of Nature".'[33]

It has correspondence courses on, amongst others, astrology, alchemy, magic, occultism, Tarot and healing; the study material is published in over twenty books by its founder C. C. Zain. It publishes its own Brotherhood of Light Egyptian Tarot; the Hermetic emphasis is clear, with Zain's book on Tarot beginning with a chapter on 'Doctrine of Kabalism [sic]', and his description of Tarot as 'the ONE standard text-book on the meaning of universal symbols'.[34] After progressing through forty-nine degrees of initiation through the courses, members then attain a fiftieth secret degree. At the heart of the Church's teaching are 'the two keys': 'King Solomon's Temple has two doors; so also, there are two doors to its oracle. He who would enter either must possess their respective keys. The door on the right is opened only with the aid of a golden key; that on the left requires a key of silver.'[35] The golden key is astrology; the silver key is Tarot.

The Church of Light has a long pedigree tracing back ultimately, once again, to Paschal Beverly Randolph, though the present-day organisation is very different from anything Randolph might have envisaged. It was founded in 1932 by

C. C. Zain, the pen-name of Benjamin Williams (1882–1951), also known as Elbert Benjamine. The Church of Light grew out of the Brotherhood of Light, a correspondence school Williams set up in Los Angeles around 1915, teaching his 210-lesson course in astrology and other esoteric subjects. That in turn was a development of the Hermetic Brotherhood of Light, which he had joined in 1900, becoming its leader in 1914. The Hermetic Brotherhood of Light, founded in 1895, grew out of the ashes of the Hermetic Brotherhood of Luxor, which had collapsed in scandal in 1886, and continued its teachings. The Hermetic Brotherhood of Luxor was founded in London in 1884 by two students of Paschal Beverly Randolph, and incorporated his teaching on sex-magic.[36]

The Church of Light, like AMORC (see p. 186) and the Fraternitas Rosae Crucis (see p. 183), has now distanced itself completely from any mention of sex-magic. Probably the only movement now still promoting Randolph's teachings on the esoteric power of sex is the Ordo Templi Orientis (see p. 212), whose founder Theodor Reuss took the teachings from his colleague Carl Kellner, who had been a member of the Hermetic Brotherhood of Light.

ROSICRUCIAN FELLOWSHIP

The Rosicrucian Fellowship was founded in 1907 by Max Heindel (1865–1919), author of *The Rosicrucian Cosmo-Conception* (1909). Heindel had been a member of the Theosophical Society (see p. 23) in Los Angeles, and had also met, on a visit to Germany, Rudolf Steiner, founder of Anthroposophy (see p. 34). It is probable that he was at least initially influenced by both.

Although its teachings are quite different from many of the other Rosicrucian-type movements, as with some other groups the Rosicrucian Fellowship claims that it is *the* American continuation of 'the original' Rosicrucians. Heindel's widow wrote:

> The Rosicrucian Fellowship, founded by Max Heindel under the direct guidance of the Elder Brothers of the Order, is the authorised representative for the present period of the ancient Rosicrucian Order, of which Christian Rose Cross, or Christian Rosenkreutz is the Head. This Order is not a mundane organisation, but has its Temple and headquarters on the etheric plane. It authorised the formation of the Fellowship by Max Heindel for the purpose of carrying the Western Wisdom Teachings to the Western people. In earlier ages the Order carried on its work through various secret societies in Europe and elsewhere; but the growth and advancement of the people of the United States have in recent years reached such a point that the Order deemed it advisable to establish an exoteric centre here for the extension of its work. The Rosicrucian

Fellowship is its latest manifestation in physical form, putting out the most up-to-date version of the Rosicrucian Teachings, in twentieth-century scientific terms, which are at the same time simple and devoid of technical abstractions.[37]

The teachings of the Rosicrucian Fellowship are a form of mystical Christianity, with correspondence courses on philosophy, spiritual astrology and the Bible. The main difference from mainstream Christianity is that it teaches reincarnation:

> that each soul is an integral part of God, which is seeking to gain experience by repeated existences in gradually improving material bodies and that, therefore, it passes into and out of material existences many times; that each time it gathers a little more experience than it previously possessed and in time is nourished from nescience to omniscience – from impotence to omnipotence – by means of these experiences.[38]

Members above the introductory student level must abstain from meat, alcohol, tobacco and mind-altering drugs. There is a great emphasis on spiritual healing through the aid of 'invisible helpers', portrayed as angelic beings.

LECTORIUM ROSICRUCIANUM

Lectorium Rosicrucianum was originally founded in the Netherlands in 1924 under the name Rozekruisers Genootschap (Rosicrucian Fellowship) by two brothers, Zwier Wilhelm Leene (1892–1938) and Jan Leene (1896–1968), and Henriette Stok-Huyser (1902–90); the last two used the writing names J. van Rijckenborgh and Catharose de Petri. Rozekruisers Genootschap was linked for a while to the Rosicrucian Fellowship in the United States, but broke this connection in 1935.

After the Second World War, when it was banned by the Nazis, it re-formed as Lectorium Rosicrucianum, the International School of the Golden Rosycross. It has centres in Britain, the United States and over three-dozen other countries, and its magazine *Pentagram* is published in 16 languages. In 2010 it has 12,500 full members (known as pupils) worldwide, 8,500 of these in Europe, though only 60 in Britain and 80 in the United States. It also has around 2,900 probationary members, 2,600 of these in Europe.[39]

More than most Rosicrucian orders, its teachings are a version of Gnostic Christianity, stressing 'the living spiritual core in the original revelations of all the great world religions and mystery schools' and imparting 'the inner knowledge which points the way to soul-rebirth and ultimately the re-establishment of the link with the Spirit of God'.[40]

Gnosticism generally teaches the contrast between the spiritual world (good) and the material world (evil). Lectorium

Rosicrucianum, which in its doctrines is close to the twelfth-and thirteenth-century Cathar religion of southern France,[41] teaches that there are two nature-orders, 'the familiar one containing both the living and the dead . . . characterised by pairs of opposites and by perishability', which it calls 'dialectics', and 'the original divine nature-order', which it calls 'statics': 'Although this interpenetrates our nature-order completely, it is not perceptible to dialectical sense organs because it is separated from our nature-order by an enormous difference in vibration.' The divine nature-order is also known as the Kingdom of Heaven, and the human heart contains a remnant of it, a Divine Spark (see p. 12 and p. 74) or Rose of the Heart, which causes us 'to seek out the original state of being "with the Father", the state of being immortally at one with God'.

Following insight into the difference between the two nature-orders, and the desire for salvation, one can achieve the rebirth of transfiguration through self-dissolution, the 'total self-surrender of the I-personality to the actualisation of this salvation'. This is followed by a new mode of life, 'under the direction of the aroused spirit-spark-atom, the newly born soul', and fulfilment, 'the resurrection in the original field of light'.

In common with other Rosicrucian movements Lectorium Rosicrucianum places a great deal of emphasis on symbols, including the golden rose on a golden cross, the circle containing a square and an equilateral triangle – 'the Circle of Eternal Love containing the *Trigonum Igneum* or Fiery Triangle and the Square of Construction' – and the Pentagram, 'ever the symbol of the reborn, new Human Being'.

As with the Rosicrucian Fellowship (see p. 190) there are strict behavioural standards; the full members, or professing pupils, abstain from meat, alcohol, tobacco and drugs.

In addition to the *Pentagram* magazine Lectorium Rosicrucianum, like many other esoteric schools, provides a wide range of books on its beliefs in English and other languages, including *Elementary Philosophy of the Modern Rosycross, The Universal Gnosis, The Egyptian Arch-Gnosis* and *The Secrets of the Brotherhood of the Rosycross*, all by J. van Rijckenborgh.

HERMETIC ORDER
OF THE GOLDEN DAWN

Like Theosophy (see p. 23) the Hermetic Order of the Golden Dawn (HOGD) is important both for the people associated with it during its relatively short existence and for its continuing effect on later movements – its 'offspring'. And like Theosophy, it was unique in its own time.

It is now generally accepted that, from a critic's viewpoint, the HOGD was founded on a lie – in fact, a series of lies. An apologist might say that, like most esoteric organisations, it was eclectic – it borrowed most of its teachings and rituals from various places, and created others out of whole cloth – and that, also like many other esoteric organisations, it fudged its origins for good reasons (see below).

The Hermetic Order of the Golden Dawn was the creation of Dr William Wynn Westcott, Dr William Robert Woodman and Samuel Liddell 'MacGregor' Mathers. (Mathers added 'MacGregor' to his name and called himself Chevalier MacGregor and the Comte de Glenstrae to bolster his romantic Scottish pretensions; his chosen motto, by which he was known within HOGD, was *S'Rioghail mo Dhream* (SRMD), Gaelic for 'Royal is my race'.)[42] All three were Freemasons, and leading members of the Societas Rosicruciana in Anglia (known by Freemasons as Soc. Ros. and open only to master masons). HOGD was the brainchild of Westcott, who (in one version of the story) was given, in 1887, a manuscript of around sixty pages by an elderly clergyman with occult interests. The manuscript contained, in an artificial language, fragments of 'Golden Dawn' rituals that clearly owed much to Freemasonry, with large elements of the Kabbalah (see p. 165), astrology, alchemy and related subjects. Westcott asked Mathers to flesh out the fragments into full working rituals, and recruited Woodman, who was then Supreme Magus of Soc. Ros., to be the third leader of the new organisation. (In one of several other versions Westcott, or someone else, found the manuscript on a bookstall in Farringdon Road, London.)

It is rather more likely that Westcott found the Cipher Manuscripts amongst the papers of Kenneth Mackenzie, who had helped Robert Wentworth Little set up Soc. Ros. in 1866. Little had asked Mackenzie to help decipher some old documents containing 'ritual information' he had supposedly once been shown in the Library of United Grand Lodge by the then Grand Secretary of English Freemasonry, who claimed to be the last surviving member of a Rosicrucian order created by a nineteenth-century Venetian ambassador to England – but we are dependent on Westcott for this story. Soc. Ros., therefore, although a new organisation, supposedly had links with an earlier Rosicrucian order. It must be noted that the esoteric historian A. E. Waite, himself a member of the Golden Dawn and leader of one of its offshoots (see below), is scathing about the veracity of both Westcott and Mackenzie; he refers to the 'recurring mendacity' of the latter.[43]

The importance of Soc. Ros. in the genesis of the Golden Dawn can be gauged from a summary of the order's aims: 'to afford mutual aid and encouragement in working out the great problems of Life, and in discovering the secrets of nature; to facilitate the study of the systems of philosophy founded upon the Kabbalah and the doctrines of Hermes Trismegistus'.[44]

Mackenzie, author of the *Royal Masonic Cyclopaedia* (1877), was a serial collector of esoteric societies; amongst others he was Grand Secretary of a fringe masonic order, the Swedenborgian Rite. When he died in 1886 his widow gave his Swedenborgian papers to Westcott, who became Supreme

Grand Secretary of the Rite – and amongst these papers were almost certainly draft rituals Mackenzie had written, probably for one of two societies he had founded or was involved in, the Hermetic Order of Egypt and the Royal Oriental Order of the Sat B'hai. Beyond little doubt these were the papers that were the Cipher Manuscripts underlying the birth of the Golden Dawn just a year later.[45]

Westcott and Mackenzie were also members of a small and short-lived alchemical research group, the Society of Eight (1883–5); Mathers joined this shortly before it faded away, becoming friendly with Westcott. Some authorities believe that the Cipher Manuscripts may have been draft rituals Mackenzie had written for the Society of Eight.

The lie came in – or was embroidered – with Westcott's 'discovery' amongst the cipher papers of a letter from one Fräulein Anna Sprengel, chief adept of a non-existent German occult order, Die Goldene Dämmerung; he contacted her and she granted a charter to the HOGD to form the Isis-Urania Temple No. 3 in London.[46] Over a period of about a year Westcott wrote letters from Fräulein Sprengel (or Soror SDA, from her Latin motto *Sapiens Dominabitur Astris* – see below); he had these letters translated into German, then back into English. The HOGD thus became a fully authorised British branch of an ancient continental order, whose teachings went back into the mists of antiquity. Rather like the dodgy antiques dealer in the BBC TV drama series *Lovejoy*, who would forge a piece of yellowed paper certifying that a six-week-old painting was a genuine antique, Fräulein Sprengel's letters gave this brand new order a provenance; it therefore had authority.

Such a practice is hardly new; the Early Christian Church was littered with gospels and epistles falsely attributed to the apostles; some of these (for example, the Second Epistle of Peter) made it into the New Testament.[47] Linguistic analysis has shown that several of Paul's epistles are unlikely to have been written by him.[48] The Athanasian Creed was certainly not written by Athanasius (293–373 CE) but about a century later, yet it reflected his beliefs, and giving it his name ensured that people would take notice of it. Much the same applies with the 'provenance' of esoteric societies.

In a remarkable letter to Israel Regardie (see p. 206) in 1933, Paul Foster Case, founder of the HOGD offshoot Builders of the Adytum (see p. 220), explained in some detail the problems he had with the Golden Dawn, including its roots: 'But that the G.D. . . . is in the authorised line of descent from such a society established in any period around the 1400s or 1500s I most seriously doubt.' He went on to discuss the wider issue of 'evidence of continuity' from previous orders:

> But the continuity is of a stream of inner relationship. Even when one encounters an organisation built on false pretence, he must encounter some truth. And those who have been in the Vault have made their contact with the True and Invisible Order, not because of the historical claims of S.R.M.D. [Mathers' HOGD motto] with reference to the G.D., but because there are actually true formulas among the hotch-potch of good and bad and indifferent which one finds in the 'esoteric' literature of the G.D. Even that ridiculous Rosicrucian imposter, Spencer Lewis, who heads the A.M.O.R.C. [see p. 186], cannot avoid getting some good stuff into his lessons, and I have known two or three persons who actually made their first contact with the real thing through his Order.[49]

In any case, although Fräulein Sprengel was a useful lie, in several ways she represented elements of the truth, or something akin to it. Kenneth Mackenzie had claimed to have been initiated into a Rosicrucian Order by some German adepts.[50] There were also links, of ideas and ideals even if not by direct organisational lineage, between the Golden Dawn, Soc. Ros. and a genuine eighteenth-century German group, the Brotherhood of the Golden and Rosy Cross. This movement is first mentioned in a document of 1710, but in 1777 its constitutions and 'traditional history' claimed that the three degrees of Freemasonry were 'a seminary or preparation for the higher curriculum of the Rosicrucian Order and as a kind of spiritual prolegomenon . . . the preparatory school of the Rosy Cross'.[51] (In reality, as its members had to be masons, it was probably no more than one of many high-sounding side degrees of Freemasonry that sprang up in the eighteenth and nineteenth centuries.) The nine-grade degree structure of the Brotherhood of the Golden and Rosy Cross, from Zelator up to Magus, is identical to that of Soc. Ros. a century later – and is carried on into the Golden Dawn, with the addition of Neophyte below Zelator, and Ipsissimus above Magus.[52]

To summarise: all three founders of the Golden Dawn were members of Soc. Ros; Westcott, who provided the Cipher Manuscripts that formed the basis of HOGD's rituals, and who created Fräulein Sprengel and her forged letters, had close links with Mackenzie who was involved (amongst much else) in the creation of Soc. Ros. from uncertain sources, and who almost certainly originated the Cipher Manuscripts. From such shaky beginnings arose arguably the most important and influential esoteric society of recent centuries.

Mackenzie is one of four people named as 'eminent adepts and chiefs' in the History lecture of the Golden Dawn, written by Westcott; the others are Eliphas Lévi (see p. 181), Jean Marie Ragon, a French occult writer, and Frederick Hockley, one of the leaders of the Society of Eight.

Fräulein Anna Sprengel may well have been based on a real person, who provides a little known but vital link between the Theosophical Society and the Hermetic Order of the Golden Dawn. This was Anna Kingsford (1846–88), briefly London president of the Theosophical Society before leaving to found her own Hermetic Society (see p. 27–28).

Westcott and Mathers, who were both members of the Society of Eight around 1885, met Kingsford around the same time, and were quickly impressed by her. In 1886 they were both speakers at Hermetic Society meetings, on the subjects of alchemy and the Kabbalah. (Other members included W. B. Yeats and A. E. Waite, both to become prominent in the Golden Dawn.)

The same year Anna Kingsford edited Valentine Weigelius's 1649 work *Astrology Theologised*, on the title page of which was the Latin motto *Sapiens Dominabitur Astris* ('the wise will rule [or be ruled by] the stars'); the same motto used by Anna Sprengel (Soror SDA) in her letters to Westcott, which began in November 1887.[53]

Westcott actually gave the very last paper to the Society; Anna Kingsford's increasingly poor health meant that the 1887 session of meetings never occurred. Kingsford died of tuberculosis on 22 February 1888, and the Hermetic Society of which she was the driving force died with her.[54]

But ten days before her death another organisation centred on Hermetic beliefs began. Whatever the intricacies and deceptions of its conception, the Hermetic Order of the Golden Dawn was born on 12 February 1888 when, to quote R. A. Gilbert, Westcott, Woodman and Mathers 'signed their pledges of undying allegiance to themselves'.[55]

By the end of the year the London temple had thirty-two members, twenty-three men and nine women; Mathers' wife Mina, who was to be enormously influential in the Golden Dawn, was the first woman to join. Mina (née Bergson) was the sister of Nobel prize-winning French philosopher Henri Bergson; she later changed her first name to the more Celtic-sounding Moina.[56] She and 'MacGregor' Mathers had an entirely celibate marriage.

In August 1890 Westcott claimed to have received a final letter from Germany saying that Fräulein Sprengel had died, and conveniently breaking off any further contact. By then the HOGD was a going concern, with three temples in London, Weston-super-Mare and Bradford, and no longer needed its fake progenitor.

The HOGD was a secret society like the Freemasons and some Rosicrucian groups in that it awarded degrees as members progressed up the ladder, but with its main emphasis being the study of magical theory and ritual. There was plenty of material they could study; French writers such as Eliphas Lévi, Papus and Etteilla (Jean-Baptiste Alliette, 1738–91) had produced books on the mystical meanings of Tarot and the Kabbalah, and much else; and there were Mathers's 'ancient' rituals to be learnt.

The degrees of the outer order of the HOGD were Neophyte 0=0, Zelator 1=10, Theoricus 2=9, Practicus 3=8 and Philosophus 4=7. But for a few (and unknown to the rest) there would later be an inner circle, the Ordo Rosae, Rubeae et Aureae Crucis (RR et AC), 'the Rose of Ruby and the Cross of Gold'. Based on the Rosicrucian symbolism of Christian Rosenkreutz, this had three degrees, Adeptus Minor 5=6, Adeptus Major 6=5, and Adeptus Exemptus 7=4. The outer order only studied the theory of magic; the RR et AC taught practical ritual magic, and was without doubt the most intensive and all-embracing esoteric school of its time.

Beyond this, at least according to Aleister Crowley,[57] was an even higher order, the Mysterious Third Order of the Silver Star, or Argenteum Astrum (AA); this had three more degrees, Magister Templi 8=3, Magus 9=2 and Ipsissimus 10=1. The adepts of this order were beyond mere humanity, existing purely as spirits on the astral plane.

The pairs of numbers refer to *sephiroth* on the Tree of Life (see p. 174); the first, in a circle, shows how far the initiate has progressed from Malkuth at the bottom of the Tree; the second, in a square, how far they are from Kether at the top. *Sap. Dom. Ast.*, as the mythical Fräulein Sprengel signed herself, was 7=4, the highest human level possible. One of her last letters to Westcott helpfully granted the three founders of the Golden Dawn the same level of initiation as herself.

Unlike Soc. Ros., the HOGD was open to non-masons and also, unusually for its day, to women. It attracted Freemasons, Theosophists, Rosicrucians and people interested in magic and mythology, alchemy and astrology, the Kabbalah, Tarot, numerology and much else – including a hugely influential slice of British artistic society. Members included the Irish poet W. B. Yeats (later a Nobel prize winner), the esoteric historian

A. E. Waite, the artist and tea heiress Annie Horniman (who would later found the Gaiety Theatre in Manchester and the Abbey Theatre in Dublin), the actress Florence Farr (mistress of Yeats and George Bernard Shaw, amongst others), and briefly, to the ultimate dismay of all of these, Aleister Crowley.

The twentieth-century occultist Gerald Yorke, who worked closely with both Crowley and Regardie, called the Golden Dawn, with its inner order the RR et AC, 'the crowning glory of the occult revival in the nineteenth century. It synthesised into a coherent whole a vast body of disconnected and widely scattered material and welded it into a practical and effective system, which cannot be said of any other occult Order of which we know at the time or since.'[58]

In 1891 Dr Woodman died suddenly, and was not replaced as a chief of the HOGD. Westcott took over his position as supreme magus of Soc. Ros., letting Mathers consolidate his position as effective head of the Golden Dawn. From 1892, when the inner order of RR et AC was introduced, to around 1896, the HOGD flourished, teaching astrology, alchemy, Kabbalah, Tarot, geomancy, Hermeticism, elements of the Greek and Egyptian mystery religions, and much more. Between each grade were detailed courses and examinations.

One of several vital aspects of the HOGD's teaching that came from Eliphas Lévi was the correspondence between Tarot and Kabbalah. In his work *Le Dogme et Rituel de la Haute Magie* (1855–6) Lévi linked the twenty-two Major Trumps of Tarot to the twenty-two Hebrew letters, the ten number cards to the ten *sephiroth* (from the four aces representing Kether to the four tens representing Malkuth) and the four suits to the four letters of the Tetragrammaton YHVH, the sacred name of God.[59]

The HOGD greatly developed Lévi's concept of correspondences. As well as the associations between Tarot and the Tree of Life there were further correspondences between the twelve signs of the zodiac, the astrological planets and the four elements; with Hindu, Greek and Roman gods; with parts of the body; with notes of the musical scale, colours, precious stones, perfumes, animals and plants, both real and imaginary; and much more.[60] Correspondences are a complex extension of the idea of sympathetic magic: if two things are related in some way, then one can be used to influence or strengthen the other. They also help the practitioner to focus his or her mind more clearly during a ritual. If they wished to invoke a particular spirit or its essence for a particular magical working, they would go through the tables of correspondences and select the relevant plants, precious stones, colours for cloths or candles, scents for incense and so on, so that everything in the ritual worked harmoniously together.

Christian churches do something similar, just with the use of colour, traditionally having the priests' vestments and the altar cloths white or gold for Easter and Christmas, red for Pentecost and other festivals, purple or violet for Advent and Lent, and green for most Sundays.

For the RR et AC Mathers and his wife Mina designed a colourful seven-sided vault covered in astrological symbols, based on the description of the vault in which the body of Christian Rosenkreutz had been discovered (see p. 179); the Adeptus Minor initiation ritual written by Mathers was based on his legend and the discovery of his uncorrupted body. The vault was 12 feet (3.7 m) across and 8 feet (2.4 m) high, with each of the seven walls 5 feet (1.5 m) wide; at its centre was a circular altar, above a coffin in which the chief adept lay during the initiation ritual for new members of the inner order. Perhaps a third of HOGD members progressed to the RR et AC, where they learned the practice of the magic whose theory they had studied in the outer order.[61]

One of the few practical rituals learned in the outer order, which has since been adopted by many esoteric groups including some Wiccans, was the Lesser Banishing Ritual of the Pentagram. This has the dual purpose of consecrating a sacred space and of raising the consciousness of the participants. The celebrant at a ritual (or an individual on his own) first makes the sign of the Kabbalistic Cross, visualising lines of brilliant white light across his body while intoning words of power in Hebrew, names of *sephiroth* corresponding to 'Thou art the Kingdom, the Power and the Glory, for ever. Amen'. Then facing each compass point in turn (east, south, west and north) the celebrant draws a pentacle in the air and speaks one of the sacred names of God. Finally, again facing each compass point, the four archangels are named, while visualising the four traditional elements.

Over the next few years the HOGD grew to over 300 members. Then things started going wrong.

In 1892 Mathers had moved to Paris, setting up a Golden Dawn temple there (the French esotericist Papus was a member), and leaving Westcott as the remaining chief of the HOGD in England. Annie Horniman, who years earlier had been at the Slade Art College with Mina Mathers, and had been funding the couple for years, largely to help further Mina's art career, fell out with them both when they wanted yet more money. Mathers had become enthused with a romantic Jacobite cause, and she was not prepared to have her money spent on that.

When Mathers imperiously demanded a written pledge of personal loyalty from every member of the inner order in 1896 she refused, and in December Mathers expelled her from the HOGD. The following spring news leaked to the authorities (very likely via Mathers) that Westcott was involved in running a secret society which practised magic; this did not look good for a man in his position as a senior London coroner. Westcott resigned from the HOGD, leaving it entirely in Mathers's hands, with Florence Farr – in no way as capable an administrator as either Westcott or Annie Horniman – running it in London. She let the teaching and examinations become a mess and lost control of any organised study in the inner order whose Sphere Group, formed by her, 'obtained astral visions by means of ritualised meditation'.[62]

Mathers's increasingly autocratic behaviour triggered a revolt from the members of the inner order in London. In response to this, in February 1900 Mathers wrote a furious and stern letter to Florence Farr, revealing the truth about the non-existent Fräulein Sprengel: Westcott 'has NEVER been *at any time* either in personal, or in written communication with the Secret Chiefs of the Order, he having *either himself forged or procured to be forged* the professed correspondence between him and them'.[63] This understandably created a storm throughout the inner circles of the HOGD, who set up an investigating committee, which Mathers promptly ordered to be dissolved. Westcott, on being questioned by W. B. Yeats, would neither confirm nor deny Mathers' accusations. As they were still reeling from this news there came yet more explosive problems.

Aleister Crowley had joined the HOGD in November 1898; by the following May he had risen to Philosophus, the highest degree in the outer order. He demanded entry to the inner circle, but was turned down on the grounds of unsuitability – or what Florence Farr, certainly no prude herself, called his 'moral depravities'. In January 1900 Crowley went to Paris to complain to Mathers, and Mathers initiated him in the first grade of the RR et AC (Adeptus Minor, 5=6), but when he returned to London the other members refused him access to papers he said he was entitled to have. In April 1900, in full Highland dress, Crowley tried but failed to take possession of the London temple on behalf of Mathers.

Woodman was dead. Westcott had resigned. Now Mathers, the last remaining founder, was expelled from the HOGD, along with Mina Mathers and Crowley. W. B. Yeats took over the order, Annie Horniman returned, and together they tried to sort out the mess that Florence Farr's less than competent leadership had caused.

The autumn of the following year, 1901, saw a widely publicised court case in which an American couple known as Theo and Laura Horos (actually Frank and Editha Jackson) faced numerous charges including conspiracy to cheat and defraud a young woman of money and jewellery, the rape of a sixteen-year-old girl, and 'procurement for immoral purposes' of both of these and a third young woman. They had set up a fake occult order, the Order of Theocratic Unity, based on the HOGD; when they were arrested the police found a number of Golden Dawn ritual books belonging to Mathers, and distorted details of the HOGD were reported in the sensationalist press accounts of the court proceedings. Mathers had apparently been completely taken in by the couple – Laura Horos, who called herself the Swami Viva Ananda, even claimed to be Fräulein Anna Sprengel, and Mathers had told Florence Farr in his letter of February 1900 that 'it is I alone who have been and am in communication with the Secret Chiefs of the Order' and that Soror SDA was in Paris with him – and had elected them honorary members of his Paris temple; but they stole a number of ritual documents from him.[64]

The lurid publicity of the Horos case would have been even more damaging to the Golden Dawn were it not that by this time the Golden Dawn, as such, was effectively finished. It split into three different organisations, from which came several people who were to be extremely important in the continuing British esoteric tradition.

A. E. Waite took over the London temple, changed the name to the Independent and Rectified Rite of the Golden Dawn, and changed the emphasis from ritual magic to a more spiritual – and more Christian – 'mystical path'. This faded out in 1914, to be replaced the following year by the Fellowship of the Rosy Cross, whose members included the Christian occult novelist Charles Williams and the mystic, poet and academic Evelyn Underhill.

Those who wanted the original HOGD emphasis on magic formed Stella Matutina, the Order of the Morning Star; these included Florence Farr, Annie Horniman, W. B. Yeats, Dr Robert Felkin (see p. 36) and Israel Regardie – who in 1937–41 published a four-volume work containing, and preserving for later groups, the teachings of the HOGD.[65] By then Stella Matutina had lost impetus and largely ceased to exist; although some criticised Regardie for publishing this secret material, many at the time (and most esotericists today) praised him for preserving it. In fact he was not the first to do so; Crowley had published some of the rituals in abbreviated form in his magazine *The Equinox* in 1909–10.[66]

In 1912 Felkin, as chief of Stella Matutina, visited New Zealand and established a temple in a building known by the Maori name Whare Ra, or House of the Sun. He was invited to return there in 1916; he moved the international headquarters of Stella Matutina to New Zealand, and remained there until his death ten years later. Whare Ra continued until 1978 – the last group with a direct line of lineal descent from the original HOGD.

Mathers had continued as leader of the 'rump' Golden Dawn; some of his followers, including Dr Edward Berridge, formed the Alpha et Omega Order, with temples in London and Edinburgh, though Mathers himself stayed in Paris; Paul Foster Case (see p. 220) joined this group in the United States in 1918 and Dion Fortune (see p. 226) joined it in London in 1919; both were to leave in 1922. Mathers died in 1918; the Alpha et Omega Order continued under Mina Mathers until her death in 1928.

Meanwhile Aleister Crowley had launched his own order based on the HOGD, AA or (probably) Argenteum Astrum (Order of the Silver Star), in 1907 (see p. 212).

The Hermetic Order of the Golden Dawn has been remarkably influential on occult thought over the last century, considering its short and troubled life. Golden Dawn historian R. A. Gilbert expresses 'a certain sympathy for Westcott and his fellows. If in no other way, then as a monument to English eccentricity the Hermetic Order of the Golden Dawn has no equal.'[67]

There are numerous versions of the Golden Dawn today. The best known is also called the Hermetic Order of the Golden Dawn, based in Florida and headed by Chic and S. Tabatha Cicero, which has an active offshoot in Britain and temples in Spain, Italy, Greece and Canada. Founded in Georgia in 1977, it is upfront in saying it 'does not claim institutional lineage to the original HOGD, but it does claim *initiatory lineage* to the

What I Believe . . .
Ritual

A means of focusing magical intent and magical energy.
Jack Gale, Magician
Retired school teacher

Ritual in my experience is probably the most moving and inexplicable part of my spiritual life. Almost no mainstream religion offers participation in ritual, and almost no religion that I've ever found offers participation in ritual which is so achingly beautiful it makes you weep – and that's what my tradition offers, like most paganism offers some form of ritual, where we each do these things; not only do we enact them but we embody them.

People say 'What is ritual?' and I say, imagine Tai Chi but with Blake's poetry, and you get some sense of that. Movement and beautiful sound and candle light and incense and symmetry and harmony, and the combination of familiar beautiful poetry with unfamiliar beautiful poetry, so the combination of the expected and the unexpected, the calming and the jarring, has the capacity to do things to the interior life.
Dr Christina Oakley Harrington, Wiccan priestess
Owner of Treadwells esoteric bookshop, London,
former university lecturer in History and
Religious History

Ritual is a set of actions which, if done properly, have something else embedded in them in the same way that a body consists of flesh and bones and things, and has a spirit indwelling it, so a ritual has something inexplicably embedded in a set of words and actions.
Gareth J. Medway, Priest Hierophant of the
Fellowship of Isis
Writer and assistant psychic

Ritual is one of the most beautiful things to do. It is an artform. It is a form of sacred drama, mystery play. Calling ritual 'Sacred Drama' gives you a different angle to approach this spiritual technique.
Ina Cüsters-van Bergen, Magister, Hermetic Order of the Temple of Starlight

I am often disappointed when I see people or groups performing rituals with little structure or preparations. Rituals require intentions, tools, acts, words and clear structures to be all planned mindfully. Even the most spontaneous ritual uses a repertoire of tools, systems, methods and skills that already exist. Rituals work on intents, not whims of fancy!
Mani Navasothy, Wiccan High Priest and founder of Hern's Tribe
Physicist

We have fragments of ancient ritual passed down to us from various sources. It's tempting to try and re-enact those rituals to gain an understanding of what they were attempting to do; and if they were working with the natural energies of the Earth, are they still working? Can we, in our modern jaded perspectives, with our modern supposed hyper-intelligence, actually glean anything from this and can we actually feel these moments in time? Yes we can, and they do work.
Terry Dobney, Keeper of the Stones at Avebury
Retired motorcycle restorer

original order through Israel Regardie'.[68] Regardie and Chic Cicero were close friends for many years.

In addition to being an order it is also a linked but separate non-profit organisation under the same name, dedicated to preserving the knowledge of the Western Mystery Tradition and promoting the teachings of the original HOGD; its website contains a wealth of material including the three Rosicrucian manifestos, articles and essays on the Rosicrucians, Kabbalah and Tarot by Westcott, Mathers and others, and the text of the complete set of 36 Flying Rolls, teaching documents written for members of the inner order by Mathers, Westcott and other HOGD leaders largely between 1892 and 1894.

The UK website says:

> Whether you consider yourself a novice, an aspiring student or an adept in your own specialist field we hope you find something within our pages that aids your progressive journey toward the light. We aim to build this site into a treasure house of knowledge disseminated by those adepts and students alike who are keen to share their knowledge and insight with a wider community.[69]

The open attitude and level of scholarship of the later Hermetic Order of the Golden Dawn mean that it is well regarded and well respected by other Golden Dawn groups, with one exception. Another American group with a very similar name insists that the only true Golden Dawn tradition is the one going back to Mathers's Alpha et Omega organisation. 'The Hermetic Order of the Golden Dawn outer order of the Rosicrucian Order of AO', headed by a former student of Cicero, David Griffin, claims that it is 'a direct lineal descendent of the original HOGD': 'You will get the authentic Golden Dawn teachings of the Alpha et Omega as it was envisioned by McGregor [sic] Mathers. Move on from the Regardie printed materials and watered-down Llewellyn books to the true, original, and advanced Golden Dawn secrets of the A.O. available nowhere else, from humble Neophyte to exalted Magus and beyond in our Third Order.'[70] Its website openly attacks a number of other

Golden Dawn and Rosicrucian groups, especially those with a Regardie heritage, and Griffin's group has had legal disputes with the Cicero group over its name. The matter appears to have been settled in the Cicero group's favour.[71]

The majority of Golden Dawn groups, however, appear to maintain a respect for each other. Some of these include the Holy Order of the Golden Dawn, based in Toronto;[72] the Order of the Golden Dawn, based in Montreal;[73] the Hermetic Sanctuary of Ma'at,[74] an internet-based 'cyber-temple' run by the Ordo Stella Matutina, based in North Carolina;[75] the Open Source Order of the Golden Dawn, which is a Thelemic development from the original Golden Dawn;[76] the Esoteric Order of the Golden Dawn,[77] which comes under particular attack by Griffin's group; and Sodalitas Rosae Crucis & Solis Alati, a Rosicrucian group drawing on several traditions, which after listing them says disarmingly:

> All these named societies and traditions have two things in common; a) they have, to a greater or lesser extent, preserved and perpetuated the western hermetic tradition, and b) they have all been involved in mud-slinging campaigns against fellow brethren/groups. The former we draw our inspiration from, seeking to continue their exalted work; the latter we strive to be conscious about, so that history does not have to repeat itself again and again.[78]

In Britain the Oxford Golden Dawn Occult Society headed by Mogg Morgan calls itself 'a freestyle ritual group';[79] for some years its offshoot LOGDOS, the London lodge of the Oxford Golden Dawn Occult Society, was 'a practical-based non-hierarchical occult group which is not bound to any specific dogma'.[80]

It is highly unlikely that *any* of today's groups of the Golden Dawn, AA or Ordo Templi Orientis (see p. 212) can trace an unbroken lineage back to the original orders, despite the claims of some of them. But the ideas, ideals and many of the teachings of the Golden Dawn have continued in a variety of esoteric movements (see p. 219ff).

ORDO TEMPLI ORIENTIS
AND THELEMA

Aleister Crowley, born Edward Alexander Crowley (1875–1947), who was brought up in a strict Exclusive Brethren home, loathed conventional Christianity, but spent his life searching for union with God. His hedonistic lifestyle, particularly his indulgence in sex and drugs, added to his reputation as 'the wickedest man in the world', a label applied to him by the popular press, which he delighted in. But despite his reputation Crowley was never a Satanist, as he has been portrayed in the media and by Christian opponents of occult movements.

After the Hermetic Order of the Golden Dawn (HOGD) expelled both Crowley and 'MacGregor' Mathers in 1900 the two were initially allies. But having gained what he wanted, initiation into the second order, Crowley also fell out with Mathers, each of the two believing himself the greater esotericist, and in 1907 he formed his own Order, A∴A∴,[81] usually thought to stand for Argenteum Astrum, the Order of the Silver Star, though Crowley never made this clear.

This was based on the HOGD; indeed, the lower grades are known as the Order of the Golden Dawn. The second level grades of Adeptus Minor, Major and Exemptus are the Order of the Rose-Cross. Unlike the HOGD, where the highest three grades were beyond humanity, in the AA the grades of Magister Templi, Magus and Ipsissimus form the Order of the Silver Star. The motto of the AA is 'The method of science, the aim of religion'. Another significant difference from the HOGD was that the grades were seen more as levels of personal spiritual growth rather than initiatory levels.

There are numerous versions of the AA today, claiming a variety of lineages; in some cases they have been incorporated into one version or another of the Ordo Templi Orientis (OTO, see below); in other cases the two organisations are separate but linked.

Crowley's life was a tapestry of adventure, art and excess. He was a mountaineer, co-leading the first attempt to scale K2 in Pakistan in 1902, and attempting the first ascent of Kanchenjunga in Nepal in 1905; he was an expert chess-player; he was a sometimes indifferent but sometimes astonishing artist and poet (he 'repeatedly asserted that his poetry was far superior to that of Yeats').[82] And he was a supreme self-publicist with (in all senses of the phrase) a wicked sense of humour.[83] From 1899 to 1913 he owned Boleskin House on the southern shore of Loch Ness; there he performed a number of magical rituals. The house has become an iconic spiritual focal point for Crowleyan followers. It was owned by Led Zeppelin guitarist Jimmy Page from 1971 to 1991, though he rarely stayed there.[84]

On his honeymoon with Rose Kelly (sister of the artist Sir Gerald Kelly, later president of the Royal Academy) they spent a night in the King's Chamber of the Great Pyramid. In Cairo some months later, in April 1904, Rose was drawn to the god Horus, and over three days Crowley received, via a spirit being called Aiwass, the text of *Liber Legis* or the Book of the Law, the foundation text of the Thelemic religion. (The Greek *thelema* means 'will, purpose, intention'.) The *Liber Legis* is the primary spiritual text of all Thelemites, whether members of the AA, OTO or other groups or none.

Liber Legis (more correctly *Liber AL vel Legis*) contains the precept 'Do what thou wilt shall be the whole of the law'.[85] This is used not only by Thelemites but also by Wiccans (see p. 293); it has become known as the Wiccan rede, usually prefixed by 'An [If] it harm none . . .' The phrase is not

Crowley's, but originated from François Rabelais nearly four centuries earlier, in his famous scurrilous satire *The Histories of Gargantua and Pantagruel*, first published in 1532. In that book, for the monks and nuns of the Abbey of Thélème:

> In all their rule, and strictest tie of their order, there was but this one clause to be observed,
> ### DO WHAT THOU WILT.
> Because men that are free, well born, well bred, and conversant in honest companies, have naturally an instinct and spur that prompteth them unto virtuous actions, and withdraws them from vice, which is called honour.[86]

The saying can actually be traced back over a thousand years before Rabelais, to St Augustine of Hippo (354–430 CE), who wrote 'Love, and do what thou wilt.'[87]

Largely perhaps because of Crowley's own hedonism, the maxim 'Do what thou wilt shall be the whole of the law' has been much misinterpreted. It was never a recipe for self-indulgence: 'You're free to do whatever you like.' The point of the original precept, before it was taken on and adapted by Crowley, was that one's will should be totally in line with the will of God, so that one acts always within the will of God.

In Thelema 'Do what thou wilt' is less to do with the will of God, as Thelema is not a monotheistic religion, as with the inner will; one esoteric researcher comments: '*The Book of the Law* suggests that finding one's true will is equal to finding one's way in the universe, one's purpose in being alive.'[88] This is perhaps most strongly (and ambiguously) exemplified in the Thelemic concept of the Holy Guardian Angel, variously seen as the higher self, the Silent Self, the 'personal genius' or one's own true divine nature.[89]

'Do what thou wilt shall be the whole of the law' was also intended by Crowley to be half of a greeting; the response should be 'Love is the law, love under will,' which fills out the meaning considerably. Thelemites often use the number 93 to represent both Will and Love; in the Greek system of *isopsephy*, equivalent to the Hebrew *gematria*, letters are assigned numerical values, and the Greek words *thelema* and *agape* (love) each add up to 93 (see p. 168).

In 1910 Crowley was initiated into the Ordo Templi Orientis, an esoteric group founded by Theodor Reuss in Germany, most likely in 1906. Reuss was also German head of a quasi-masonic occult order, the Rite of Memphis and Misraim (see p. 34), and there were elements of this, and of the Swedenborgian Rite (see p. 196), in the OTO. Among the borrowed ideas were teachings on sex-magic, taken via Reuss's friend Carl Kellner, a member of the Hermetic Brotherhood of Light, from Paschal Beverly Randolph (see p. 184 and p. 189), a maverick American Rosicrucian who believed that sex-magic was the hidden secret at the heart of both Rosicrucianism and Freemasonry. The origins of the OTO – like its later history – are blurred and confused.[90]

In 1912 Reuss made Crowley head of the order in Britain, granting him the illustrious title of 'Supreme and Holy King of Ireland, Iona and all the Britains in the Sanctuary of the Gnosis'; Crowley promptly changed the focus of the British OTO, making it Thelemic, with the Book of the Law to be used as its Volume of Sacred Law in every lodge.[91] Reuss and Crowley began to fall out. When Crowley unilaterally appointed a North American head of the OTO, Reuss initiated H. Spencer Lewis, granting him a charter to form an American lodge; Lewis was to go on to found the Rosicrucian order AMORC (see p. 186). By 1921 the feud between Reuss and Crowley had developed to the extent that when Lewis asked Reuss, 'What connection has Crowley with your organisation?' Reuss replied 'Dissolved.' A few months later Crowley wrote to Reuss that it was his 'will to be OHO [Outer Head of the Order] and Frater Superior of the Order and avail myself of your abdication – to proclaim myself as such'.[92]

When Reuss died in 1923 Crowley proclaimed himself head of the OTO worldwide, though many members, especially in Germany, ignored this. Although there were a number of

OTO lodges in Britain, Europe and the United States (some following him, others not), he never managed to organise and unite it into a successful order.

In 1920 Crowley set up an esoteric community in a small house near Cefalù, a fishing port on the north coast of Sicily. He named it the Abbey of Thelema after Rabelais's creation, and lived there with two of his mistresses, their children and a few others, studying and performing ritual magic. The 'abbey' was also called Collegium ad Spiritum Sanctum, the College of the Holy Spirit; this was a clear reference to the Rosicrucian heritage behind Crowley's study and work, with the aim that it should benefit mankind (see p. 179–80).

But the Abbey of Thelema had major problems. Crowley's baby daughter Anne Leah (Poupée) died, and her mother Leah Hirsig miscarried her next child. In 1923 a young Oxford undergraduate died there, probably after drinking contaminated water from a nearby spring rather than, as reported, from drinking the blood of a sacrificed cat; his wife, returning to England, gave a very negative interview to the *Sunday Express*, which had already been attacking Crowley. Mussolini's government threw Crowley and his followers out of Sicily exactly three years after they had first gone there.

Crowley continued his study and practice of ritual magic (which he always spelt 'magick', partly to differentiate it from stage magic, and partly with the K standing for *kteis*, Greek for female genitalia) throughout his life. Amongst other works he wrote the *Gnostic Mass* and the *Hymn to Pan* (1913), the influential *Magick in Theory and Practice* (1929) and *The Book of Thoth* (1944), his own idiosyncratic version of Tarot, painted under his instruction by Lady Frieda Harris (see p. 176). Shortly before his death Crowley initiated Gerald Gardner, later to be the founder of Wicca, into the VII degree of the OTO, and granted him a charter to initiate others (see p. 291). Aleister Crowley died in a boarding house in Hastings in December 1947. According to one esoteric authority: 'At the time of his death in 1947 the OTO consisted of a handful of

European lodges that rejected his teachings completely, and one lodge in Pasadena, California [see p. 363], that went out of existence a few years later.'[93]

Since Crowley's death there have been numerous different versions of the OTO claiming different lineages.[94] Although Gerald Gardner had probably never performed any OTO rituals he was the highest level initiate in Europe. He met Karl Germer, whom Crowley had appointed in 1942 to succeed him as Outer Head of the Order after his death, to discuss the future of the OTO, but Gardner was in poor health at the time and did not continue with this.

Kenneth Grant (1924–2011) had briefly been a student of Crowley when working as his secretary from 1944, and had been initiated into the AA. In 1951 Germer gave Grant a charter to run the OTO in Britain, but when Grant made changes to the ideas and working of the order Germer expelled him. Despite this Grant continued leading what became known as the Typhonian OTO. In the 1950s Germer also initiated Herman Metzger, who then ran the OTO in Switzerland.

Germer died in 1962 without naming a successor. Metzger claimed to be the new Outer Head of the Order but was not generally accepted; he died in 1990. A further group, followers of the Brazilian Marcello Ramos Motta (1931–87) called themselves Society OTO; but as Motta, though a member of AA, had never actually been initiated into the OTO they were not a major force.

In 1969 an American Second World War veteran, Grady McMurtry, asserted his leadership as 'Caliph of the OTO' based on documents of emergency authorisation from Crowley, whom he had met when stationed in Britain, and incorporated the OTO in California in 1970.[95] In a series of court cases over the years reminiscent of the legal battles starting in 1928 between Fraternitas Rosae Crucis and AMORC over the name Rosicrucian (see p. 186–7), but with a markedly different outcome, the Caliphate OTO has successfully challenged the right of any other group to call itself the Ordo Templi Orientis or to use the initials OTO; it also secured the copyright in Crowley's writings. Kenneth Grant's group is now called simply the Typhonian Order. The Albion OTO, a small British group founded in 2003 by a former Caliphate member, ceased to exist in 2008.[96] A variety of other OTO-type groups avoid the problem by simply not having OTO in their name.

The Caliphate OTO is thought to have between 2,000 and 3,000 members worldwide, with fewer than 100 in Britain. The majority of Thelemites are actually outside the OTO, either in an assortment of small groups (often very antagonistic to each other) or quite independently, many while also members of other esoteric schools or religions.

The founder of the original OTO, Theodor Reuss, was made a patriarch of the Gnostic Catholic Church by the French esotericist Papus in 1908. When Reuss made Crowley British head of the OTO in 1912 he also passed on the leadership of the Gnostic Catholic Church in Britain. However, as Reuss did not have a valid lineage of the Apostolic Succession until his reconsecration in 1919 it is unlikely that Crowley had the Apostolic Succession himself, even if Reuss had consecrated him (see p. 62–4).

Today there are numerous versions of the Gnostic Catholic Church linked to and with the same leaders as the various competing versions of the OTO and the AA, and claiming valid lineages going back to Crowley. As the Gnostic Catholic Church is Thelemic rather than Christian, a lineage to Crowley is considered more important than a lineage to Christ through the Apostolic Succession.[97] They all perform the Gnostic Mass written by Crowley in 1913.

SCHOOLS OF OCCULT SCIENCE

The original Hermetic Order of the Golden Dawn (HOGD, see p. 195) may have self-destructed, but numerous groups have continued its legacy, calling themselves Hermetic or Western Mystery Tradition societies, or Schools of Occult Science. A selection of these are described here.

Most of them follow the Rosicrucian ideal of improving society through improving the individual. For their correspondence courses these schools generally charge enough to cover the printing and administration; although this can mount up over several years, it is generally considerably less expensive than most personal development movements, which take a different approach to self-knowledge and self-improvement (see p. 147).

The word 'occult' raises immediate accusations of evil from Christian critics; for example: 'The millions involved with occultism are ignorant of the real nature of these mysterious and dangerous areas of investigation, and refuse to turn to the one source of truth regarding the kingdom of darkness.'[98] In contrast, one influential twentieth-century occultist, Dion Fortune (see p. 226), has described occultism as 'a noble quest for the soul, a true crusade against the Powers of Darkness'.[99] It is worth recalling that 'occult' simply means 'hidden'.

Many esoteric schools are able to trace a clear organisational lineage back to the HOGD, unlike the more spurious lineages claimed by many Rosicrucian groups, HOGD itself and today's Golden Dawn groups (see p. 183–4, p. 197–8).

BUILDERS OF THE ADYTUM

The Builders of the Adytum (BOTA) is an American offshoot of the Hermetic Order of the Golden Dawn (HOGD, see p. 195), and almost certainly the oldest one still continuing. It was founded by Paul Foster Case (1884–1954) who had been interested in the esoteric since his childhood. Case joined the New York branch of Mathers's group Alpha et Omega in 1918 and quickly rose through the ranks to praemonstrator, the leader responsible for teaching members. Then, as others did, he fell out with Mina Mathers who had become head of Alpha et Omega after her husband's death. She accused him of teaching the principles of sex-magic in the outer order: 'I regret that anything on the Sex question should have entered into the Temple at this stage for we only begin to touch on sex matters directly, in quite the higher Grades.'[100]

For his part, Case had his doubts about Mina Mathers's leadership ability. Some years later, in a long and detailed letter to Israel Regardie about his problems with the Golden Dawn, Case wrote that Mina Mathers, 'then began to display extraordinary misunderstanding of the American situation. She encouraged a Frater in Chicago to initiate anybody possessed of $10 (by mail), and soon the country was flooded with Neophytes who had never seen the inside of a Temple.'[101] At the end of 1921 Mina Mathers asked him to resign as praemonstrator, and in 1922 he left the order.

Case founded the School of Ageless Wisdom in 1923, providing occult correspondence courses; in 1938, with a move to Los Angeles where it is still based, this became the Builders of the Adytum. BOTA's background in HOGD is clear in its concentration from the very start on Tarot (see p. 175) and Kabbalah (see p. 165), but Case was not comfortable with the ceremonial ritual magic of the inner order of HOGD. In his 1933 letter to Regardie he wrote:

> What I object to in the G.D. is the subtle mixture of really poisonous material with so much that is of value. And to get rid of the poison has been my principal undertaking for more than ten years.
>
> The consequence has been that I have been obliged . . . to formulate the rituals anew. But there is no pretence to the sort of historical continuity that is offered by Lewis, or Plummer, or Clymer, or the G.D., or any other 'true Rosicrucian Order'.[102]

(H. Spencer Lewis was the founder of AMORC, George Winslow Plummer [1876–1944] the co-founder and leader of Societas Rosicruciana in America, and R. Swinburne Clymer the founder of Fraternitas Rosae Crucis.)

In a slightly earlier letter Case writes that he is glad to find that the chiefs of another Golden Dawn offshoot 'put the emphasis rather on the work itself than upon any notion of "apostolic succession" from the "original" Rosicrucian Fraternity'.[103] Although BOTA does have a clear lineage, at least back to the Golden Dawn, it stresses that this is less important than the fact that its teachings have stood the test of time.

> Builders of the Adytum is an authentic Mystery School in the Western Tradition. Its teachings are based on the Holy Qabalah and the Sacred Tarot, and have been handed down from one group of initiates to another since ancient times. However, BOTA does not claim value on the grounds of being old, but because its instructions have met the tests of centuries of practical application.[104]

After Case's death in 1954 he was succeeded by Dr Anne Davies, who further extended his teachings until her own death in 1975.

BOTA is now run by a board of stewards. Most of the books supplied by BOTA are by Case or Davies, but they also recommend Dion Fortune's *The Mystical Qabalah* (see p. 226). The school offers correspondence courses in Tarot, the Kabbalah, spiritual alchemy, esoteric astrology and other related subjects. BOTA's introductory booklet *The Open Door* says that these:

> constitute an interlocking system of studies and practices which has served as the foundation of the Western Mystery training for many generations and they are treated as such by BOTA. The particular potency of this system lies in its use of symbols, which are a universal language that directly instructs subconsciousness with its pictorial wisdom, regardless of language differences.[105]

'Pictorial wisdom' clearly includes Tarot. Like several other offshoots of the Hermetic Order of the Golden Dawn, BOTA has published its own design of Tarot (very similar to the Rider-Waite-Smith pack), the images symbolising the deep esoteric truths taught by the movement. The cards are black and white, and members are encouraged to colour them to bring out their personal interpretation of the symbolism and their own relationship with them. Case writes in *The Book of Tokens: Tarot Meditations*:

> When you colour your own cards, they take on the character of your personality. They are inseparably linked with you! The attention you must give impresses their patterns upon the cells of your brain – builds the details of the designs into your consciousness. And making the TAROT KEYS a part of yourself is one of the most practical secrets of all occultism. It is the necessary foundation for all advanced Tarot practice.[106]

In its booklets BOTA address the issue of the secrecy of esoteric or occult teachings:

> In ancient times the teachings were held within a very strict code of secrecy because the world, not being ready for them, sought always to destroy what it did not understand. With the advance

of civilisation and the abatement of oppression, many more now understand what previously was comprehensible only to the few and it was decided by those responsible for the guardianship of the Wisdom Teaching that much of it would be given to the world openly.[107]

Hitherto, the great practical secrets have been guarded carefully from spiritual dilettantes and have only been given to duly initiated men and women under the strictest pledges of secrecy. In the past, this secrecy has been necessary because of the ecclesiastic and legal restrictions upon freedom of thought and worship. Today such close secrecy is no longer necessary. Much may now be given out openly which formerly could be imparted only in private and by word of mouth.[108]

After completing two introductory courses members may be initiated into a group known as a Pronaos for 'a practical work of harmonisation with cosmic Principles';[109] BOTA have Pronaos groups across North America and elsewhere. They also have study groups where members and non-members can study and meditate together.

As with similar schools the philosophy is practical; the aim is that as the member 'continues with the process of self-unfolding, he gradually increases mastery of himself, first in small things, then in greater'.[110] Progress can only be made if there is sincerity, desire and willingness to work.

For you to be successful in our Work, your personal goals must correspond to those of the Order: personal enlightenment, self-transmutation and service to Life. To only desire healing and wealth is not enough and will surely result in failure. So we seek those individuals who are well motivated that will persist in our Work and not just skim the surface. BOTA does not offer to remake your world for you. It does offer you the keys to knowledge that will enable you to do it for yourself, with the inner help that linkage with a true Mystery School confers.[111]

'Adytum' is Greek for 'the innermost part of the Temple, the *Holy of Holies, that which is not made with hands*'. The name Builders of the Adytum 'indicates that we propose to help you build the *Inner Temple* wherein conscious contact with the Higher Self may be made and your true spiritual heritage may be realised'.[112]

There may well also be physical improvements in a member's life, such as health and wealth, as a result of their studies, but these should not be the reason for joining. However, if they are as powerful as BOTA indicate, they should certainly not be dismissed:

> The practical work of BOTA, which includes study, meditation, imagery and ritual, initiates a series of subtle but important changes in your inner world, not the least of which is an expansion of your conscious awareness. Even a slight increase in this area has a remarkable effect on your mental/emotional capacities. Your intelligence increases and you become more aware of your motivations. You become more observant, which improves your memory. Your ability to anticipate future effects of present causes is enhanced, improving your discrimination in making choices. Objectivity is increased, aiding the ability to think more logically and clearly, which increases control over your environment and helps you define your goals.[113]

The list is remarkably similar to L. Ron Hubbard's claims about a 'Clear' (see p. 360–1), except that his techniques are psychological in nature, while those of BOTA and other mystery schools are spiritual. Their expression here is also akin to many of the goals of personal development or self-help courses and seminars, which have always had a greater appeal in the United States than in Britain.

But the main aim is to enable the initiate to be raised to a higher state of consciousness; other terms used include 'an awakening' and 'illumination', or an awareness of the God within.

BOTA's teachings are not tied to a particular national mythos, nor its members to a particular nationality; based in Los Angeles the school is international, with centres throughout the United States and Canada, and in South and Central America, New Zealand, France, Spain, Germany and the UK. Unusually, it also doesn't require members to relinquish membership of any other orders. There are around 4,000 members worldwide; members must be over twenty-one.

In common with most occult schools BOTA has suffered from members splitting away over the years: 'There are many who believe they have a clearer vision of the needs of the Inner School. They form their own groups sometimes in violation of their oath. This is not something we monitor except to note that they violate their oaths.'[114] The largest offshoot is the Fellowship of the Hidden Light or Fraternitas LVX Occulta (FLO), set up in 1982 when a senior member of BOTA, Dr Paul A. Clark, left with several other high level initiates. FLO uses Paul Foster Case's teachings on Tarot and Kabbalah, but also includes some of the HOGD ceremonial magic which Case had dropped in BOTA.

Like most occult schools FLO has a series of correspondence courses leading members through different levels of the movement. Clark explains:

> The breakdown of the curriculum is on four levels: Probationary, which acts as an outer court; the Lesser Mysteries or outer order, where serious transformation of the personality is undertaken; the Greater Mysteries or inner order where disciplines designed to forge a conscious link with the higher self is undertaken. The third order or supreme mysteries are reserved for those highly evolved souls who guide our work. I am the Steward, or 'Servant' who acts as the visible head. I make no claim to be a member of the third order. I am simply a servant of the other members of our order from Probationer up. I am simply a student who is striving to assist others as I try to understand myself.[115]

The third order thus appears to be similar to the third order of the HOGD.

The Fellowship of the Hidden Light has groups in the United States, Canada, Britain, Australia, France, Spain and Japan.

SOCIETY OF THE INNER LIGHT

Dion Fortune (1890–1946) was born in Wales into a Christian Science family as Violet Mary Firth; she took her pseudonym from her family motto, *Deo, non Fortuna* – 'By God, not by chance'. She had visions from her childhood, and joined the Theosophy movement for a while (see p. 23); from them she took the idea of the Masters, but she saw them as spiritual rather than physical beings.

In an early job, when she was twenty, she felt that she was under psychic attack from a female superior who sought to completely demoralise her; she set out to discover how she could defend herself, resulting in one of her most significant works, *Psychic Self-Defence* (1930). She studied psychology, particularly the works of Freud and Jung, and worked as a lay psychoanalyst.

Fortune's visions continued. In one she met Jesus and the Comte de Saint-Germain (see p. 65), and learnt about her past lives. She began doing trance work in 1922. She joined the HOGD offshoot Alpha et Omega (see p. 207), run by Mina Mathers. With some like-minded friends she also joined the Christian Mystic Lodge of the Theosophical Society in 1925, 'as a means of counteracting the Theosophical Society's Star of the East movement to promote Krishnamurti as the new World Teacher', says Gareth Knight, Fortune's biographer.[116] They resigned from this in 1927 and founded the Community (soon renamed the Fraternity, and later the Society) of the Inner Light, initially meeting in a hut in Chalice Orchard at the foot of Glastonbury Tor in Somerset. In the same year she was ejected from Alpha et Omega by Mina Mathers.

From 1927 to 1938 she worked with her husband, a Welsh doctor, Thomas Penry Evans. With Evans as her priest she developed her study and practice of magic, a blend of esoteric Christianity, Kabbalah and Tarot, with some strong Pagan elements; her twenty-four books, including six occult novels, are read and recommended today by both esoteric and Neo-Pagan movements, though the Society of the Inner Light stresses that she was never a witch, and downplays the Pagan aspects of her work.

When Evans left her in 1938 (they were divorced in 1945) Fortune took a lower profile, partly because her publishing activities were curtailed by wartime paper rationing. She continued her researches into Arthurian and Grail material; she was also instrumental in mounting a magical defence of Britain during the Second World War.[117] According to an introductory leaflet, 'over the years [she] produced teaching on a wide range of metaphysical subjects, including masculine and feminine relationships, the esoteric orders and their work, the training and work of an initiate, the Arthurian legends, principles of esoteric healing, and much else besides.'[118]

The Society has changed some of the emphasis of its teachings over the years, in part depending on who was running it. It was strongly influenced for a while by Alice Bailey's teachings on the Secret Masters (see p. 37); it picked up on the Alexander technique for improving physical posture; it even dabbled briefly, 'for purely practical reasons', with Scientology's E-Meters (see p. 361–2). However, its founder's teachings continued to be of prime importance.

The Society of the Inner Light is 'a registered charity based on the Christian religion',[119] and indeed, from 1961 to 1991 the Christian side was given greater emphasis, says Knight, who writes: 'a very powerful Christian dynamic burst into the group in 1960/1 and one which was sufficiently powerful to cause many sparks to fly and various members to disperse and go their separate ways'.[120] Knight was one of those who left, to set up his own esoteric movement, the Gareth Knight Group.

However its emphases have changed over the years the Society of the Inner Light has remained a school within the Western Mystery Tradition:

> The principle work of the Western Esoteric Tradition is expansion of consciousness. It deals with the 'ground of all being', unmanifest, beyond time and space, which differentiates countless modes of being in evolving through a manifest universe. The purpose of these modes of being is to realise the Divine Intention . . . [which] is concerned with the true purpose and destiny of each one of us. To achieve this we train our members in the Qabalah, Bible and with ritual, as well as daily usages, including meditation.[121]

Its main source books are Dion Fortune's *The Mystical Qabalah* and *Cosmic Doctrine*. As with other British esoteric schools there is a great emphasis on mythology, particularly Celtic and Arthurian mythology; Fortune herself was closely linked with Glastonbury.

Following initial training the Society teaches three different paths, the Mystic, the Hermetic and the Path of the Green Way:

> On the Mystic Path the ego casts everything aside that separates it from God. It seeks to know even as it is known; and as the mind cannot know God, it even casts away the mind to enter into the Divine Union. All that is not God to it is dross; and it purges and repurges the soul until nothing remaineth but pure spirit.
>
> This is a steep and narrow way, though swift and sure.

The Path of the Green Way seeks God in nature, in his works:

> For the god within, being lifted up and exalted to ecstasy with a divine inebriation, perceives the God Without in hill and herb and elemental force . . .
>
> And it is an inebriation of the soul, not of the flesh. An inebriation of colour, sound and motion that lift the senses out

of the flesh into a wider vision, for Dionysius is a Messiah as well as the Christ, and the soul can transcend the mind by sublimating the senses as well as by renouncing, and some find God on this Path as truly as by the Way of the Cross.

The Hermetic Path is a middle way between the other two: 'Use the mind God gave you to reach up and realise the things of the spirit upon the one hand, and reach down and control the things of the senses on the other, and thus you shall stand equilibrated between them, as the Initiated Adept.'[122]

Like most other esoteric schools the Society stresses the difficulty of the work, almost to the point of actively discouraging people from becoming members. It also lays great stress on moral living, courteousness, good citizenship, self-discipline, responsibility and other similar virtues. It will not accept members who are homosexual or bisexual 'since much of the work of the Group is concerned with polarity, as generally understood and at every level'.[123]

The Society is quite specifically British in emphasis. At one time its *Work and Aims* booklet insisted on certain qualifications for potential members:

Born and raised in the United Kingdom.
Raised with experience in the British tradition, i.e. fairy tales, nursery rhymes and folk stories; full knowledge of the legends and myths of our history . . .
A good knowledge of British history with no conflicting beliefs from other religious or cultural training or experiences.
A love of things British.[124]

After a one-year correspondence course 'designed to give an adequate knowledge of the Tree of Life of the Qabalah', members progress through three degrees, the 'Lesser Mysteries', which, says a newer edition of *Work and Aims*:

are broadly based upon traditional Masonic symbolism. These are designed to develop and strengthen character, to give experience of ceremonial working, and to develop the visionary powers of the mind as a means toward attaining higher consciousness . . .

Those who successfully pass through this process . . . may elect to move on to the 'Greater Mysteries', which are concerned with developing consciousness at the level of the Evolutionary Personality and ultimately the Spirit. This is the level of the Adept as a natural progression from that of the Lesser Mystery initiate. Here specialised work may be undertaken under the direction of the inner plane hierarchy.[125]

Two former members of the Society of the Inner Light, W. E. Butler and Gareth Knight (see p. 231), have produced very significant books in the esoteric tradition. When the Society dropped to only a couple of dozen members in the late 1990s, Knight was asked back to help get it on its feet again: 'A new Warden and council of management had taken control of the Society in 1990 and now encouraged me to rejoin and advise on ways to restore some of the old grades system and practices.'[126] This meant Knight having to leave his own movement, now renamed the Avalon Group (see p. 240). With access to manuscripts in the Society of the Inner Light's archives, he has co-authored or edited two 'new' Dion Fortune books,[127] as well as writing her biography.

SERVANTS OF THE LIGHT

Servants of the Light (SOL) was founded in 1973 by W. E. Butler (1898–1978) and is based in Jersey; the Helios correspondence course, which led up to its formation, was founded by Butler and Gareth Knight (b.1930) in 1964. Both were former members of Dion Fortune's Society of the Inner Light (see p. 226). Butler, who wrote a number of significant works on the Western Mystery Tradition, was an ordained priest in the Liberal Catholic Church (see p. 56), once led by Charles W. Leadbeater, who helped turn the Theosophical Movement more towards esoteric Christianity (see p. 30). Butler's successor as SOL's Director of Studies is Dolores Ashcroft-Nowicki (b.1929).

Servants of the Light is organised on standard lines of progression. A six-lesson foundation course 'gives the SOL Supervisors the chance to evaluate students and their ability to work in a disciplined fashion'.[128] The Entered Novice takes a fifty-lesson main course over four or five years; the first six lessons, written by Gareth Knight, are based on *The Art of True Healing* by Israel Regardie, a former member of Stella Matutina (see p. 206), while the remaining lessons, written by W. E. Butler, use Gareth Knight's *A Practical Guide to Qabalistic Symbolism* as a reference text for the Tree of Life.

Butler created a course in which, after a period of mental and spiritual self-cleansing, the student builds up a mental world for himself and then populates that world, in increasing detail, with the self-discoveries made along the way. This powerful method of learning implants the essence of the Tree of Life within the student himself, making it a living point of contact with the spiritual world.[129]

By the tenth or twelfth lesson, if progress is satisfactory, the Novice becomes a Fellow within the Fellowship of the SOL; this is the First Degree.

To progress to the Second Degree, during the main course students must attend three ritual magic workshops, at Beginners, Intermediate and Advanced level. The Second Degree correspondence course takes forty-four weeks; at some point during this time the Fellow may be offered initiation, becoming a Frater or Soror of the Fraternity of the SOL. Fraters and Sorors help to teach Novices and lead Fellows in their ritual work.

Beyond this is a Third Degree, by invitation only. All that is made known publicly is that 'the work involves worldwide communications with other Schools and Orders, that much of the work is of an advanced Inner-Plane nature, and that Third Degree members are known as Councillors'.[130]

Servants of the Light, like most mystery schools, has outer and inner levels; the outer level (i.e. visible to the outside world) is the First and Second Degrees. From these are drawn the members of the Inner Court. SOL is a 'contacted' school:

> By contacted, we mean those schools that are in close psychic touch with the overshadowing Hierarchy on the Inner Planes. It is in this Inner Group that the real power resides; and from there it is mediated in various ways to its counterpart on the physical level. The SOL *is* so contacted, and its inner powers are slowly becoming available to those who come within its sphere of influence.[131]

It sees the esoteric sciences as 'the Western equivalent of the Eastern Yoga systems. The Western system is just as effective and noble as the Eastern systems, and they both lead to the same ultimate goal: integration of the psyche and soul and a direct knowledge of the spiritual realities which underlie manifestation.'[132]

The main emphasis of the teaching for Novices and Fellows is on the Kabbalah, whose Tree of Life was described by Dion Fortune (see p. 226) as 'the mighty, all-embracing glyph of the soul of man and the universe':[133]

> Without this composite system, it is probable that the Western Tradition would have been entirely destroyed. Owing to its simplicity, however, the glyph is easily committed to memory; and because of its profundity, from this sparse simplicity can be derived a complete and satisfying philosophy and knowledge of life in both its inner and outer aspects.[134]

SOL see the Kabbalah as:

> the foundation of the Western Mystery Tradition . . . the great body of philosophy to be found in the religion texts of the Jews, including the Old Testament of the Bible, particularly the Pentateuch. It can also be seen in the vast complex of astrological, alchemical and occult symbology that has come down to us, as well as in the Rosicrucian and Masonic myth – including the Tarot, which is indigenous to the West.[135]

The Western Mystery Tradition, sometimes called the Hermetic Tradition, also has clear links with Egyptian and Greek thought from around the time of Christ – the Gnostics and Neo-Platonists. SOL's 'contact' is from the ancient esoteric School of Alexandria, from the Temple of On, or Heliopolis. The Third Degree is also known as the House of the Amethyst.

> The House of the Amethyst is one of the outer names of the great Alexandrian Fraternity, the Fraternitas Alexandrae, which has its existence on the Inner Planes, and of which the SOL is an earth-level expression. The Fraternitas Alexandrae is the inner fountainhead from which all our teaching ultimately stems. It is

a withdrawn Order under whose authority the whole school works, teaches and has its existence.[136]

This emphasis on the ancient School of Alexandria is echoed elsewhere in esoteric movements (see p. 293 and p. 302).

SOL also encourages its members to become familiar with mythology, particularly but not solely Celtic mythology and the Arthurian cycle – the Matter of Britain. 'Any mythological knowledge you acquire will not be wasted. The ability to cross-index the legends and god forms can be of immense value in the understanding of the ancient past.'[137] During the course students must make a detailed study of at least two pantheons in addition to their native tradition. The school sees:

> an urgent need for seekers of all ages to resume the Quest of the Grail. The need for sound esoteric training is more urgent than it has ever been.
>
> We do not claim, as others do, that the occult way holds all the answers to the world's ills; but we do claim that it has a part to play in the eventual victory over them. We believe, sincerely, that the ancient traditions hold a timeless key which may be applied to modern life and its problems. We aim to train dedicated men and women who will help others to achieve the inner serenity that is their birthright.[138]

SOL has added to the number of esoteric Tarot packs (see p. 176) with its own Servants of the Light Tarot. Despite SOL's heritage, for once this doesn't claim to be a copy of Mina Mathers's pack, or even to contain the true symbolism of the HOGD (see p. 195); instead, Dolores Ashcroft-Nowicki has worked together with two artists to produce a pack which reflects the esoteric teachings of her school. Her book, *Inner Landscapes*, uses the SOL Major Arcana for 'pathworking', or guided meditational journeys.

In 2009 much of the administrative running of SOL, previously carried out by Dolores Ashcroft-Nowicki and her husband Michael Nowicki, was passed on to a three-person

Administrative Resource Council (ARC), 'leaving Dolores free to concentrate on broadening and refining the SOL Teachings' such as creating a third degree of studies and re-writing other SOL courses, says Stephen Tanham, one of the ARC officers.[139]

In total over the last 40 years SOL has had nearly 7,000 students; at any time SOL usually has about 1,000 active students in twenty-three countries, making it one of the largest and most influential esoteric movements of the early twenty-first century. It actively encourages its lodges to take different approaches; for example, it has an Arthurian lodge, a Craft lodge and lodges based on women's mysteries and esoteric Christianity. It also has five daughter schools in different countries including Germany, Trinidad and Mexico (see p. 236). 'They each have their own focus and specific way of delivering the Qabalistic-centric teachings that lie at the heart of the SOL, in all its forms,' says Tanham. He explains that this diversity of symbolic and ritualistic models is deliberate, 'based on Ernest Butler's original vision that SOL would model itself on (and indeed is linked on the Inner Planes with) the original schools and academies of Alexandria, during the golden age prior to the burning of the libraries and the imposition of Christianity.'[140]

'We're trying to recreate the ideas of Alexandria where every belief system was welcome so that they could interact and inform each other of what they do and how they do it,' says Dolores Ashcroft-Nowicki.[141]

FRATERNITY OF THE GOLDEN CIRCLE

Fraternidad del Círculo Dorado (Fraternity of the Golden Circle) began in Guadalajara, Mexico, in 1986–7 as an esoteric study-group focusing on the research and practice of the Western Mystery Tradition. It based its teachings on the Golden Dawn and BOTA (see p. 195 and p. 220), and also used W. E. Butler and Dion Fortune's books (see p. 226). In 1990 they made contact with Dolores Ashcroft-Nowicki and began studying the Servants of the Light (SOL) course (see p. 231): 'After working for three years with students from Spain and Latin America, it became evident that the school needed to provide teachings and practices adapted to the Hispanic lifestyle. This was a turning point in the course the school would undergo in the following years.'[142]

Led by Jorge Nájera and Alejandra Mora, the Fraternity, now formally an independent daughter school of SOL, concentrates mainly on 'an updated and more modern vision of the mysteries' – mystic Kabbalah, esoteric astrology and Tarot – with advanced programmes in Kabbalistic ritual magic, Egyptian ritual magic and mental alchemy.

Its stated purpose shows that the Fraternity is firmly within the 'original' Rosicrucian tradition:

The motivation behind Fraternidad del Círculo Dorado is to aid sincere spiritual seekers who search for the Eternal Wisdom and whose highest goal is to be at the service of Light. The purpose of the school is to spread the teachings of the Western Mysteries and to provide the magical and occult training needed for men and women to incorporate spiritual principles into their lives that will contribute to expand their consciousness, manifest general wellbeing, health and wealth, therefore, building towards unity and fraternity amongst human beings.

The Fraternity of the Golden Circle has nine lodges or temples and a daughter school of its own founded in 2009, Templo del Sol Interno (Temple of the Inner Sun), which is based on the Egyptian tradition.

TEMPLE OF STARLIGHT

Most members of the Servants of the Light (SOL, see p. 231) pursue their spiritual development within SOL, but some eventually branch out and found their own esoteric school. The Temple of Starlight (or Ordo Templi Lucis Asterum) was founded in 2003 by Ina Cüsters-van Bergen in Rotterdam, the Netherlands. Although its founder was a third degree initiate of SOL this is not an acknowledged daughter school but an independent venture – though Cüsters-van Bergen is clearly conscious of the importance of her esoteric lineage: 'Her lineage comes from Moina Mathers and J. W. Brody-Innes of the Alpha et Omega Lodge of the *Stella Matutina* Temple of the Golden Dawn: through Dr. Theodore Moriarty, Dion Fortune, who was the founder of the Society of the Inner Light, and through W. E. Butler and Dolores Ashcroft-Nowicki of the Servants of the Light.'[143]

The school is firmly within the Western Mystery Tradition: 'There are so many rich and beautiful traditions in the West. Not only Wicca and Druidry, but also Arthurian, Egyptian, Babylonian, Greek, etc. And technical systems like Alchemy, Magic, Kabbalah, Astrology etc. And on top of that the ability to be able to let them meld together into one big system.'[144]

A trained therapist, she also integrates psychotherapy, hypnosis and neuro-linguistic programming into her teachings. But it is the esoteric spiritual path which is the heart of her school.

My mission is to teach, and help to bring our beautiful spiritual tradition back into society again. In our Western culture Gnostic spirituality has suffered a lot. Our tradition was so wounded during the times of the inquisition, and later when being thrown from the universities at the time our society split religion and science. One of my missions is to bring it back to mainstream society: to be one of the ambassadors, to give it back its proper place in society. Some of the students in my school do not feel free to tell other people that they are working in this tradition. We have people who work at universities, and they are simply not able to tell that they are working in this tradition, because there is a taboo on spiritual practice in some professions, it would endanger their professional position: and this in a society which claims to be free![145]

AVALON GROUP

When Gareth Knight left the Society of the Inner Light (see p. 228) in the 1960s he initially helped set up the Helios Group, a correspondence course which eventually transformed into Servants of the Light (see p. 231). He started his own school, gave lectures on guided visualisation and ritual work, based on what he had learned in the Society of the Inner Light, and wrote a number of books. In the mid-1980s he set up the Gareth Knight Group, 'a small ritual group base consisting of my more promising students'.[146]

In 1998 he was called back to the Society of the Inner Light to 'advise on ways to restore some of the old grades system and practices'. He handed over his own group to Wendy Berg, who had worked with him for many years, and it was renamed the Avalon Group in 1999.

The group's course shows its origins in the Society of the Inner Light; it consists of three streams, Hermetic/Kabbalist Magic, Green Ray/Faery/Elemental/Natural Magic and Devotional/Esoteric Christian (see p. XXX). The textbooks for the first two degrees are both by Gareth Knight: *A Practical Guide to Qabalistic Symbolism* and *The Secret Tradition in Arthurian Legend*. It describes its aims:

> Our aims are to bring about changes in consciousness, and to foster an increased awareness of the spiritual realities.
>
> To co-operate with those who work on the Inner Planes in fostering harmony and balance amongst all creation, whilst developing our own full potential as human beings.

To engage in magical ritual as a means of impressing upon the collective unconscious the perfect patterns which are in accordance with Divine Will.

Most of the offshoots from the Society of the Inner Light, including the Servants of the Light, say that they are a 'contacted group'. The Avalon Group's website gives a clear explanation of this:

This means that the outer group which the world sees is, like an iceberg, only a part of the complete whole, and the outer group are aware of this. The outer group operates like the earth terminal of an electric circuit in the overall scheme of things, but the greater vision and guidance of its work comes from higher level inner beings who are not physically incarnate ...

A fundamental skill, then, is to learn how to contact and communicate with these higher level teachers ...

Students in the physical group practise techniques from their first year of training which will enable them to raise consciousness at will. As part of the process, these same techniques also 'open' the (non physical) 'heart', as described in numerous mystical texts.[147]

LONDON GROUP

Like the Servants of the Light and several other groups, the London Group stems from the Society of the Inner Light (see p. 226), which its founder Alan Adams joined in 1954. He founded the London Group in 1975 and led it until his death in 1998; it was based in outer London until 2000, when it relocated to the Midlands of England. Adams, under the name Charles Fielding, wrote *The Practical Qabalah* and co-wrote a biography of Dion Fortune.

The London Group, like its forerunners, is rooted firmly in the Western Mystery Tradition: 'A notable feature of religions of the past is that typically each had an inner and outer aspect. The outer form became the religion of the masses, while the inner form contained deeper teachings offering a direct path to personal experience of the inner realities and an opportunity to help in the spiritual evolution of humanity.'[148]

It is clear from the group's literature and website that the inner personal development of its members is not an end in itself, but provides 'an opportunity to help in the spiritual evolution of humanity':

Any genuine school of the Mysteries gives out teaching with one end in mind – namely, that the principles learned are lived out in the day-to-day life of its members, and that, like yeast in a mass of dough, right thinking and ethics based on cosmic law, are set to work in the local communities and broader global village we inhabit. It is surprising just how much even a single such 'archetypical pattern' can help to redress the chaos so prevalent in the world today.

As with a number of other groups this is firmly in the spirit of the Rosicrucian manifestos (see p. 179–80).

The Outer Court correspondence course has four sections: 'The first of these outlines the vocabulary the group uses and introduces the key foundational techniques of the Western Mysteries, as practised by the group. The second two sections provide a good solid grounding in the practical Qabalah with a Jungian influence. The fourth and final section introduces the principles of the Modern Mysteries.' On satisfactory completion of this course the candidate may be invited to join the Inner Group.

The London Group stresses the practical nature of its work: 'Our keynote is "action". We have no room for arm-chair philosophers. We welcome innovation and use many techniques to help individuals become truly themselves. There are many ways of service and many groups seeking to put Aquarian Age ideals in action. There is no shoe to fit all sizes and shapes, and an esoteric group is no different.'

Some esoteric schools appear to the outsider to be rather conservative, even a little old-fashioned in their transmission of what are, after all, traditional teachings. The London Group emphasises that it 'passes on that tradition in a contemporary form suitable for use in the twenty-first century'. It also gives the impression of being rather more flexible than some other schools: 'We hope this outline of our aims and training methods has been informative. If we are not what you are seeking, then at least we may have helped you to know more clearly what it is you do seek! There is no "one way", but there is a best way for each and every one of us.'

The London Group itself had an offshoot, the Dallas Group (also called the Star and Cross and the Celtic Christian Church, Texas), co-founded by Hans W. Nintzel who, until his death in 2000, was director of RAMS, the Restoration of Alchemical Manuscripts Society, based in Richardson, Texas.[149]

CHAOS MAGIC

Chaos magic (sometimes spelt 'magick') is a fairly new development in 'occult science'. Its name originally springs from chaos theory in quantum physics and also, perhaps, from what might seem to outsiders to be the chaotic approach to practising it, in comparison with the careful application of tried and tested magical ritual from existing traditions. It could be considered a postmodern approach to the theory and practice of magic.

Many of those interested in esoteric religion, including both Hermetic occultism and Neo-Paganism, are well educated and well read. Just as most Wiccans have now come to accept that theirs is actually a new religion, very largely created about half a century ago rather than in the mists of antiquity (see p. 285), so those interested in ritual magic have come to accept that even the most traditional magical rituals were 'invented' at some point. Much of today's occult science traces directly back to the Hermetic Order of the Golden Dawn (see p. 195), and much of its ritual, rather than being carved in ancient stone, was actually created by 'MacGregor' Mathers and others little more than a century ago.

Chaos magicians, accepting that, as one says, 'It's all made up anyway', are happy to experiment, and to make things up themselves, more relevant to their own lives, circumstances and interests – and to the present day rather than Victorian, Renaissance, medieval or Ancient Egyptian times. Rather than invoking the angels who guard the four cardinal points by their traditional Hebrew names, they might instead call on John, Paul, George and Ringo. Instead of working with the traditional elements of Air, Water, Earth and Fire, when a certain British girl group was at its height in the mid-1990s some had a spicier alternative and called on Posh, Sporty, Scary and Baby. (Those who also wanted to work with the invisible fifth element of Spirit would have added Ginger.)[150]

There is clearly a playfulness in the attitude of Chaos magicians; in their best-known saying (originally ascribed to Hasan-i-Sabbah, the first master of the Assassins), 'Nothing is True. Everything is Permitted'.[151] One of the founders of Chaos magic, Peter J. Carroll, puts it this way: 'Chaoists usually accept the meta-belief that belief is a tool for achieving effects; it is not an end in itself.' But like all esotericists and Neo-Pagans their study and ritual work has a serious purpose: to know oneself, to develop spiritually and to change the world around them. The attraction of Chaos magic is summed up by Carroll: 'Chaos Magic for me means a handful of basic techniques which must be adhered to strictly to get results, but beyond that it offers a freedom of expression and intent undreamt of in all previous forms of magic.'[152]

Peter Carroll and Ray Sherwin are generally seen as the founders of Chaos magic, both as a concept in 1976 and as a movement, the Illuminates of Thanateros (IOT), in 1978. Carroll has written a number of foundational books, including *Liber Null* (1978), *Psychonaut* (1981) and *Liber Kaos* (1992). A later significant writer in the field is Phil Hine, with *Prime Chaos* (1993), *Condensed Chaos* (1995) and *Pseudonomicon* (1996). The title of the last is a play on the *Necronomicon*, the fictional grimoire in the stories of horror writer H. P. Lovecraft; Hine's book outlines some of his 'ideas concerning the magical possibilities of the Cthulhu Mythos'.[153]

Some of the ideas behind Chaos magic can be found in the writings of the co-author of the *Iluminatus!* trilogy, Robert Anton Wilson (1932–2007), and in the work of the artist Austin Osman Spare (1886–1956). The later Gnostic novels of science-fiction writer Philip K. Dick (1928–82) have also been cited by some Chaos magicians as an influence.

Chaos magicians come from many backgrounds, from ritual sex-magic groups such as the Ordo Templi Orientis to Wiccans and Druids exploring different paths. Many work alone or in twos and threes, but as Carroll writes:

> others have worked in concert in a loose configuration of allied groups. The Magical Order of the IOT has in practice functioned as a highly creative Disorder. This creative disorder has spawned, among other things, a structure known as 'The Pact'. The Pact is, in contradistinction to the usual implications of such a name, a friendly society for mutual support and encouragement in the field of magic. The Magical Pact of the IOT represents another phase of the current of Chaos Magic in which its practitioners elect to work as an integrated force.[154]

Although Chaos magic, both within and outside the IOT, is clearly a significant part of modern occultism, some of its leading theorists and practitioners see it as something beyond what they consider the hidebound and superstition-ridden orders of more traditional occultism. In *Psybermagick: Advanced Ideas in Chaos Magic*, Carroll, apparently only partly tongue-in-cheek, adapts Diderot's famous aphorism about kings and priests: 'Magic will not be free from occultism until we have strangled the last astrologer with the entrails of the last spiritual master.'[155]

But at the same time many Chaos magicians draw on teachings and techniques from other areas of esoteric religion. In his book *Chaos Ritual* Steve Wilson outlines a way of developing a personal, individual magical system by utilising ideas from both Sahaja Yoga and shamanism. Wilson prefers the term Results Magic rather than Chaos Magic;[156] 'Whether it works or not, for me, has always been of paramount importance,' he says.[157] He explores what he calls the Great Contradiction, 'how to induce the spontaneous, how to force freedom, how to control the chaotic', referring to artist and magician Austin Osman Spare's work with 'sentient sigils', 'based on the idea of encapsulating a desire in a form unintelligible to the conscious mind and then forcing it into the unconscious by deliberately forgetting it. Then, Spare assumed, the unconscious would do whatever necessary to make the sigilised wish come true.'[158]

Chaos magic deliberately subverts the tropes of traditional occultism. In ceremonial magic as practised by the Golden Dawn and similar groups, and based in part on masonic rituals, every word and gesture is pre-ordained and no deviation is allowed; Wilson's book shows how spontaneity can be brought into ritual magic, developing and changing the ceremony while it is actually taking place.

Such subversion is characteristic of what is sometimes known as Left-Hand Path occultism. This is not a euphemism for 'Black Magic', which is very largely the creation of horror writers like Dennis Wheatley, but a precise definition is hard to find. The phrase comes from the Tantric term *vama-marga* (left-path).

The concept can be found in Hinduism and Buddhism, where for centuries some holy men have flouted societal conventions by eating forbidden foods, living in graveyards or being naked in public. Legends of the Assassins suggest that under two of their leaders, Hasan II and Muhammad II, they abandoned two of the strongest prohibitions of Islam, the drinking of alcohol and the eating of pork.[159] An historical precedent in the West is the largely medieval idea of Lords of Misrule, Feasts of Fools, Abbots of Unreason and even Boy Bishops, where for one day of the year the rulebook was ignored and the usual strict conventions were overturned.

Left-Hand Path magicians do not follow rigid rituals laid down years ago; they do not submit to authority in their magical work. They are individualistic and reject moral absolutes, and their magical work may be more for their own benefit than society's – self-empowerment rather than healing, for example. Chaos magicians and Thelemites tend to be Left-Hand Path; so are the very few occultists who are genuine Satanists.

SATANISM

Satanism, as it is usually perceived, is effectively a Christian creation; it has nothing to do with modern witchcraft, Neo-Paganism or the vast majority of esoteric movements. Satan, or the Devil, is part of the Christian religion – though as some Christian sects such as the Christadelphians point out, the biblical evidence for him as a personal being, though it is there, is slight. The Devil in Christianity is a carry-over from Gnostic Dualism, which has some of its roots in Zoroastrianism; this gives the neat contradiction, still present in Christianity, that although there is only one God – monotheism – he has an evil opponent; this is almost, though not quite, ditheism, the difference being that Christianity has changed the Devil from an evil God into a powerful but limited fallen angel.

Most good Bible dictionaries[160] reveal that there is no simple identification in the Bible of the Devil equals Satan equals Lucifer; instead there is talk of demons and devils, and also of 'the satan' meaning 'the adversary or accuser' as in a court of law. The terms sometimes seem interchangeable. One Christian authority accepts the lack of clear identification: 'We can only conjecture, therefore, that Satan is a fallen angel.'[161] Another points put that the theme of Lucifer as the fallen angel 'actually owes more to the influence of Milton's *Paradise Lost* than to any direct biblical references'.[162]

The identification of Lucifer with the Devil is thought to be a mistake made by St Jerome in the fourth century CE, which is still with us; Lucifer, far from being a proper name, is simply Latin for 'light-bearer' or 'light-bringer' (the Hebrew original means 'the bright one'), a term sometimes applied to the morning star, the planet Venus. (In Victorian times matches were known as lucifers, without any demonic inferences being drawn.) The 'name' only appears once in the Bible, in Isaiah 14:12. Historically it refers to the king of Babylon[163] but allegorically, according to the Evangelical *New Bible Dictionary*, 'the true claimant to this title is shown in Revelation 22:16 to be the Lord Jesus Christ in His ascended glory', and not the Devil at all.[164]

Effectively, the Devil as we usually think of him is a piece of Christian folklore. The concept of the Devil with horns, a tail and cloven hooves is entirely medieval in origin, rather than biblical. The medieval mind was intensely superstitious, and the medieval imagination intensely fertile. Consider Hieronymus Bosch's painting, *The Garden of Earthly Delights* (c.1500), which shows that while the Renaissance brought great changes in art, culture and much else, the effects of the medieval mindset were slow to fade away. Arguably they are still with us today, for example in Christian 'deliverance ministry'.

As for Satanism, with its black masses, rituals and incantations, this is almost entirely the bastard child of nineteenth-century occultism and the darker side of the Romanticism of the period, Gothic and decadent – and fictional. J. Gordon Melton, one of the United States' most respected authorities on alternative religions, and an ordained Methodist minister, points out that practically everything we know about Satanism and Black Magic actually comes from the pens of Christian writers: 'Though none had ever seen a Satanist ritual or met a real Satanist, these Christian writers described their practices in great detail. That is to say, the Satanist tradition was created and sustained by generation after generation of anti-Satanist writers.'[165] Satanic Ritual Abuse (see p. 255) was simply a recent version of the same process.

Esoteric researcher Gareth J. Medway has established that reports of black masses in front-page splashes in the tabloid press over the years simply recycle the same details – which he traced back to a collection of folk tales and fairy stories by Jean-François Bladé, *Contes Populaires de la Gascogne*, published in 1886. As Medway points out, other stories in the same collection concern: '"Fairies, Ogres and Dwarves," dragons, a wicked stepmother or two, "The Sleeping Beauty" and "The Sea That Sang, the Apple That Danced, and the Little Bird Who Told All."'[166] Despite its origin, this story of the black mass is reproduced as factual by several well-known authors on the supernatural including Montague Summers (see p. 64), Rollo Ahmed and Peter Haining, leading other writers to assume that it must therefore be true.

That is the fictional portrayal of Satanism, though often presented as real. There are genuine Satanists, but before examining them it is worth mentioning a few groups of people who are sometimes confused with Satanists.

Some are small groups of teenagers who, inspired by the album covers, lyrics and stage trappings of heavy-metal bands, have read Aleister Crowley, or more likely have read *about* Crowley, because his works are not an easy read; then for kicks, borrowing from horror films and novels, they have tried their own imaginative recreation of Black Magic rituals in a graveyard.

Some supposed Satanists are the minority of paedophiles who dress up their perversion with pseudo-Gothic religious trappings, either to instil more fear in their victims, or to increase their own pleasure in their actions, or perhaps, by some warped psychological reasoning, to justify their actions to themselves (see p. 260).

There is a very small subset of people interested in esoteric studies who might sometimes use the terms Satanism or Luciferianism as synonyms for their seeking after hidden knowledge. Although this might seem a strange definition, it fits in with the Garden of Eden story of the tree from which the serpent persuaded Eve to eat the fruit: 'For God doth know that in the day ye eat thereof, then your eyes shall be opened, and ye shall be as gods, knowing good and evil . . . the woman saw that the tree was . . . a tree to be desired to make one wise' (Genesis 3:5–6). They are looking for knowledge and perhaps power – but they are not real Satanists either, in the sense of worshipping the force of evil.

There are, however, a few who proudly and openly take the name of Satanists, and who follow their own Satanic religion – though most of these are basically anti-Christian or pro-hedonist rather than being actual worshippers of Satan. Probably the best-known recent Satanist of this type was Anton LaVey (1930–97), founder of the Church of Satan in San Francisco in 1966 and author of *The Satanic Bible* (1969). His aim was to make carnal desires a proper object of celebration. LaVey courted publicity, and was often photographed performing rituals over a 'living altar' – a naked woman.

'Satanism is a blatantly selfish, brutal religion,' says Burton H. Wolfe in his introduction to *The Satanic Bible*. In the book LaVey lists nine Satanic statements, including:

1. Satan represents indulgence, instead of abstinence!
4. Satan represents kindness to those who deserve it, instead of love wasted on ingrates!
5. Satan represents vengeance, instead of turning the other cheek!
8. Satan represents all of the so-called sins, as they all lead to physical, mental or emotional gratification![167]

As one anthropologist has said of LaVey's writing, 'Here Satan clearly represents an idealised, empowered self rather than an external evil.'[168]

In the mid-1970s the Church of Satan became less centralised and more low-key. It was still in existence at the time of LaVey's death in October 1997. The Church of Satan website illustrates that the emphasis is still the same:

we are the first above-ground organisation in history openly dedicated to the acceptance of Man's true nature – that of a carnal beast, living in a cosmos which is permeated and motivated by the Dark Force which we call Satan . . . We Satanists are our own Gods, and we are the explorers of the Left-Hand Path. We do not bow down before the myths and fictions of the desiccated spiritual followers of the Right-Hand Path.[169]

In 1975 Michael Aquino, a former Lt Colonel in the US Army, and a number of other members broke away from the Church of Satan in protest at what they saw as its corruption and publicity-seeking, and set up the Temple of Set. In their beliefs the Egyptian god Set is broadly equated with Satan. Professor Jean La Fontaine writes: 'While the "official view" is probably that he is a person, a "real being", he is not worshipped but approached as a friend.'[170] The movement's website suggests less of the Church of Satan's emphasis on indulgence, and more of a link with earlier occult ideas for self-knowledge and self-development through ceremonial magic: 'The Temple of Set determined to preserve the principle of individualism, but to add to it the evolutionary "higher self" aspirations of Aleister Crowley's pre-O.T.O. philosophy of *Thelema* [see p. 214]. Glorification of the ego is not enough; it is the complete *psyche* – the entire self or soul – which must be recognised, appreciated, and actualised.'[171]

The number of members of either group is difficult to ascertain, but it is certainly nowhere near as high as either tabloid newspaper stories or the groups themselves claim. According to a 1995 study by British academic Graham Harvey, in all there were fewer than 100 actual Satanists in Britain, in six organised groups;[172] while La Fontaine reckons that: 'the figures for those committed to, or seriously interested in, Satanism in Britain are likely to be between 100 and 250 – certainly no more than 400, which is negligible in a population of about 60 million'.[173]

This conflicts with figures from the 2001 UK Census, in which 1,525 people wrote in 'Satanist' as their religion; but as historian and magician Dave Evans points out, 390,000 people wrote in 'Jedi Knight', casting a little doubt on such self-identification.[174] As he suggests elsewhere, 'one must consider the responses of young adults wishing to merely shock or pose' – or as he calls them, 'fashion-Satanists'. Evans also refers to 'philosophical satanists' who have 'been attracted by the individualist, self-agency approach' of books like *The Satanic Bible*, or may 'simply be bohemians, hedonists and dilettantes who might enjoy the shock value or fashionable *kudos* of having such a book on display in their homes, rather than being magical practitioners *per se*'.[175]

Just as unlikely is the figure extrapolated from a survey carried out in 1989 by the Sorcerer's Apprentice bookshop in Leeds. They handed out *The Occult Census* to customers in their shop, and distributed it to their mailing list and to other shops and magical groups. They found that 4 per cent of respondents said they had a committed belief in Satanism. It is obvious that this does not suggest that 4 per cent of the UK population are Satanists; the population being sampled were occultists or people interested in the occult, who make up a small minority of the overall population. In fact, the survey is an object lesson in the dangers of careless interpretation of statistics. It cannot even be taken to suggest that 4 per cent of occultists in Britain are Satanists; the Sorcerer's Apprentice shop sells considerably more 'Satanic' merchandise than most occult shops do, meaning that a significantly higher proportion of its customers are interested in Satanism.[176] The survey was also geographically skewed, with 33 per cent of its respondents coming from the north of England, which only has 22 per cent of the national population.[177] One further point worth noting is that in the relevant question respondents were asked to give their level of interest in sixteen esoteric areas from Astrology to Spiritism, and many showed a Serious Interest or Committed Belief in more than one; Committed Belief was 46 per cent of all respondents for Paganism, 42 per cent for Witchcraft, 37 per cent for Healing, and 35 per cent each for Divination and Ritual. With just 4 per cent Satanism had by far the lowest percentage of all.

The survey's own interpretation of its results emphasises that 75 per cent of its respondents have no interest whatsoever in Satanism, and a further 15 per cent only a 'curious interest'; the Sorcerer's Apprentice concludes: 'Almost anything connected with Witchcraft or the Occult is considered Satanism by the ignorant but this is not so . . . The predilection of the Christian Church to pass off all aspects of Occultism as Satanism can now be seen for the propaganda exercise it has always been.'[178]

Numbers of Satanists in the United States and other countries are unknown; La Fontaine concludes that 'there is no doubt that there is an international movement, albeit tiny'.[179]

SATANIC RITUAL ABUSE

In February 1995 eight children were returned to their families in Ayrshire, Scotland. They had been 'taken into care' by social workers five years earlier, after some of the parents had been accused of ritually abusing them[180]. The parents were innocent of any such behaviour.

In the late 1980s and early 1990s Britain was shaken by case after case of so-called Satanic Ritual Abuse (SRA), in a number of places including Rochdale, Nottingham and the Orkneys. Around the country children were taken away from protesting families – in all, 211 children over 4 years.[181] A vast amount of distress was caused to the children and their parents.[182] Some discomfort was also caused to thousands of practising Neo-Pagans who, in the headline-conscious eyes of journalists, were synonymous with witches who were synonymous with Satanists. The air was thick with accusations, Christian spokespeople and social workers monopolised radio interviews – but almost no one was actually prosecuted.

Eventually it all faded away. Even the then Chief Constable of Manchester, James Anderton, widely referred to at the time as 'God's spokesman' for his openly Christian beliefs, said there was not enough evidence to sustain a prosecution. Some social workers were reprimanded for being over-zealous – in particular one who had questioned children in both Rochdale and the Orkneys – and the children were, in some cases after several years in foster care, returned home.

The entire concept of Satanic Ritual Abuse stemmed originally from the unsubstantiated claims of first one, then several women in the United States to have been victims of Satanic cults, in some cases 'teenage brood mares' of babies for sacrifice by such cults.

The first significant book was *Michelle Remembers* by Dr Lawrence Pazder and Michelle Smith (1980); Pazder was Michelle's psychiatrist, and later her husband. Michelle's story was horrific. From the age of five, in 1955, she had been subjected to Satanic abuse; she had been kept naked in a cage with snakes; she had been put in a car with the corpse of a woman and the car had been deliberately crashed. Kittens had been mutilated, babies had been sacrificed and she had been forced to drink blood at the altar of Satan. And much more.

Horrific if true; but it was a horror story. In fact Pazder had encouraged his already disturbed patient to believe and embroider her darkest fantasies. Therapists at the time often tried to 'recover the lost memories' of their patients through hypnosis – an idea now largely, though not yet completely, discredited.

The second major book was *Satan's Underground* by Lauren Stratford (1988). She was the classic 'teenage brood mare', being raped by a Satanic cult and giving birth to three babies that were killed on film or sacrificed in front of her; before that, when she had refused to take part in rituals, she had been locked in a metal drum with the bodies of four sacrificed babies.

Two years later her entire story was shown to be false by a Christian magazine, *Cornerstone*; her Christian publishers, Harvest House, withdrew her book. Lauren Stratford was actually Laurel Willson, who had a lifelong history of mental illness, self-harm and making allegations of sexual abuse. Despite her exposure as a fake she published two more books as Stratford before, in 1998, reinventing herself once more as Laura Grabowski, a Holocaust survivor.[183] And despite her exposure as a fake, *Satan's Underground* is in print again from a different publisher and is still being championed by people who want to believe in Satanic baby-killing cults. Laurel Willson died in 2002.

These were not the only such stories. In the early 1990s one psychotherapist claimed 'that 10,000 babies were being bred each year in America especially for satanic sacrifices', and a British counter cultist, Maureen Davies (see below) 'worked out that there were probably 3,000 sacrificial babies born in Britain each year'.[184] No one ever seemed to ask two obvious questions: why did no one notice that their daughters, sisters, friends or pupils were repeatedly pregnant, and where are all the bodies?

As touched upon in the Michelle Smith case above, 'Satanic Ritual Abuse' is closely linked to another phenomenon of the last few decades: adult women going to a therapist because they are suffering from depression, anxiety or other problems, then through their therapy discovering that they had repressed their memories of being sexually abused as children by their fathers, priests or teachers. In the United States especially, families have been riven apart as, completely out of the blue, adult daughters have accused their fathers of abusing them years, sometimes decades earlier. A number of men have been prosecuted on no evidence other than the formerly repressed memories of the 'victims', stories obtained under therapy, sometimes including hypnotic regression.

Psychiatrists, doctors, social workers and the police are now becoming wary of the dangers of False Memory Syndrome, whereby an already disturbed person can be led, through hypnotic regression, group therapy or other forms of counselling, to remember in graphic detail events in their lives which never occurred. In some cases there is actually clear evidence disproving the 'memories', such as the alleged abusers being in another state at the time of the supposed abuse, and one case of a woman who claimed to have been raped by Satanists 'countless times', but was later found still to be a virgin.[185] Mark Pendergrast, who has studied False Memory Syndrome intensively, writes of 'clients in psychotherapy who are desperately seeking to locate the source of their unhappiness. If the therapist has let them know, either subtly or directly, that they can expect to find scenes of sexual abuse while under hypnosis or through guided imagery, they are likely to do so.'[186]

The American anthropologist Sherrill Mulhern, who taught for many years at the Université de Paris, has produced disturbing evidence suggesting that certain therapists first draw out their patients' fantasies, and then encourage them to believe them.[187] The therapists' validation strengthens their patients' belief, whatever it might be. Once the narrative is fleshed out, it becomes a new memory, indistinguishable from a genuine one.

In passing, the idea of False Memory Syndrome also throws considerable doubt on accounts gained through therapy, and especially through hypnotic regression, of both past lives and alien abduction. Many psychologists now believe that rather than revealing true memories, hypnosis simply reinforces the subject's belief, whether it be fact or fiction.

The formulation of religious myth by creating a narrative interpretation of a subjective personal experience could be seen as a related phenomenon (see p. 118).

In the United States the best-known case of 'ritual child abuse' was the McMartin Preschool in Manhattan Beach, California. In 1983 a deeply religious and psychologically unstable mother came to believe, with no evidence, that her two-year-old son had been anally abused by a teacher at the preschool. She shared her worries with other parents, leading to lengthy inter-rogation of the children at the preschool.

In response to their questioning the children said, amongst much else equally bizarre: that they had been taken to Palm Springs in either an aeroplane or a hot air balloon, been sexually abused, then returned to the school; that they had been flushed down toilets, travelled down sewers, been sexually abused, then returned to the school; been taken through trapdoors in the classroom floors into underground tunnels to rooms where they were abused; that they were forced to ride naked on a horse, watch the mutilation and killing of animals, were buried in coffins, were abused by the side of a road and were forced to engage in Satanic rituals, including the ritual murder of infants and the drinking of a baby's blood; and that they saw flying witches, film stars and local politicians.[188]

In retrospect it is unbelievable that this 'evidence' led to a six-year criminal trial costing $15 million. In the end no one was found guilty of any offence – but the teacher originally accused had spent five years in jail, other staff had also been imprisoned, and the lives of the children, their parents and the teachers at the preschool had been scarred, perhaps for life.

Throughout the 1980s stories of Satanic Ritual Abuse were believed by a few childcare specialists in the United States, and in 1987 a small group of fundamentalist Christians and SRA-believing psychotherapists there passed the idea of Satanic Ritual Abuse across the Atlantic to Britain. It was taken up by a few British social workers and some Christian spokespeople, leading to the distressing accusations and seizing of supposedly abused children in Nottingham, Rochdale, Ayrshire, the Orkneys and other places.

In Britain, just as in the McMartin Preschool case, young children were repeatedly and intrusively questioned until they gave the 'right' answers; any answers that in any way suggested abuse were clear proof ('Believe the child'), while answers denying abuse (by far the majority) meant that the children were 'in denial'; stories about flights in hot air balloons and long journeys down tunnels were ignored. One of the Orkneys children said years later that she had 'been subjected to hours of intense questioning and was bribed with sweets to tell social workers what they wanted to hear'.[189]

Some of the statements by supposed experts were little more than hysterical fantasies, and almost all were without any foundation in fact; in some cases they were clearly faith-based rather than evidence-based. For example, Maureen Davies, one of the leaders of the Evangelical Christian counter-cult organisation the Reachout Trust, said in a newspaper article: 'The Reachout Trust is aware of some 30 satanic ritual abuse rings operating in

Britain.'[190] She attacked the prestigious Duke of Edinburgh Award because its curriculum included the game *Dungeons and Dragons* which, she said, 'is really witchcraft or Satanism dressed up and called fantasy' and is 'actually just a way of promoting witchcraft'. She also asserted that 'teenagers are prepared to be murdered and to commit suicide for their belief system in reincarnation'.[191]

Although the over-the-top nature of statements such as these, which were widely reported in the press, caused many people to discount their reliability, such 'experts' were still consulted by the police and social workers, and took in many people. Even the respected left-wing feminist journalist Bea Campbell OBE was a leading advocate of the reality of Satanic Ritual Abuse.[192] In sociological terms it was a classic moral panic.

But as Shawn Carlson, the author of an American report on SRA, wrote: 'Never attribute to Devil-worshipping conspiracies what opportunism, emotional instability and religious bigotry are sufficient to explain.'[193]

A detailed report by social anthropologist Professor Jean La Fontaine in 1994, funded by the Department of Health, concluded that there was no evidence whatsoever for SRA.[194] Out of eighty-four cases she considered, three showed some form of ritual trappings, but these did not resemble the typical allegations of 'Satanic Ritual Abuse'. This is clear in the official abstract of her report: 'Organised abuse accounts for a small minority of all cases handled by child protection teams. However, no evidence was found that the sexual and physical abuse of children was part of rites directed to a magical or religious objective. In the three substantiated cases of ritual, not satanic, abuse, the ritual was secondary to the sexual abuse.'[195] In other words some paedophiles, for their own reasons, have on a few occasions cloaked their abusive behaviour with some sort of ritual, but this is not the same thing as genuine Satanists abusing (let alone sacrificing) children as part of their religious rites.

The Reachout Trust began to accept the reality rather than the myth. In 1999 founder director Doug Harris said: 'Are there instances of abuse that are wrapped up in satanic ritual – yes. But if you mean that every witches' coven sacrifices children – no.'[196] Even that was not correct, because in fact 'there was no evidence of devil worship – whether in pretence or in reality' in any abuse cases.[197] But the same year in their magazine *Reachout Quarterly* they stated, in response to criticism: 'Reachout Trust has not been increasingly focused on the campaign against satanic abuse. They have always been focused on a positive outreach to cults, occult and new age. Maureen Davies indeed became more focused and that was why we agreed together that it would be time for her to leave as that was not the purpose of Reachout Trust.'[198] By 2010 an article on their website stated that 'we do not support the myth of SRA – just the opposite'.[199]

Satanic Ritual Abuse scares have occurred in other countries: Canada in 1985, the Netherlands in 1986, and in Scandinavia, Australia and New Zealand. In each case, it seems, the scares followed in the wake of SRA 'experts', social workers or Fundamentalist Evangelicals, visiting these countries. This is not a new phenomenon; as the Spanish explorer Alonso de Salazar Frías wrote in 1611 in criticism of the Inquisition: 'I have observed that there were neither witches nor bewitched in a village until they were talked and written about.'[200]

Effectively, accusations of Satanic Ritual Abuse were a modern equivalent of the medieval Christian belief that Jews ate babies, and of the sixteenth- and seventeenth-century witch-hunts. The stories, whether taken from adults recovering 'repressed memories' during therapy or from children interviewed by SRA-believing counsellors, contain many recurring features, leading anthropologists and religious scholars to identify the 'transmission of the mythology from place to place'.[201] Massimo Introvigne, an Italian scholar on religious movements, comments: 'Although some Satanists have been guilty of real crimes, Satanic Ritual Abuse is largely an urban legend perpetuated by a fraction of social workers and child psychologists who have done a lot of damage.'[202]

What I Believe . . .
Initiation

I'd differentiate between induction into a group and initiation into the mysteries. There is no such thing as self-initiation; what is really meant by that misleading term is self-dedication, seeking initiation. Initiation is not when you go to the mysteries, but when the Mysteries come to you.

Stuart Inman, 1734 practitioner
Artist and teacher

A flight of steps; it never ends; it's a series of stages throughout one's life, or more accurately lives, indicating a change and a deepening of one's working relationship with the otherworld. An initiatory ceremony would take me up a notch. But initiation often takes place outside magical circles, outside the accepted idea of ritual in some cases; sometimes initiation may be brought about by personal circumstances.

Jack Gale, Magician
Retired school teacher

It's important because at a certain stage you have to assent to what is going to happen to you, and what initiation does is: it puts you on the spot, and it makes you go in your heart, and you have to ask yourself a very deep question: 'Do I want this or don't I?' Because in magic, the one fundamental is: you do it because you want to and not because somebody makes you do it. And it's only by going through that experience that you can actually work with magic.

Dr Paul Newman, Wiccan with interest in
Eastern spirituality
Sessional Lecturer in Mathematics,
University of London

A 'rite of passage' into a new life (and usually a new community).
Oberon Zell-Ravenheart, Co-founder, Church of All Worlds

My initiation for me meant a commitment to my past; it also equally importantly meant that I was embraced by a community of people who'd made that same commitment and we now all had that in common. It also meant that I went through something I could never, ever describe and turned my inner life upside down, and quite frankly put me in touch with spiritual beings, that I couldn't begin to describe to anybody.
Dr Christina Oakley Harrington, Wiccan priestess Owner of Treadwells esoteric bookshop, London, former university lecturer in History and Religious History

I think ultimately what initiation is about is gaining a freedom, either a freedom through knowledge, a freedom through some sort of passing through the veil, whatever it is. When one is initiated one has gained further insight, it's a new insight, and that insight has to be liberating, otherwise it's not an initiation.
Dr Michael York, Shaman Retired Professor of Cultural Astronomy and Astrology, Bath Spa University

A singular event to mark a process of awakening which is really an ongoing process.
Dr William S. Redwood, Esoteric Researcher and Lecturer

One of the children from the Orkneys case, who was separated from her family from the age of six to thirteen, many years later described how she had been questioned by the social worker who had also been involved in the Rochdale case.

> I was terrified of her. She was very intimidating, very controlling. I was always small when I was a child but she would lean over me. She got very angry. She would want me to agree with what she was saying.[203]

> We kept telling them that we had not been abused, but they wouldn't listen. The interview techniques used were designed to break us down.[204]

There have been two positive outcomes from the moral panic of SRA. First, the guidelines for interviewing children have been redrawn extensively to minimise the danger of either intimidating or in any way leading the children in their answers. Second, psychologists have been able to bring to the attention of social workers and others the phenomenon of False Memory Syndrome, when impressionable or disturbed adults can be led, through therapy, to 'remember' things in their lives that never happened. Some psychologists are also casting doubt on the whole concept of repressed memories.

But despite this the story continues to recur. In February 2000 BBC News reported allegations in a tabloid newspaper by London psychotherapist Valerie Sinason that 'children are being bred for sacrifice and sexual abuse, kept in cages, forced to eat human flesh and excrement, and made to watch abortions and murders. Today. In Britain.'[205] Sinason specialised in treating 'multiple personality disorder'; her revelations came from her patients' stories. No other evidence was provided.

There is no doubt in reality that Satanic Ritual Abuse, as such, is a modern myth. The danger is that the publicity that accompanies each new resurgence of the scare, including lurid stories on the internet, could blind us to the very real cases of non-Satanic, non-ritual child abuse which occur every day.

NOTES FOR PART TWO

1   http://www.kabbalah.com, http://www.kabbalahcentre.co.uk.
2   George 1995: 62, 173–5, 263–4.
3   Coincidentally the word 'cabal' was the initial letters of five of
     King Charles II's most powerful ministers, Sir Thomas Clifford,
     Lord Arlington, the Duke of Buckingham, Lord Ashley and
     Lord Lauderdale.
4   Any 'alternative history' book that asserts unequivocally that
     Jesus was an Essene may safely be ignored.
5   The Moody Blues's 1968 concept album *In Search of the Lost
     Chord* is a Sixties psychodelic expression of that perennial
     quest.
6   This is described by Tarrés's former lover Patrice Chaplin in her
     fascinating autobiographical account of the uncovering of the
     secrets of Girona, *City of Secrets* (Chaplin 2007); her own
     Kabbalistic journey is recounted in Chaplin 2010. See also
     Barrett 2007c; Barrett 2010b.
7   See Barrett 2007a: 73ff.
8   See, for example, the list of correspondences of the Builders of
     the Adytum: http://www.botaineurope.org/en/corresp.html.
9   Servants of the Light introductory booklet: 3.
10   Bogdan 2007: 123.
11   Pollack 1989: 137.
12   Builders of the Adytum introductory booklet: BOTA 1989.
13   Rider was the publisher. This is usually known as the Rider-
     Waite pack, but I am following the movement to give equal
     weight to the artist.
14   Waite 1911: 68.
15   Waite 1938: 194.
16   Waite 1911: 68.
17   The texts of the first two manifestos are given in an Appendix in
     Yates 1972: 235–60; the third is summarised in Yates 1972:
     60–64. The full texts are available online at http://levity.com/
     alchemy/fama.html, http://levity.com/alchemy/confessi.html
     and http://levity.com/alchemy/chymwed1.html.
18   See Barrett 2008a: 56–9.
19   For a more in-depth look at both the origins of Rosicrucianism
     and several present-day Rosicrucian Orders see Barrett 2007a,
     Chapters 2 and 4.

20   Gilbert 1987b: 89.
21   http://www.soul.org/Warning.html.
22   http://www.soul.org.
23   Leaflet: *The Rosicrucians*, Beverly Hall Corporation, n.d.
24   Deveney 1997: 395.
25   Deveney 1997: 142–3.
26   Poesnecker 1996: 88, 89, 91, 104.
27   http://www.soul.org/Warning.html.
28   Quoted in King 2002: 144.
29   http://www.soul.org/Warning.html.
30   The figures of 250,000 members in 1990, falling to 200,000 in 1998, are given by Philip Charles Lucas in Melton and Baumann 2002: 47.
31   Booklet: *An Introduction to AMORC*, 31st edition, n.d.
32   Booklet: *Mysticism . . . What it is, What it does, What it offers*, (Crowborough, E. Sussex: AMORC, n.d).
33   http://www.light.org/who-we-are.cfm.
34   Zain 1987: 37.
35   http://www.light.org/kabbalah-and-the-two-keys.cfm.
36   This brief summary is based largely on the respective entries in Greer 2006: 149–50, 274–5, 275–6, 487–9.
37   Heindel, n.d.: 16–17.
38   http://www.rosicrucian.com/differ.htm.
39   Hans Rieuwers, Lectorium Rosicrucianum, in correspondence with the author, 2 November 2010.
40   Unless otherwise stated all quotations are from H. C. Steinhart, then General Secretary of Lectorium Rosicrucianum, in correspondence with the author, 12 July 1995, 30 October 1995 and 22 November 1999.
41   See Massimo Introvigne, 'Lectorium Rosicrucianum: A Dutch Movement Becomes International', CESNUR '97 International Conference, Amsterdam, at http://www.cesnur.org/testi/ RosyCross.htm; Stoyanov 2000: 187–215; and O'Shea 2000.
42   Cavendish 1984: 39; Cavendish 1990: 143; Drury 2000: 42; compare the spurious chivalric titles of 'speculative historian' Laurence Gardner and George King, founder of the Aetherius Society.
43   Waite 1924: 566.
44   Quoted in Regardie 1989: 17.
45   Greer 2006: 277–8, 373–4, 569–70, 634–5.

46 No. 1 was supposedly the mother temple in Germany, and No. 2 was supposedly a previous British temple, defunct since the death of its chiefs (Gilbert 1986: 30–31).

47 Ehrman 2005: 31; Alexander and Alexander 1999: 752; Barton and Muddiman 2001: 1271.

48 Kenny 1986.

49 Letter from Paul Foster Case to Israel Regardie, 10 August 1933, at http://szermeno.intuitwebsites.com/files/QuickSiteImages/letter2.pdf.

50 Waite 1924: 565.

51 Waite 1924: 442.

52 Waite 1924: 446; Jackson 1994: 73.

53 Sources on Anna Kingsford: http://hermetic.com/dionysos/abk.htm, http://www.hogd.co.uk/gd_history_ciceros.htm.

54 Gilbert 1987a: 3.

55 Gilbert 1997: 21.

56 For consistency she is referred to as Mina throughout this book, except in quotations. 'Mathers' on its own refers to 'MacGregor' Mathers throughout.

57 'Crowley is really the source for this info, and we believe it is somewhat suspect. (We have no info from Mathers or Westcott on this matter).'– Chic and Tabatha Cicero, Hermetic Order of the Golden Dawn, in correspondence with the author, 22 October 2010.

58 In Foreword to Howe 1972: ix.

59 Lévi 1995: 124–9.

60 The tables of 'a few of the principal correspondences' take up twenty-one pages in Appendix V of Aleister Crowley's *Magick in Theory and Practice* (New York: Castle, 1929).

61 For a rare photograph of a full-sized modern reconstruction of the Golden Dawn Vault of the Adepti see Barrett 2008a: 111.

62 Gilbert 1987b: 113.

63 Quoted in Gilbert 1997: 51.

64 Gilbert 1997: 7–20, 50–52.

65 Regardie 1989. Strictly speaking these were the teachings of Stella Matutina rather than the Golden Dawn.

66 Bogdan 2007: 127.

67 Gilbert 1986: 200.

68 http://www.hermeticgoldendawn.org.

69 http://www.hogd.co.uk/home.htm.

70 http://www.golden-dawn.com/eu/index.aspx.

71 'October 2010 – The Ninth Circuit Court of Appeals recently ruled in our favour': the HOGD Fund page on http://www.hermeticgoldendawn.org; http://courtlistener.com/ca9/UHk/the-hermetic-order-of-the-gold-v-david-griffin/.

72 http://www.golden-dawn-canada.com.

73 http://www.horustemple.com.

74 http://www.ritual-magic.com.

75 http://www.ordo-stella-matutina.com.

76 http://www.osogd.org.

77 http://www.esotericgoldendawn.com.

78 http://www.rosae-crucis.net.

79 http://www.mandrake.uk.net/ogdos.htm.

80 http://www.lawbright.com/logdos/.

81 Known as 'honour points', the three dots are the standard typographical style for the initials of a number of esoteric movements, including some masonic societies, but for simplicity it will not be followed hereafter.

82 Davis: 23.

83 This is the briefest of outlines; there are numerous readily accessible detailed biographies of Crowley.

84 Weston 2009: 225.

85 http://www.oto-uk.org/liber220.

86 François Rabelais, *The Histories of Gargantua and Pantagruel*, The First Book, chapter 57; Rabelais 1955: 159.

87 Augustine of Hippo, *On the First Epistle of John*.

88 Esoteric researcher Ken Eakins in correspondence with the author, 6 November 2010.

89 For some discussion of the complexity of the term see Ed Richardson, 'The Holy Guardian Angel: a tricky little devil', at http://www.philhine.org.uk/writings/ess_hga.html. Thelemite Steve Wilson points out (in correspondence with the author, 9 November 2010) 'that "the knowledge and conversation of the holy guardian angel", from the Abra Melin magic system, was chosen by Crowley to represent the supreme state in a ridiculous way, to mock the idea that, without first attaining it, we can really know what is meant by "enlightenment", "nirvana", "moksha" etc.'

90   One useful site for source documents on the origins and history of the OTO and related groups is http://user.cyberlink. ch/~koenig/, but it should be noted that Koenig's research is heavily criticised by supporters of the Caliphate OTO.

91   This terminology highlights the masonic origins of at least parts of the OTO.

92   http://user.cyberlink.ch/~koenig/white.htm.

93   Greer 2006: 448.

94   Massimo Introvigne and PierLuigi Zoccatelli say: 'At present, there are more than one hundred rival "Crowleyan" OTOs (in addition to several "pre-Crowleyan") throughout the world' (Melton and Baumann 2002: 986).

95   http://www.oto-uk.org/history.

96   http://www.lashtal.com/nuke/PNphpBB2-viewtopic-t-2998. phtml.

97   http://hermetic.com/sabazius/history_egc.htm.

98   DeHaan 1972: 10.

99   Fortune 1994: 4.

100   Letter from Mina Mathers to Paul Foster Case, 1921, at http:// www.golden-dawn.com/eu/displaycontent.aspx?pageid=160- biography-paul-foster-case.

101   Letter from Paul Foster Case to Israel Regardie, 10 August 1933, at http://szermeno.intuitwebsites.com/files/QuickSiteImages/ letter2.pdf.

102   Ibid.

103   Letter from Paul Foster Case to Israel Regardie, 15 January 1933, at http://szermeno.intuitwebsites.com/files/QuickSiteImages/ letter1.pdf.

104   https://www.bota.org/about_us/about.html.

105   BOTA introductory booklet: BOTA 1989: 6.

106   Case 1989: 1.

107   BOTA n.d.: 2.

108   BOTA 1989: 2.

109   http://www.botaineurope.org/groups/tgre.html.

110   BOTA 1989: 1.

111   Ibid: 2.

112   Ibid: 2 (italics in original).

113   Ibid: 43.

114 Soror QI, Publication Steward, BOTA, in correspondence with the author, 16 September 2010.

115 Dr Paul A. Clark, Steward of the Hidden Light, in correspondence with the author, 23 September 2010.

116 Gareth Knight, author of *Dion Fortune and the Inner Light* (Loughborough: Thoth Publications, 2000) in correspondence with the author, 10 February 2000.

117 Evans and Sutton 2010: 34–41.

118 Leaflet: *The Society of the Inner Light: Work and Aims*, 2000 edition.

119 The secretariat of the Society of the Inner Light, in correspondence with the author, 7 February 1995.

120 Knight 2002: 19.

121 Introductory booklet, *The Society of the Inner Light: Work and Aims*, n.d.: 2.

122 Ibid: 13, 14, 16.

123 Ibid: 10.

124 Ibid: 27–8.

125 Leaflet: *The Society of the Inner Light: Work and Aims*, 2000 edition.

126 http://www.angelfire.com/az/garethknight/aboutgk.html.

127 Dion Fortune and Gareth Knight, *The Circuit of Force* (Loughborough: Thoth, 1998), and *Principles of Hermetic Philosophy* (Loughborough: Thoth, 1999).

128 Servants of the Light administrative officer Stephen Tanham in correspondence with the author, 25 August 2010.

129 Ibid.

130 http://www.servantsofthelight.org/courses/third-degree.html.

131 Introductory booklet, *Servants of the Light School of Occult Science*, n.d.: 6.

132 http://www.servantsofthelight.org/aboutSOL/sol-faq.html.

133 Fortune 1987: 17 (chapter 3, paragraph 13).

134 Booklet: *Servants of the Light School of Occult Science*, n.d.: 3.

135 Ibid: 3.

136 http://www.servantsofthelight.org/courses/third-degree.html.

137 Booklet: *Servants of the Light School of Occult Science*, n.d.: 4.

138 Ibid: 6.

139 Stephen Tanham in correspondence with the author, 24 August 2010.

140 Ibid.

141 Dolores Ashcroft-Nowicki in conversation with the author, 20 August 2010 – a few days before, aged over 80, she set out on her annual seven-week tour of the United States.

142 All quotations are from a Fraternidad del Círculo Dorado introductory leaflet, n.d.

143 http://templeofstarlight.eu/content/ina-c%C3%BCsters-van-bergen-magister-and-director-studies.

144 Ina Cüsters-van Bergen in conversation with the author, 26 May 2010.

145 Ibid.

146 http://www.angelfirc.com/az/garethknight/aboutgk.html.

147 http://www.avalon-group.org.

148 All quotations are from http://www.thelondongroup.org.uk.

149 http://www.ramsdigital.com.

150 This paragraph is based on a discussion between three chaos magicians and the author at Talking Stick, London, 19 January 2000.

151 Quoted in Harvey 1997: 100; also printed at the foot of each page of the magazine *Chaos International*. The original Assassins quotation was probably 'Nothing is forbidden; everything is permitted'.

152 This and the previous quotation are from Peter Carroll, 'Chaoism and Chaos Magic, A Personal View', at http://www.sacred-texts.com/bos/bos283.htm.

153 http://www.philhine.org.uk/books/index_mine.html.

154 From Carroll 1992: Appendix 4, quoted at the Psychonomicon website, http://www.firehead.org/~pturing/occult/chaos/pcarroll/liber_kaos.htm#ch2.4.

155 Carroll 2000: 46.

156 Following the usage of Ray Sherwin, who was one of the co-founders with Peter Carroll of Chaos Magic and the Illuminates of Thanateros.

157 Steve Wilson in conversation with the author, October 2010.

158 Wilson 1994: 19, 21.

159 See Barrett 2007a: 35–8.

160 For example J. D. Douglas (ed.), *The New Bible Dictionary* (London: Inter-Varsity Fellowship, 1962); Alan Richardson (ed.), *A Theological Word Book of the Bible* (London: SCM

Press, 1957); William Smith, *Smith's Bible Dictionary* (New York: Pyramid, 1967).

161 Smith 1967: 607.

162 Barton and Muddiman 2001: 450.

163 Pfeiffer and Harrison 1963: 622.

164 Douglas 1962: 755.

165 Melton 1992: 109.

166 Medway 2001: 88.

167 LaVey 1969: 21.

168 Woodman 1998: 134.

169 http://www.churchofsatan.com/home.html.

170 Jean La Fontaine, 'Satanist and Pseudo-Satanist Groups' in Blécourt et al. 1999: 102.

171 http://www.xeper.org/pub/gil/xp_FS_gil.htm.

172 Harvey 1995: 283–96.

173 Jean La Fontaine, 'Satanist and Pseudo-Satanist Groups', in Blécourt et al. 1999: 108.

174 Evans 2007: 79–80.

175 Dave Evans, 'Speculating on the Point 003 Percent? Some Remarks on the Chaotic Satanic Minorities in the UK', in Petersen 2009: 216, 217.

176 Evans 2007: 72.

177 Evans in Petersen 2009: 214.

178 *The Occult Census* 1989: 17.

179 Jean La Fontaine, 'Satanist and Pseudo-Satanist Groups' in Blécourt et al. 1999: 109.

180 *Independent*, 14 April 1991, cited in Medway 2001: 246–8.

181 Parker 1993: 288.

182 A harrowing TV drama by Michael Eaton, *Flowers of the Forest* (BBC2 1997), was based on a number of such cases.

183 http://www.cornerstonemag.com/features/iss090/sideshow. htm; http://www.holysmoke.org/sdhok/sideshw2.htm; http://www.cornerstonemag.com/features/iss117/lauren.htm.

184 Parker 1993: 311.

185 Medway 2001: 342.

186 Pendergrast 1996: 106.

187 Sherrill Mulhern, 'Satanism and Psychotherapy: a rumour in search of an Inquisition', in Richardson et al. 1991: 145–72.

188 http://www.law.umkc.edu/faculty/projects/ftrials/mcmartin/
mcmartinaccount.html; http://www.religioustolerance.org/
tunnels.htm; http://www.religioustolerance.org/ra_mcmar.htm.

189 *Scotsman* (11 September 2006).

190 Maureen Davies in the *Western Mail* (14 August 1989), cited in
Gilbert 1993: 153.

191 Maureen Davies in a public lecture, 'Report on American Trip',
cited in Gilbert 1993: 87, 108.

192 http://www.dramatis.hostcell.net/BCOBE/bcobe.html#CampbellB.

193 Carlson and Larue 1989: 16.

194 See La Fontaine 1998 and Blécourt et al. 1999.

195 Abstract of J. S. La Fontaine, *Extent and Nature of Organised
and Ritual Abuse* (London: HMSO 1994) at http://www.ncjrs.
gov/App/publications/Abstract.aspx?id=157278.

196 Doug Harris, founder director of the Reachout Trust, in conversation with the author, 9 December 1999.

197 Professor Jean La Fontaine in correspondence with the author,
20 September 2010.

198 *Reachout Quarterly*, 57 (Autumn 1999), 5.

199 http://www.reachouttrust.org/articleView.php?id=250.

200 James S. Amelang, 'Between Doubt and Discretion: Revising the
Rules for Prosecuting Spanish Witches', in Lottes et al. 2008: 79.

201 Jean La Fontaine, 'Satanic Abuse Mythology' in Blécourt et al.
1999: 131.

202 Massimo Introvigne, director of CESNUR, in correspondence
with the author, 4 February 2000.

203 *Guardian* (21 October 2006).

204 *Scotsman* (11 September 2006).

205 *Mail on Sunday* (13 February 2000), 42–3.

Part Three:
Neo-Paganism

'Neo-Paganism', to quote Oberon Zell, founder of Church of All Worlds, who is said to have coined the term, is 'a revival and reconstruction of ancient Nature religions adapted for the modern world.'[1]

As this book has demonstrated throughout, there are many connections and cross-fertilisations between Neo-Pagan movements and both New Age and esoteric/Hermetic movements. In a similar way to the Society of the Inner Light (see p. 226) and other esoteric organisations, some Neo-Pagan groups focus on the Matter of Britain, particularly Glastonbury, the Grail and the mythic power of Merlin,[2] and on British folklore and even fairytales for part of the mythology used in their study and ritual. It is interesting therefore to discover that the esoteric writer A. E. Waite, who often has a reputation for pedantry, even for being curmudgeonly about the validity of other people's esoteric movements, edited a small book of poetry about fairies three years before he joined the Hermetic Order of the Golden Dawn (see p. 195). In his fascinating and often delightful introduction to the book he claims that the derivation of the word 'fairy' from 'a debased Latin verb, *fatere*, to enchant, was common in mediaeval times'. Of particular note to present-day Neo-Pagans he writes: 'the original fairy of Frankish poetry and fiction was simply a female initiated into the mysteries and marvels of magic. Such was the mighty Morgan la Fay, the mystic sister of King Arthur.'[3]

So female Wiccans (see p. 285) and Druids (see p. 316) today are, in that sense, a continuation of the British and European fairy tradition.

It is arguable that one of Neo-Paganism's greatest strengths is its diversity. Though there is sometimes rivalry and mutual criticism between different traditions and groups of Neo-Pagans, whether Druids or witches (often known as 'bitchcraft'), there is probably far more commonality between them, and mutual support in the face of opposition, than there is between the many variations and offshoots of Christianity. On the whole Wiccans, Druids, Heathens and others respect each others' paths; they are happy to learn from each other, meeting together socially, sometimes even sharing rituals.

What probably most links the movements in this part of the book is their focus on and respect for nature, in terms of the physical land and the plants and animals on it, the turning of the seasons and in many cases the spirits or deities of nature.

There are also many overlaps between the movements in this part. The use of shamanic trance, for example, can sometimes be found in some Wiccan or Druid groups.

SHAMANISM

Shamanism is perhaps the oldest spiritual activity of all. It is usually associated with small village societies outside the industrialised Western world, such as in Siberia or the more remote areas of South America, but in recent years it has become a major part of contemporary Earth-based spirituality or nature religion, closely associated with Neo-Paganism.

Modern shamans, like the shamans of early religion, usually work alone. They are able, through trance or visions, to enter the spiritual world and communicate with the beings there, working magic or bringing healing back to those in their care. Because shamanism is based on individual experience there is no single set of beliefs – each shaman finds his or her own way – but there are many courses in learning how to be a shaman. One shaman, Leo Rutherford, describes briefly what shamanism is about:

> Shamanism is the oldest tradition on Planet Earth of healing, maintaining balance and harmony in society and the individual, and keeping our connection with Mother Earth and All Creation. A shaman knows that all things are alive, lives both in this world and the spirit world, and has understanding of the inner realities. What I like to call contemporary shamanism is the application of these ancient timeless ways to our situation of the present, be it urban, suburban or whatever. Our outer world may be different, but our human inner landscape has the same components it always did. Our outer health and wholeness (holiness) depends on our inner state and the balance between matter and spirit.[4]

The shaman is one who crosses between worlds. 'Using rhythmic drumming, dance and song the shaman experiences a consciousness-shift which enables her to let her soul journey to what is traditionally known as the Spirit World,' says shamanic teacher Jonathan Horwitz.[5] He refers to shamans as 'stone-age psychotherapists', and healing, both physical and psychological, is probably the main part of the shaman's work.

One of the most prominent schools of shamanism is the Scandinavian Centre for Shamanic Studies in Denmark, founded by Horwitz in 1986, which holds courses throughout Europe. Its basic course is on 'The Shaman's Journey', fundamental to the shaman's work; it also teaches courses on, amongst others, shamanic singing, healing, counselling and helping people who are close to death.

Although the shamanic path is independent and individual, American shaman and academic Michael York says that the shaman has a very definite social role.

> It works two ways: the shaman serves the community but the community also is the anchor for the shaman and keeps her or him from getting lost permanently in the otherworld. The community the shaman serves draws the soul traveller back from what might otherwise amount to sheer madness or insanity. But the function that the shaman is basically working on is healing, for the community and individuals.

York sees healing as physical, spiritual and psychological. 'All of that. What is health? Wholeness!' In fact the words health, heal, hale, holy, whole and holistic all come from the same Old English root: *hal, halig*. 'The completion, the totality, of the community is what the shaman serves,' says York. He works in the European or more broadly Indo-European tradition, including the Roman, the Greek and the Vedic, and also the Northern, Germanic tradition. 'Shamanism itself is a tool, and so I use a shamanic tool or technique,' he says. 'Shamanism concerns the development of multiple perspectives; it's shifting from the ordinary perspective into an otherworld perspective or at least some kind of a different perspective. Ultimately the shaman tries to create a portfolio of different viewpoints or perspectives, which allows one then to see things from those multiple viewpoints, leading to different understandings.'[6]

Other shamans work together. In the UK, the London Open Drumming Group, which was set up in 1997, aims to 'provide a safe working environment to practise core shamanic techniques'. It is not for beginners, but is open to people who have already done a course in core shamanism or have done shamanic counselling with a teacher known to the organisers:

> Within the core shamanic framework the shamanic journey, song, dance art and craft have been some of the forms the group have used to explore personal creativity, healing and personal development. The group has also worked with ceremony and ritual for both personal and community healing. Whatever form the work takes we are always looking to deepen our relationships with our spirit helpers and teachers and to bring the power and wisdom available in the spirit world to this reality.[7]

Shamanism, like other Neo-Pagan paths, is in close touch with nature. Jonathan Horwitz comments:

> As I see it, one of the greatest challenges to the new generation of shamans is to re-establish the contact between human beings and the other inhabitants of the Earth, to network nature, to stop the slaughter of the environment we share, to find out what can be done – spiritually, ritually, and practically – with the damage which has already been done, and to learn once again that the Earth will nourish us – physically and spiritually – if we allow her to do it.[8]

But urban shamans like Ross Heaven show in books like *The Journey to You* and *Spirit in the City* that there is also a major role for shamanism in today's busy city life.[9]

WITCHCRAFT

Today's witches rarely match the popular image of the toothless old hag living in her hovel. They live in the country and the city, in all Western countries; they are likely to be well educated and many of them are professional people; they are old and young; and they are as likely to be men as women. Male witches are called witches; terms such as 'warlock' and 'wizard' belong only in fantasy novels.

One point must be made clearly here. Witchcraft has nothing to do with Satanism (see p. 248); witches do not worship Satan. This is still the most common misunderstanding that witches (and other Neo-Pagans) have to cope with, particularly from the media but also, more worryingly, sometimes from schools and social services. Organisations such as the Pagan Federation and Pebble (see p. 341 and p. 343) have done much in recent years to change such perceptions at a government department and local authority level; but that has had little effect on the tabloid newspapers, which have a field day with stories such as a Pagan policeman being allowed to take Pagan holidays instead of Christian ones, with a typical story beginning: 'Pagan police officers have been given the right to take days off to celebrate festivals where they leave food out for the dead and take part in "unabashed sexual promiscuity".'[10]

The terms 'witch' and 'witchcraft' cover a wide range of things, no doubt contributing to popular confusion. Today they tend to be used to describe at least three very different types of people in addition to present-day Neo-Pagan witches: witches in medieval and Renaissance times; witches in the Bible; and women identified as witches in some West African countries today. These will be considered briefly in reverse order before moving on to today's Neo-Pagan witches.

Horrifyingly in the twenty-first century, reports occasionally reach the news in the West of women in rural areas of some African countries being accused by their neighbours of being witches, and being burned to death, sometimes with a petrol-soaked tyre around their necks. In recent years a version of this has arisen in Britain.

It can be difficult for people to lose the undoubted power of traditional tribal beliefs, even when they are now Christians and are living in the West. In 2005 the Metropolitan Police in London set up a unit called Project Violet specifically to deal with the problem of young West African children being accused of being witches because of behavioural problems such as disobedience or bed-wetting. Parents, advised by their pastors in Evangelical Christian, often Pentecostalist, churches, are led to think that their children have been corrupted by *kindoki* or *ndoki*, a form of black witchcraft widely believed in by villagers in the Congo, Nigeria, Angola and other countries.

The children, both boys and girls, are largely aged eight to eleven, but some are as young as five.

To drive the evil spirit out, the child might be beaten, burned or harmed in other ways, such as having hot peppers rubbed into their eyes or their genitals. Some children are sent back to Africa to be put through such ceremonies to deliver them from the evil spirits; others are dealt with in their homes and churches in Britain. Although in Britain such treatment is clearly seen as child abuse, the Congolese, Nigerian and Angolan parents and pastors believe that they are delivering their children from evil spirits and protecting themselves from the harm that such spirits can cause.

Such 'deliverance ministry' in Christian Churches is controversial enough with adults, let alone with children. Through

Project Violet, West African pastors in London who appreciate the severity of the problem help to identify occurrences of it, and to educate pastors and parents about it.[11]

Witches in the Bible are usually condemned, as in the well-known Old Testament verse 'Thou shalt not suffer a witch to live' (Exodus 22:18). Some Pagan writers in the late twentieth century suggested that the word 'witch' might have had the sense of 'one who poisons wells'; if so, such a penalty would have made some sense for nomadic peoples living in a desert. In fact this was a modern myth; the word used in Exodus, with a Hebrew root meaning 'muttering', meant someone who performs incantations. Some Evangelical Christians use this Old Testament injunction to justify their condemnation of Neo-Pagan witches today.

Numerous scholars have explored how and why people were accused of witchcraft in medieval and Renaissance times, but the meaning of 'witchcraft' was generally consorting with the devil in one way or another. It is now generally recognised by scholars that such witchcraft, with all its demonic trappings, rather than being any sort of reality was very largely the imaginative creation of the Church.[12] Torture was an efficient means of ensuring a confession to whatever charges the inquisitors brought. Historian Robin Briggs is blunt:

> At the risk of disappointing many people in search of sensational discoveries or retrospective legitimation, one simple point must be made. Historical European witchcraft is quite simply a fiction, in the sense that there is no evidence that witches existed, still less that they celebrated black masses or worshipped strange gods. There were plenty of people who dabbled in the occult, in search of wealth, power or revenge, but none of these thought themselves members of a satanic sect.[13]

It is extremely unlikely that any of these 'witches' would have recognised anything in common with today's European and American witches. The closest would have been cunning folk, who sold people charms, prayers and remedies for falling in love, safe childbirth and recovery from sickness – and also the thing of which they were most accused, curses.

Around 1486 two Dominican monks wrote the *Malleus Maleficarum* (The Witch Hammer). The book, which became the textbook of the Inquisition, is full of accounts of how succubi and incubi pass semen between men and women. It also puts the burden of witchcraft largely on women: 'they are more credulous . . . naturally more impressionable . . . they have slippery tongues . . . they are weak . . . since they are feebler both in mind and body, it is not surprising that they should come more under the spell of witchcraft.'[14] Modern witches might tend to disagree.

The book's authors, both men, both highly educated Dominicans, displayed a fear and loathing of women which was not uncommon at the time amongst educated religious men.[15] Women, it was believed, had the power to emasculate men, not just metaphorically but physically; the book contains numerous accounts of men claiming a witch had stolen their penis. Here is an early account of multiple Bobbittism:

> And what, then, is to be thought of those witches who in this way sometimes collect male organs in great numbers, as many as twenty or thirty members together, and put them in a bird's nest, or shut them up in a box, where they move themselves like living members, and eat oats and corn, as has been seen by many and is a matter of common report? It is to be said that it is all done by devil's work and illusion, for the senses of those who see them are deluded in the way we have said. For a certain man tells us that, when he had lost his member, he approached a known witch to ask her to restore it to him. She told the afflicted man to climb a certain tree, and that he might take which he liked out of a nest in which there were several members. And when he tried to take a big one, the witch said: You must not take that one; adding, because it belonged to a parish priest.[16]

As well as being a delightful story, this clearly illustrates the authors' fear of women. Five centuries later in the late twentieth and early twenty-first centuries some men have feared that they were being emasculated not only by feminism, with its ideal of the New Man, but also by Wicca, with its emphasis on the Goddess. There are all-women areas of Wicca, sometimes known as Dianic Wicca, but most Wicca, as with other Neo-Pagan movements, is firmly balanced between the female and the male. Outsiders may only notice the Goddess, because of the difference from the male Judaeo-Christian God; but the majority of Neo-Pagans, both women and men, venerate both Goddess and God.

To quote Shan Jayran, Clan Mother or Priestess of the 1980s London-based group, the House of the Goddess: 'So what does this mean for men? It means a third way, neither bully nor wimp, but powerful, wild, loving, sexual and supportive with room for doubt and uncertainty. This is very much the cutting edge of the Craft today.'[17]

To return to the medieval persecution of witches, there is an interesting argument that the Inquisition could not have had so much 'success' in identifying witches if ordinary people had not been willing to turn in their neighbours. In an age of superstition, if your child was ill or your cow died, you might well put the blame on a woman in your village whom you had insulted or cheated a few months earlier, and who might have got her own back by cursing you.[18]

Another reason for grass-roots public opinion turning against the formerly respected wise-women or herbalists could perhaps be to do with the Black Death, which swept Europe between 1347 and 1350, killing as many as a third of the population. If people asked their local herbalist or wise woman for a potion to protect or cure their family and were given, for example, an infusion of willow bark (the forerunner of aspirin), it would have had little effect against the plague. If you ask for help and your loved ones die, you are apt to lose faith in – or even to blame – the person whose help you sought.

WICCA

Although the words are often used interchangeably, Wicca is not simply a synonym for witchcraft, used to avoid many of the negative connotations of the latter word. It actually applies to organised witchcraft in a form only devised in the 1950s, and which is classed by sociologists of religion as a new religious movement.[19]

The word 'wicca' is usually traced back to a Saxon root meaning 'to bend', sometimes to a word meaning 'wit', as in knowledge or understanding, and sometimes, though with less justification, to a word for 'wise', as in 'wise-woman' (in France a midwife is still known as a *sage femme*). It is thought probable that the original pronunciation was 'wicha' rather than today's standard pronunciation of 'wikka'.

Sometimes, instead of witchcraft or Wicca, it is known as 'the Craft' – interestingly, the same word used for the three main degrees of Freemasonry, perhaps indicating one of the roots of Wicca, which also has three degrees.

To a very large extent modern witchcraft is the creation of a retired British civil servant, Gerald Gardner (see below). Before him, however, and providing at the time the powerful backing of academic study, came the Egyptologist Dr Margaret Murray of the University of London. Murray argued persuasively in *The Witch-Cult in Western Europe* (1921) and *The God of the Witches* (1931) that medieval witches did not worship the Devil but were followers of an old, pre-Christian Pagan religion, 'which appears to be the ancient religion of Western Europe'.[20] Murray called this worship Dianic, after the goddess Diana.

It is likely that Murray's research was sparked off by the American journalist and folklorist Charles Leland's book *Aradia, or the Gospel of the Witches* (1899). This supposedly presented the *Vangel* or gospel of a secret religion of witches in Tuscany, gathered for Leland by a young Italian woman called Maddalena. She had herself 'inherited a family trove of charms and invocations which were intended to heal, break curses and invoke spirits, and of tales',[21] and Leland hired her as his research assistant to track down more of the same. A great deal of doubt has now been thrown on the reliability of Leland's work by, amongst others, historian Professor Ronald Hutton.[22]

Murray was also influenced by the anthropologist Sir James Frazer's monumental work *The Golden Bough: A Study in Magic and Religion* (originally 1890; the 12-volume edition was published in 1906–15),[23] in which he argued that kings had been sacrificed throughout history to symbolise the cycle of death and rebirth. But Frazer was an armchair anthropologist who drew all the material in his mammoth work from previous textbooks and from accounts by missionaries of the 'primitive' peoples they worked amongst, rather than by going out into the field himself.[24]

Frazer's work has been much criticised by later anthropologists and sociologists, and his major conclusions have been shown to be historically invalid. However, *The Golden Bough* was influential on Robert Graves's work of poetic myth *The White Goddess* (1948, revised 1952, 1961) – which itself added to the confusion of myth and history, especially about the goddess in Celtic literature, for those trying to find an historical underpinning for Neo-Pagan beliefs. Scholars now point out that there is actually no evidence whatsoever for a religion of one goddess; early Pagan religions were pantheist rather than female monotheist.

Margaret Murray's theory of the ancient witchcraft religion has also been criticised on many scholarly grounds. Richard Cavendish, historian of the esoteric, states, 'This brilliant and ingenious theory is unfortunately full of holes and has been demolished time and again.'[25] This did not stop the Oxford University Press splashing on the 1970 US paperback of Murray's *The God of the Witches*, 'The findings she sets forth, once thought of as provocative and implausible, are now regarded as irrefutable by folklorists and scholars in all related fields.'[26] That is simply false.

Folklorist Professor Jacqueline Simpson is one of several scholars who have demonstrated how Murray came up with her theory, then selected evidence to support it. For example, Murray found just one reference to a coven having thirteen witches, then manipulated the figures by including or ignoring numbers of people to 'prove' that other covens had thirteen witches – thus creating a modern myth.[27]

Whatever the factual truth, Murray's thesis, with the added weight of Graves's *The White Goddess*, which contained more poetic than historical truth, became received wisdom for Wiccans for a few decades, making it possible for them to say they were recreating the old religion, not creating something out of whole cloth. In her seminal work *Drawing Down the Moon*, Margot Adler quotes American Druid and author Isaac Bonewits (1949–2010):

> Graves is a sloppy scholar. *The White Goddess* has caused more bad anthropology to occur among Wiccan groups than almost any other work. It's a lovely metaphor and myth and an inspirational source of religious ideas to people, but he claimed it was a work of scholarship and that people were to take what he said as true. There are still a few groups of Neo-Pagans who use Graves and Murray as sacred scripture.[28]

In fact Graves's book has numerous errors in history, archaeology and philology, and its idea of a Celtic Moon Goddess has probably contributed more historical error to Neo-Pagan beliefs about the Celts than anything else (see p. 300).

The Dianic Wicca of the 1970s and 1980s, founded by Hungarian-born American feminist Zsuzsanna Budapest, stemmed very much from Murray's thesis; it is a religion of the Goddess, and very much a religion for women. It could be argued that Dianic Wicca, and similar religious movements, are historically as much a spiritual expression of the feminist movement as anything else – but they have contributed to the propagation of bad scholarship and unhistorical 'history' both within Neo-Paganism and in wider cultural understanding.

Unfortunately feminist fervour led to the popularisation of another widely believed myth about historical witches, what Gerald Gardner had called 'the Burning Times', in which it was claimed that nine million European women had been killed by fire. This completely fictional figure was first plucked out of the air by an American women's rights activist in 1893;[29] its unquestioned acceptance eighty years later by some feminists and by a section of the wider Neo-Pagan movement was a populist rallying call. As Hutton writes: 'The figure which Gage had provided for the death-toll of those executions – of nine million – provided a symmetrical counterpart to that of the Nazi death-camps'[30] – or as another historian put it wryly, 'gendercide rather than genocide'.[31]

Most historians now believe that perhaps as many as 40,000–50,000 died in total during the centuries of the Inquisition, and 20 to 25 per cent of these were male.[32] Many died by other means than fire.

There has now been a considerable amount of academic work on the genuine roots of Wicca,[33] showing that it stems as much from nineteenth-century Gothic Romanticism as from anywhere else, and casting major doubts on the scholarly accuracy of Leland, Frazer, Murray and Graves.

Wiccans, like Druids and other Neo-Pagans, are largely middle class, well educated and well read, and tend to be very self-aware. Most of them today have taken this scholarship on board, but say that the validity or otherwise of Murray and other early 'authorities' doesn't actually matter to them. Murray's thesis can be treated as a 'foundation myth'; it was useful to kick-start the new religion of Wicca, but now their religion is established enough to stand on its own two feet. They readily accept that their religion is a modern synthesis from many roots.

However, the influence of these books should not be under-estimated. They may have been trounced by scholars for their methodology and their many factual inaccuracies, but they had a remarkable effect on poets and Pagans, and forged the future of Neo-Paganism for the remainder of the twentieth century and into the twenty-first. As occultist Paul Weston writes: 'these ideas affect some people very deeply. They inspire extraordinary outbursts of strange creativity in a liminal zone where their power demonstrates how in some way they do contain truth, vital truths that feed the imagination and spirit.'[34]

From the 1930s onward there was a handful of what might be called 'middle-class parlour room' groups around England – not only in the New Forest (see below) but in Cumbria, Alderley Edge in Cheshire and elsewhere – which were effec-tively practising varieties of Neo-Pagan witchcraft. Witchcraft researcher Ethan Doyle-White has shown that these groups had a focus on the Horned God and either a Moon Goddess or a Triple Goddess; that they held four annual festivals (rather than the eight celebrated in Gardnerian Wicca from 1958); that their rituals were influenced by both ceremonial (such as Golden Dawn) and folk magic; and that they called themselves witches. 'They brought all of these elements together and independently created their own magico-religious traditions and groups,' says Doyle-White. 'Because of these similarities they can all be described as aspects of the same one religious phenomenon.'[35]

From this milieu emerged the person who founded the new religious movement that became Wicca (though he spelt it Wica), a retired colonial official, Gerald Brosseau Gardner (1884–1964). Before working for the Malayan customs service he had managed tea plantations in Ceylon, North Borneo and Malaya. He retired to England in 1936, and in 1938 moved to the New Forest in Hampshire, southern England, where he discovered the Rosicrucian Theatre in Christchurch. This was linked to the Rosicrucian Order Crotona Fellowship, a mystical order founded in Liverpool in 1924 by an actor, G. A. Sullivan, and Mabel Besant-Scott, daughter of Annie Besant, leader of the Theosophical Society (see p. 23). It moved to Dorset in 1935. The aim of the Rosicrucian Theatre was to introduce people to mystical concepts through drama, but it was not successful, only actually lasting for one season, the summer of 1938. The Rosicrucian Order Crotona Fellowship had the distinction of attracting both Gerald Gardner and Peter Caddy, one of the founders of the Findhorn Foundation (see p. 92).

Among the Rosicrucians, Gardner claimed, was a wealthy old lady known as 'Old Dorothy', later identified as Dorothy Clutterbuck. She led a witch coven of the Old Religion, and in September 1939 Gardner was initiated into it at her home. In his history of modern pagan witchcraft, *The Triumph of the Moon* (1999), Professor Ronald Hutton casts doubt on Gardner's account. Dorothy Clutterbuck did indeed live in Christchurch, in a mansion with her husband, a former Justice of the Peace. They were dedicated Anglicans, deeply committed to the Conservative Party, and held society garden parties. None of that would necessarily invalidate Gardner's story. However, Hutton has had access to some of her diaries (though unfortunately not for 1939), containing daily poems, of which he says: 'Absolutely none of them – including those at the time of the four major witch festivals – have any relevance to paganism or the occult.'[36] And although she was involved with a theatre group, it was a different company, not the Rosicrucian Theatre. For these and other reasons Hutton concludes that Gardner used Dorothy's name as a cover for another lady he called 'Dafo' (Edith Woodford-Grimes), who was his close friend and ritual partner – and the leading lady of the Rosicrucian Theatre. But as for Old Dorothy's witches' coven, he finds no reliable evidence; accounts by other writers are all second- or third-hand, he says, and recycle the same details, with some distortions, as in Gardner's own account.[37]

It should be said that other researchers, particularly Philip Heselton,[38] disagree with Hutton's conclusions.

Whatever the truth about the New Forest coven, any idea that it was a continuation of the 'Old Religion' – Gardner repeatedly writes 'They say that in the old days . . . In ancient times . . .' etc.[39] – appears to be his own foundation myth, a fake 'provenance' providing lineage and therefore both credibility and authority to his new movement (see p. 197). Australian scholar David Waldron has a harsher verdict: 'Certainly, Gardner's attempt to credit himself with a PhD, and his portrayal of Witchcraft as an authentic existing system based on anthropological empirical research, was a rather shameless way of gaining credibility for his newly formed Wiccan movement.'[40] In the wake of the abolition of British legislation against witchcraft in 1951 Gardner published two books, *Witchcraft Today* (1954) and *The Meaning of Witchcraft* (1959). The first book contained an introduction by Margaret Murray, and a chapter entitled 'There have been witches in all ages'.

Gardner had a lifelong interest in folklore, magic and the esoteric. He was a Freemason, and an initiate of Aleister Crowley's Ordo Templi Orientis (see p. 216), first meeting Crowley in May 1947, a few months before he died. His creation of modern witchcraft was a blend of uncertain history, folklore, masonic structure and magical rituals owing much to Crowley and hence to the Hermetic Order of the Golden Dawn (see p. 195). It is likely to be the case that the Crowleyan aspects of Wicca did not, as often supposed, come directly from Crowley to Gardner in 1947, but from works published decades earlier.[41]

Wicca also had quite a major sexual element; Gardner was into both naturism and flagellation. Ritual scourging may have been dropped by most Wiccan covens, but many still perform their rituals 'skyclad' (naked) – though usually, in Britain's uncertain climate, indoors. Gardner claimed that clothes blocked magical energy, and a common explanation is that nakedness in rituals removes all distinctions of class and wealth. Historian Ronald Hutton suggests two perhaps deeper reasons:

One was that it demands a high degree of trust and confidence between members of a coven, and so provides a powerful test for the evidence of harmony and unity, without which the rituals cannot be effectively worked. The second was that ... it conveys a very powerful sense that something abnormal is going on; that the participants in the circle have cast off their everyday lives and limitations and entered into a space in which the extraordinary can be achieved.[42]

There is also an undoubted sexual element to Wiccan ritual, emphasising the power of sexual polarity; in the Great Rite, intercourse is symbolised by the plunging of an athame (ritual dagger) into a chalice.

Moving back to the London area in 1946, Gardner founded his own coven at Bricket Wood, Hertfordshire. Dafo was his first high priestess, but left in 1952 when Gardner began seeking publicity.[43] She was replaced by Doreen Valiente (1922–99), whom Gardner initiated in 1953, and who was to become one of the most prominent and influential Wiccans of the twentieth century.

Valiente rewrote much of Gardner's ritual in his hand-written *Book of Shadows*, the first version of which was known, somewhat archaically, as *Ye Bok of ye Art Magical*. Its original contents came from a variety of sources, many of them going back to Crowley and the Golden Dawn. Hutton writes:

Gardner initially passed off the whole body to Doreen Valiente as those of the old witch religion. When she spotted that many passages in them derived from other sources, such as Crowley, he answered that the ceremonies of the New Forest coven had been 'fragmentary' by the time that he discovered it, and so he was obliged to flesh them out with borrowings from other texts in order to make them viable for revival.[44]

Valiente removed much of the clearly 'borrowed' material (including from Crowley) from the *Book of Shadows*, and rewrote the ritual in her own poetry and prose. The various versions of the *Book of Shadows* used by the majority of Wiccans today derive from Valiente's rewriting and restructuring of Gardner's book. A number of Wiccan rituals use poems written by Valiente, and she also adapted material in Leland's *Aradia* to write 'The Charge of the Goddess' (see below).

One of Crowley's lines survived, however: his 'Do as thou wilt shall be the whole of the Law' (itself taken from Rabelais, see p. 214) became the 'Wiccan Rede', 'An [If] it harm none, do what ye will'.

In 1957 Doreen Valiente, like Dafo, left Gardner because of his publicising of Wicca in the media. He had also that year introduced thirty 'Wiccan Laws' which, amongst other things, limited the power of the High Priestess, suggesting that when she gets older she should 'gracefully retire in favour of a younger woman'.[45] She went on to found her own coven, basically on Gardnerian principles though without his 'Wiccan Laws'. From 1964 to 1966 she was a member of Robert Cochrane's Clan of Tubal Cain, a very different form of modern witchcraft (see p. 303). Valiente continued to hold a prominent position regarding Wicca until her death, writing several influential books on the Craft.

Alongside Gardnerian the second main branch of Wicca is Alexandrian, named in part after the great school and library of Alexandria in Egypt (see p. 233–5 and p. 302) and in part after its founder, Alex Sanders (1926?–88). There are many different versions of who Sanders was initiated by, and when. He claimed in a biography to have been initiated by his grandmother in 1933 when he was seven, and to have copied her *Book of Shadows* when he was nine. In an illustrated article about a witchcraft ceremony in the *Manchester Evening Chronicle & News* in September 1962 he claimed he had been initiated for a year. But it appears that he was not actually initiated until March 1963.

Just two years later, having managed to antagonise most of the Gardnerian leaders (Gardner himself died in 1964) he was claiming to be 'King of the Witches', acclaimed so by (in two separate

What I Believe . . .
Other States of Consciousness

I do feel that thinking too much prevents intuition to surface or magical energy to flow. Changing state of consciousness, even slightly, is so important, before we can do magic. Personally I've experienced it after prolonged drumming, trance dancing, alcohol or even ritual sex with my partner.
Mani Navasothy, Wiccan High Priest and founder of Hern's Tribe
Physicist

There's no doubt that that's the key. Even performing a very quick ritual like the Lesser Banishing Ritual of the Pentagram puts you in a different mood. Some extreme moods, or trances as some people call them, are extremely profound indeed.
Steve Wilson, Thelemite
Civil Servant

Other states of consciousness . . . are useful ways to support spiritual development.
Dr William Bloom
Author and educator in a holistic and modern approach to spirituality

Everybody is in an alternative state of consciousness every time they dream. If you're trying to do anything psychic you need to get into a state where as far as possible you disassociate yourself from the outside world. It's one of those things that is very difficult to describe but it's quite easy to recognise when you experience it. Also sometimes it happens the other way: a being from outside can try and contact you.
Gareth J. Medway, Priest Hierophant of the Fellowship of Isis
Writer and assistant psychic

They are all important when they happen. Very often they are brought about by apparently external circumstances, not planned, not part of a ritual.

Jack Gale, Magician
Retired school teacher

The capability to bring up stuff from the subconscious mind, and transforming that content to a higher level: that is the essence of the Great Work.

Ina Cüsters-van Bergen, Magister, Hermetic Order of the Temple of Starlight

There are powerful traditional techniques and sacraments which abet shamanic journeying 'between the worlds' of alternate subjective realities.

Oberon Zell-Ravenheart, Co-founder, Church of All Worlds

There is a consciousness from which our relative states of consciousness arise. The three fundamental states of consciousness, waking, sleeping and dreaming, are projections of one consciousness which exists in its own right, it is not an epiphenomenon of the brain or anything like that, it is pre-existent to matter in my view, and we partake of some small part of that.

Outside of that context of the fourth state of consciousness which involves the other three, there are subdivisions within consciousness, and there is no doubt that you can go into a strange place, because I do this fairly regularly, and that for us is used as a tool to communicate with the divine. So it would be the basis of oracular work.

Dr Paul Newman, Wiccan with interest in Eastern spirituality
Sessional Lecturer in Mathematics, University of London

claims) 1,623 witches in 127 covens. Both figures are thought to be as fictional as his childhood initiation by his grandmother.

With his much younger wife Maxine, who had apparently studied in a Gurdjieff group for some years,[46] Sanders popularised witchcraft in the 1960s; his followers had a flamboyant style, which may or may not have been good for the new religion, but which certainly caught the headlines. From its start Alexandrian witchcraft was a more eclectic version than Gardnerian, including a greater emphasis on ceremonial magic and on Kabbalah. It gained publicity and credibility early in its history with the publication of *What Witches Do: A Modern Coven Revealed* by one of its members, Stewart Farrar – who with his wife Janet went on to write many more books on witchcraft. (It was Farrar who coined the term Alexandrian in 1971.)[47] Maxine Sanders, who separated from her husband in 1973, became a widely respected leader of Wicca.

Wicca is an initiatory religion with three degrees, as in Freemasonry; in a typical coven (which need not be thirteen people; see p. 287) the High Priest and High Priestess are often second-degree rather than third-degree; some of the other coven members may also be second-degree, allowing for more flexibility in rituals, but most will usually be first-degree.

One of the best-known definitions of Wicca comes from Janet and Stewart Farrar, who did much to publicise the religion with books such as the aforementioned *What Witches Do*, *Spells and How They Work* and *A Witch's Bible: The Complete Witch's Handbook*. They write:

> Wicca is both a religion and a Craft . . . As a religion – like any other religion – its purpose is to put the individual and the group in harmony with the divine creative principal of the Cosmos, and its manifestation at all levels. As a Craft, its purpose is to achieve practical ends by psychic means, for good, useful and healing purposes. In both aspects, the distinguishing characteristics of Wicca are its Nature-based attitude, its small group autonomy with no gulf between priesthood and 'congregation',

and its philosophy of creative polarity at all levels, from Goddess and God to Priestess and Priest.[48]

Wiccans, along with most Neo-Pagans, observe eight annual festivals: the summer and winter solstices, 22 June and 22 December; the spring and autumn equinoxes, 21 March and 21 September; Imbolc (in Christian terms, Candlemas), 2 February; Beltane (May Eve/May Day), 1 May; Lammas (Lady Day), 2 August; and Samhain (Hallow'een), 31 October.

Most Wiccan groups in their rituals use the 'Charge of the Goddess', which has been called 'the nearest thing the Craft accept as a statement of faith common to all'.[49] There are many different versions of the Charge today; here enough extracts are presented to demonstrate its style and content, the roots of Goddess worship under many different names, and the life-affirming nature of Wiccan belief.

Charge of the Goddess

Listen to the words of the Great Mother, who of old was called Artemis, Astarte, Athene, Diane, Melusine, Aphrodite, Cerridwen, Diana, Arianrhod, Isis, Brighde and by many other names ...

Whenever ye have need of anything, once in the month, and better it be when the moon is full, then shall ye assemble in some secret place and adore the spirit of me, who am Queen all Witches ...

And ye shall be free from slavery; and as a sign that ye be really free, ye shall be naked in your rites; and ye shall dance, sing, feast, make music and love, all in my praise. For mine is the ecstasy of the spirit, and mine also is joy on earth, for my law is love unto all beings.

Keep pure your highest ideal; strive ever towards it, let naught stop you or turn you aside; for mine is the secret door which opens upon the door of youth, and mine is the cup of the wine of life, and the cauldron of Cerridwen, which is the Holy Grail of immortality.

I am the gracious Goddess, who gives the gift of joy unto the heart of man ...

Nor do I demand sacrifice; for behold, I am the Mother of all living and my love is poured out upon the earth . . .

I am the beauty of the green earth, and the white moon among the stars, and the mystery of the waters, and the desire of the heart of man.

Call into thy soul; arise, and come unto me; for I am the soul of nature who gives life to the universe . . .

Let my worship be within the heart that rejoices; for behold, all acts of love and pleasure are my rituals. And therefore let there be beauty and strength, power and compassion, honour and humility, mirth and reverence within thee . . .

And thou who thinkest to seek for me, know thy seeking and yearning shall avail thee not unless thou knowest the mystery; that if that which thou seekest thou findest not within thee, thou wilt never find it without thee. For behold, I have been with thee from the beginning; and I am that which is attained at the end of desire.

Blessed be.[50]

OTHER VARIETIES OF WITCHCRAFT

Wicca is usually thought of as a 'small group' religion, though its rituals, pathworkings, visualisations and so on are also practised alone by members of covens. But not all witches are members of covens. With the publication over the years of a variety of books on the beliefs and practices of the religion, including versions of the *Book of Shadows*, there has been a growth in 'solitaries', sometimes known as hedge-witches, who are self-initiated and who work alone.

In Britain the largest umbrella organisation specifically for witches is the Children of Artemis.[51] Originally a ritual group in its own right, around 1995 it became a public membership organisation and an information point, helping people interested in Wicca to find a local group or coven that might suit them; it stopped this service in 2003, because not enough covens were accepting trainees and too many people were looking for one. In place of this it runs a one-day introductory course in Wicca, and also has a 'Covenstead forum' on its website, 'where covens can advertise they have vacancies and members can request contact with a coven in their area'.[52]

Children of Artemis publish a regular magazine, *Witchcraft & Wicca*, run regular pub meetings in Croydon, south London, and organise the annual Witchfest, a one-day festival with speakers, workshops and musicians. Children of Artemis has faced criticism from some British Neo-Pagans for being glossy and commercial, appealing to 'teen witches'.

In contrast, much of British witchcraft is still based on small groups; some work within established Wiccan traditions but others are more eclectic, branching out experimentally. One example of the latter is Hern's Tribe, a small 'outdoor tribal and ritual exploration group' led by Mani Navasothy and April Jonquil, initiated priest and priestess in Gardnerian Wicca. Even though it is based in London it does most of its work outdoors in woods, sometimes camping for several days.

Since 2006 they have also run the Tamesa London Circle, performing rituals by the River Thames. In 2010 they set up Hern's Tribe Albion Mysteries, a more open group exploring British mythological figures such as Robin Hood, King Arthur, Morgan le Fay and the Lady of the Lake, and teaching ancient skills including flint-knapping, preparing animal skins and skulls, and shamanic dream quests and totemic work.[53]

Today the vast majority of British witches accept their religion's modern beginnings; any holding to the supposed ancient origins of their beliefs is more in the heart than the head, poetry rather than history. In contrast some American witches insist on the ancient Celtic origin of their beliefs and rituals, usually with their hereditary transmission over generations (see below). They follow the example of the early scattered groups of the 1930s and idealistic Neo-Pagan youth of the 1960s, people yearning for the romanticism of their Celtic heritage – ignoring the inconvenient fact that, as one researcher says, 'the term "Celt" was, although based upon an ancient Greek word, largely reinvented by 19th century nationalists who gave it a whole new meaning; in effect then, the Celts, as we now understand them, were never real'.[54]

So, for example, Lady Sheba (Jessie Wicker Bell, 1920–2002), born in Kentucky, claimed that witchcraft had been practised in her family for seven generations. She published her own *Book of Shadows* in 1971, to much the same criticism for breaking her oaths of secrecy faced by Israel Regardie when he published the Golden Dawn rituals in 1937–41 (see p. 206).

Her book included versions of the 'Charge of the Goddess' and the 'Wiccan Laws' amongst much else. She claimed it had been handed down to her by her grandmother, but it has been shown to be a poor copy from a Gardnerian *Book of Shadows*.

Similarly, and equally prominent in American Neo-Paganism, Rhuddlwm ap Gawr (William Wheeler) claimed to have been inducted into an ancient Welsh tradition preserved by the Llewellyn family:

> Since 1282, the Tribe of Dynion Mwyn and the Clan of Y Tylwyth Teg has existed in relative obscurity. Our belief is that the Llewellyn family kept its secrets as the old ways were slowly dying out in Great Britain . . .
>
> When Rhuddlwm first met Sarah Llewellyn in 1965, there were less than a hundred practitioners of *The Welsh Tradition of Dynion Mwyn* in England, Wales, Scotland, Canada and America. Today, there are literally thousands.[55]

Similar hereditary claims are made by some American druids (see p. 324).

According to Neo-Pagan scholar Chas S. Clifton some of the supposedly ancient Welsh teachings passed on to Gawr bear a marked resemblance to Lady Sheba's version of Doreen Valiente's original text.[56] Other writers and leaders in witchcraft, including historian Aidan Kelly, have openly accused Gawr's movements of plagiarising their work.[57] Another writer who it is claimed has been plagiarised by Dynion Mwyn is Roy Bowers, aka Robert Cochrane (see p. 303). In response to criticisms the websites of the Association of Cymry Wiccae, Camelot-of-the-Woods Community, Dynion Mwyn, the Universal Federation of Pagans and other linked organisations connected to Rhuddlwm ap Gawr continue to promote their ancient origins, whilst hitting back at their critics with very personal counter-accusations.[58] Such very public and sometimes vitriolic disputes are reminiscent of the antagonism between some American Rosicrucian organisations (see p. 181 and p. 186–7).

Other American Neo-Pagan movements work more in the mainstream of Wicca and the Western Mystery Tradition. Gardnerian Wicca was introduced to the United States by Raymond Buckland (born in London, 1934), who met Gardner shortly before his death. He founded his first coven in Long Island in 1964; daughter covens then spread across the United States. In 1968 he founded the Buckland Museum of Witchcraft and Magic, now housed in New Orleans. In 1974, tired of the egotism and infighting he found in Gardnerian Wicca, he left it and developed his own system, Seax-Wica or Saxon witchcraft. This honours the Germanic deities, so could in some ways be seen as a blend of Wicca and Heathenry (see p. 330), though it does not claim to be a modern revival of an ancient religion as Heathenry is. In contrast with Gardnerian Wicca the teachings of Seax-Wica are all open (first published in Buckland's book *The Tree* in 1974), and the organisation is democratic, with priests and priestesses of a coven elected for a year-and-a-day. Buckland himself was always seen as the founder, not the leader. The author of numerous occult books, Buckland retired from active group work in the 1990s.

A different example of American witchcraft is the Assembly of the Sacred Wheel, a group of Wiccan covens spread across the mid-Atlantic region of the United States, each with a different focus, such as seership, healing or self-development; the founding coven began in 1984. Its elders are author Ivo Domínguez Jr, artist Helena Dominic and Michael Smith, a priest who works with Egyptian deities. It practises a syncretic form of Wicca 'and draws inspiration from Astrology, Qabala, the Western Magickal Tradition and the folk religions of Europe'.[59] With other groups it is promoting the campaign for the New Alexandrian Library, a research and reference library in Delaware, 'to preserve and to protect all forms of esoteric knowledge'[60] (see also p. 233–5, p. 293).

CLAN OF TUBAL CAIN AND 1734

As with many other Neo-Pagan and esoteric movements the origins of these two separate but closely linked groups of organisations are complex and not fully clear; this has been made worse by the different versions of history related by different factions today. The account given here is only a simplified outline; some of its details are disputed by one of the three Clan of Tubal Cain groups, which asserts that it is the only valid one.

1734 witchcraft and the Clan of Tubal Cain (CTC) both originate, at least in part, with the teachings of Robert Cochrane, the writing name of Roy Bowers (1931–66). Like several others he claimed to be an hereditary witch, this time through his great-grandfather; it is more likely that the coven he founded around 1951 was one of the several independent witchcraft groups that sprang up around England (see p. 289). His Clan of Tubal Cain was named after the biblical inventor of metal-working (Genesis 4:22), as Cochrane was at one time a smith working in a foundry; Tubal-Cain is also the recognition word in the third degree of Freemasonry.[61]

His group in southern England worshipped not the Horned God and the Triple Goddess, says Shani Oates, Maid of one of the CTC groups, but, 'the horn god, as in the sense of the horns worn by Moses . . . and the female Creatrix is a Triune deity, most closely expressed as the embodiment of Truth, Love and Beauty – the Gnostic Triple Mothers, not in any sense even remotely connected to the Goddess of popular neo-paganism'.[62]

Cochrane's group took the inspiration for their beliefs very much from Robert Graves's heavily poetic *The White Goddess* (see p. 286). Without the input of Gerald Gardner's personal tastes the members wore robes rather than working naked, and they did not practise scourging. They also did not have an equivalent of the *Book of Shadows*, and used different correspondences (see p. 171) between the cardinal points and the four traditional elements. They were an outdoor movement, doing their rituals often around a fire in clearings in woods, on hilltops and in caves, and are sometimes described as more shamanic than Gardnerian witchcraft.[63] Historian Ronald Hutton writes that Cochrane, 'laid great emphasis upon witchcraft as a mystery religion, with an elaborate symbolism which he expounded with considerable skill, and an ingrained sense of the age, majesty and fearsome power of its pagan deities'.[64] Oates, however, differentiates it from Neo-Pagan witchcraft, stressing that Cochrane 'asserted frequently that his belief and tradition were and are *not pagan*, furthermore, its deities are **not pagan**, the names given for ease of association in public are but masks for their real identities that remain undisclosed outside fully inducted members'.[65]

Doreen Valiente, having left Gardner's coven in 1957, joined Cochrane's in 1964. She later described him as 'perhaps the most powerful and gifted personality to have appeared in modern witchcraft'.[66] Cochrane was aware of the irony of newly forged 'ancient' traditions; he wrote in *Pentagram* magazine, the magazine of the Witchcraft Research Association:

> It is said by various 'authorities' that the Faith of the Wise, when they do believe in its existence, is a simple matter: a pre-Christian religion based upon whatever Gods and Goddesses are the current vogue – full of simple, hearty peasants doing simple, hearty peasant-like things . . . things that in some cases complex, nervous sophisticates also enjoy doing in urban parlours. Consequently we have an interesting phenomenon: civilised sophisticates running round behaving like simple peasants – and simple peasants who have never heard of such things![67]

Although there was much in Cochrane's version of witchcraft that Valiente preferred to Gardner's version she objected to his criticism, and often outright derision, of Gardnerian witchcraft; it was this (along with discoveries of his deceptions about his 'hereditary' background) that eventually caused her to leave two years later. Around the same time both *Pentagram* magazine, edited by a friend of Cochrane, and the Witchcraft Research Association, led by Valiente, folded.

When Cochrane began an affair with another Clan member his wife left the coven, which shortly afterwards split up. In June 1966, on Midsummer Eve, Cochrane took an overdose of belladonna and tranquillisers, dying nine days later.

The different versions of Robert Cochrane's teachings survive almost entirely from his articles in *Pentagram*, the recollections of a member and later leader of his Clan, Evan John Jones (1936–2003), and Cochrane's letters to three people, including a six-month correspondence with a US Air Force sergeant, Joseph B. Wilson, beginning in December 1965.[68] Wilson, who never met Cochrane, established a movement in the United States known as 1734, the name coming from 'a riddle based on numerical values of the goddess' in the chapter on sacred alphabets in Robert Graves's *The White Goddess*.[69]

> 1734 was developed by Joe Wilson based in part on various poetic philosophical references in Cochrane's correspondence with him. But that was just one of three sources of the ideas in 1734, the others being Ruth Wynn Owen of the Welsh tradition Y Plant Br'n, and Joe's teacher [Sean Armstrong]. Cochrane's letters are *part of* the underlying philosophy of 1734.[70]

Two early followers of 1734 in the Los Angeles area were Ann and Dave Finnin, who founded the Roebuck Tradition in 1976 (Graves's original title for *The White Goddess* was *The Roebuck in the Thicket*); this was later incorporated as the Ancient Keltic Church. Impressed by the book *The Rollright Ritual*, they contacted its author, the occultist William G. Gray, who allowed them to make copies of all of his correspondence with Cochrane. In 1982 they visited England for the first time and met Evan John Jones, who told them all his memories of Cochrane. The following year he invited them to become members of the Tribe of Tubal Cain, and they set up the Clan in California, linked to but separate from the Roebuck Tradition. In 1987 Jones asked the Finnins to become the heads of the Clan, the Maid and Magister, granting them authority over any other groups and all other members including himself.[71]

However, Jones continued to develop his ideas over the following years, introducing elements such as mask work; in correspondence with other people, according to Ann Finnin, 'he was now saying that if we were not doing the mask work we were not doing the real thing, but this was not what he had originally said. So there was confusion: what *is* the real Clan of Tubal Cain?'[72]

As the CTC doctrines under Jones continued to change, in 1998 he appointed a new Maid in Britain, Shani Oates. She and her Magister have continued to run that version of CTC, based on Jones's later teachings, since his death in 2003.[73] The teachings have now developed so much from the 1980s version that they include Gnostic Luciferian ideas.[74]

In 2005 a former member of this Clan, Carol Stuart Jones, set up another Clan of Tubal Cain; according to its website she was also inducted as a Maid in 1998,[75] though this is disputed by Oates. Although Ann Finnin was appointed Maid over ten years before herself, Oates also rejects the legitimacy of the Finnins' group.

There are now three versions of the Clan of Tubal Cain: the Finnins' group in the United States and two groups in Britain. Carol Stuart Jones's group says: 'Each of the three branches of the Clan of Tubal Cain hold bone fide lineage, complete autonomy, and without a shadow of doubt, we each have our own very particular interpretation and development of Roy, and John's, original vision.'[76] In contrast Oates insists that there can only be one Maid of the Clan of Tubal Cain, that her group is the only legitimate one and that the other two are illegitimate and spurious.[77]

Ann Finnin, Maid of the American group, says that for them the issue with Oates is not just about who is the 'genuine' inheritor of the tradition and who is not. She stresses 'serious doctrinal issues with [Oates's] interpretation of it', and says that her group and Jones's group 'are practising one interpretation of the tradition and she is practising another and that the two interpretations are very different'.[78] In September 2010 Jones and her Magister gave their oaths to the Finnins and joined their lineage. Ann Finnin wrote: 'We have attended several workings with their Clan and have discovered that, despite the distance between us and the decades that have elapsed between their training with Evan John Jones and ours, both our Clans work so similarly that it is undeniable that we are all practising the same basic tradition and spring from the same spiritual roots.'[79]

To complicate the picture further, members of Cochrane's original group continued after his death under the name of the Regency. This held public meetings in Queen's Wood, Highgate in north London, from 1966 to 1979, after which it continued to hold private meetings.[80]

In addition to these, several 1734 groups exist, on both sides of the Atlantic, following Joseph B. Wilson's teachings based in part on those of Cochrane.

All of these groups are considerably smaller than their online presence might suggest; but Robert Cochrane's legacy has been included here largely to show that not all of the witchcraft of the last half century stems from Gerald Gardner.

The troubles in the Clan of Tubal Cain have been covered at some length as an illustration of schism and diversity within religious groups, displaying at least three frequently observed factors: doctrinal differences between the groups as they follow teachings from different periods in the movement's development; one group insisting on its sole legitimacy; and personal clashes with anger, bitterness and accusations of lies and libel. All of these are often the norm rather than the exception in the development and evolution of religious movements – not just Neo-Pagan and esoteric movements[81] (see p. 4) – and throughout this book the uncertain origins of a number of groups have been discussed. Whether one faction is more or less legitimate than any other stemming from the same origins is only relevant within the doctrinal worldview of those groups; from an objective viewpoint, all the groups exist, and they may be observed and described without any distinction of validity.

CHURCH OF ALL WORLDS

A number of new religions – the Aetherius Society (see p. 119), the Raelians (see p. 127), Scientology (see p. 357), even the Mormons – have what outsiders might see as science-fictional elements to their mythology. The Church of All Worlds (CAW) is perhaps the only religion for which an SF novel is a prescribed text. Although a form of Neo-Paganism, it bases much of its teaching and ritual on Robert A. Heinlein's classic *Stranger in a Strange Land*.

CAW began in 1962 when Tim Zell (b.1942), Lance Christie and their then girlfriends, all students at Westminster College, Fulton, Missouri, formed a 'water-brotherhood' called Atl. As in the novel its members were based in 'nests', spiritual and living communities, and greeted each other with the phrase 'Thou art God'.

CAW incorporated in 1968, 'becoming the first of the Neo-Pagan Earth religions to obtain full Federal recognition,' says Zell, who headed the religion.[82] The same year also saw the first incarnation of *Green Egg* magazine. In 1979 Zell changed his first name to Otter, then in 1994 to Oberon; for a short period in the mid-1990s his surname was G'Zell, and in 1996 it changed to Zell-Ravenheart.[83]

Christie, a lifelong environmental activist – he was one of the co-founders of Earth First[84] – continued with Atl (or ATL) in one form or another; for some years it was the Atlan Foundation, and in 1998 he founded the Association for the

Tree of Life. He remained actively involved with CAW until around 1975, writing articles for *Green Egg*; he remained in contact with Zell after that, and took part in CAW reunions.

CAW has no particular dogma or creed: 'We are essentially "Neo-Pagan", implying an eclectic reconstruction of ancient Nature religions, and combining archetypes of many cultures with other mystic, environmental and spiritual disciplines . . . Some of our individual paths include Shamanism, Witchcraft, Vodoun, Buddhism, Hinduism and Sufism, as well as science fiction, transpersonal psychology, bodywork, artistic expression and paths of service.'[85]

Heinlein's phrase 'Thou art God' encapsulates CAW's belief in the immanence of divinity. A question in the CAW Membership Handbook, 'Does CAW accept the divinity of Jesus?', is answered, 'Certainly. Why should he be left out? We accept the Divinity of every living Being in the universe!'[86]

Zell is credited both with popularising if not coining the term Neo-Pagan and (independently of James Lovelock) with originating the Gaia Hypothesis, 'which theorises that the Earth is a single living organism'.[87]

As with many Neo-Pagan groups, CAW's beliefs are spiritual, environmental, personal and social. Zell writes:

> We concentrate on healing the separations between mind and body, men and women, civilisation and nature, Heaven and Earth. We are fairly all-embracing in promoting general Pagan and Gaian lifestyles and values. We advocate basic feminist and environmentalist principles, including freedom of reproductive choice, ordination of women as priestesses, sacred sexuality, alternate relationships, gay and lesbian rights, legalisation and utilisation of hemp products, protection and restoration of endangered species, wilderness sanctuaries, green politics, space exploration and colonisation, etc. We are also engaged in restoring ancient Mysteries and rituals, such as the Eleusinia and Panathenaia.[88]

CAW developed slowly and gradually, with a number of ups and downs over the years. From 1976 to 1985, for example, Zell and his wife Morning Glory moved from St Louis, where CAW was then based, to California, leaving the organisation of the Church and coordination of the nests to others; the Church effectively disintegrated, and *Green Egg* magazine folded. In 1985 Zell began to reorganise CAW, relaunching *Green Egg* in 1988 – only to lose control of the magazine in 1996.

Compared to many religious organisations, CAW is honest about its failings. 'We try to learn from our mistakes and not make them again,' says Zell.

> Most of our most glaring mistakes have been due to either ignorance or arrogance. Mistakes of ignorance can be cured with additional knowledge. Mistakes of arrogance have been far more painful, and humbling. We have had to eat considerable crow as we have evolved over the years. We will probably continue to make mistakes, for we are fallible creatures (a pack of monkeys, actually!) and sometimes our mouths overload our brains. Hopefully we will also continue to get better, but I seriously doubt we will ever attain infallibility![89]

In the early 1990s the Church had a path of progression from Seeker, an ordinary member, to Scion, those who help run subsidiary branches, to Clergy, ordained priests and priestesses with, usually, several years of training and personal spiritual development before being ordained.

CAW's membership at its height was around 650, with over three dozen nests or branches scattered across the United States and Australia (where it was the first legally recognised Neo-Pagan religion), though not in the UK. It had 'protonests' in Germany, Switzerland and Austria.

As with all US religious organisations, the Church of All Worlds was established as a corporation, with legally established bylaws. One of these reads:

> To honour Oberon Zell for his many years of service to the Church of All Worlds, and to acknowledge him as co-founder of the CAW, and in recognition of his well-known abilities as an

excellent representative of the larger primate family, he shall be known as the Primate, and shall hold this position for life unless he no longer desires to, or if through illness or incapacity he can no longer adequately demonstrate his capability to perform its duties and functions to the membership and the Clergy Council . . .[90]

In 1998 Zell took a year-and-a-day sabbatical from this role as Primate, at the same time as a major reorganisation of the Church took place. The headquarters moved from California to Ohio, and many of the administrative jobs which Zell had performed were taken on by other people in the Church; he remained an active priest in the Church, leading major ceremonies, but was no longer involved in its organisation. At the time one member suggested that 'voice and vision should be his major role'.[91]

Without Zell's active involvement, once again CAW lost both impetus and members. In August 2004, following a divisive internal dispute, CAW's board of directors decided to close down the Church for financial and legal reasons.[92] The following spring Zell formed a new board with himself as president, and CAW began what he called its Third Phoenix Resurrection.[93] Co-founder Lance Christie became actively involved in CAW again. Christie wrote in 2005:

> In brief summary, CAW was designed to bring into consciousness among people the eco-spiritual values they want to express in their lives, and ATL was designed to do the engineering of the technics which will permit them to engage in 'right livelihood' according to Gaian values when they seek to do so.
>
> Both Oberon and I have wandered up some blind alleys and barked our shins on our share of furniture during our life curricula, but when comparing notes we both find that our dedication to the 'right action' expressed in these designs has not changed or wavered in 35 years. What has changed is how much our understanding of what works and what doesn't is enriched, and the degree to which our understanding of the ecological paradigm and its meme family has achieved consciousness, from decades of experience and learning from our mistakes.[94]

Around the same time, in 2004, Zell set up the Grey School of Wizardry as a real-life online version of J. K. Rowling's fictional Hogwarts.[95] By 2010 it had over thirty faculty members and over 600 students, with a curriculum including amongst much else wizardry, nature studies, magical practice, psychic arts, healing, alchemy and cosmology. Initially it was intended to be an equivalent to a junior high school, but soon took adult students as well, and they are now the majority. Zell and his wife Morning Glory are headmaster and headmistress of the school, though it is completely separate from CAW; its faculty comes from a wide range of esoteric movements.

Both Zell and Morning Glory suffered serious health problems in the first decade of the twenty-first century. Without their active involvement in the past CAW has tended to lose its way. Many new religions falter, some collapsing altogether, when their founder is no longer with them.[96] Zell comments on the future of CAW: 'I've been taking pains to select and train my successor as Primate (Luke Moonoak), and I'm confident that the CAW Tradition will continue indefinitely. Though the actual organization may have yet more Phoenix immolations and resurrections in ages to come'.[97]

The mission of CAW is: 'to evolve a network of information, mythology and experience to awaken the divine within and to provide a context and stimulus for reawakening Gaia and reuniting Her children through tribal community dedicated to responsible stewardship and the evolution of consciousness'.[98] Linked organisations are heavily involved in ecology, particularly forestry and scholarly research into history and mythology.

From the start CAW aimed for communal living, even if a community is only a handful of people. But it was always something more than a bunch of spiritually minded hippies living in a commune. Living in a community (or nest), there is more opportunity to put their beliefs into practice.

Since we are concerned with the emergent evolution of a total new culture and lifestyle, and since we perceive no distinction between the sacred and the secular, we consider every activity to be essentially a religious activity. For us, recycling is as much a religious duty as prayer and meditation . . . We recognise that the essence of a religion is in the living of it.[99]

But specifically religious or spiritual activities are an important part of their lives.

The religious aspects include maintaining household altars and shrines (in a Pagan household, every horizontal flat space becomes an altar, just as every wall becomes a bookcase!), meditations, conversations with the Gods, to rituals and celebrations, especially those of the great Sabbats of the Wheel of the Year. These latter often include great theatrical productions, with sets, costumes, props and music, wherein people take on the personas of Gods, Elementals, and other Archetypal beings.

What Zell says about magic is fairly typical of many Neo-Pagan groups:

The practice of magic is a major component of virtually all Pagan traditions, including CAW. We define magic as 'probability enhancement'. I don't think it is possible to separate out the magical from the religious, as it all seems a continuum. Magical practices run the gamut from simple 'Kitchen Witch' spells and charms – mostly concerned with individual healings, blessings, transformations, and other small workings; through 'Circle Work' involving raising group energy for healings, community service, weather working, etc.; to larger group workings to save the planet – protecting endangered forests, people and species, etc.[100]

One point which separates CAW from many other religious groups, Neo-Pagan or not, is their free approach to sexuality. Zell and his wife have long had an open relationship with other partners; Morning Glory coined the term polyamory, which is now widely used for multi-partner relationships. In 1996 Zell,

Morning Glory and their polyamorous family adopted the joint surname Zell-Ravenheart.

The relaxed attitude to sexuality and social nudity in the Church of All Worlds can also be found in Robert Heinlein's *Stranger in a Strange Land*, and much of the terminology and symbolism of CAW is borrowed from Heinlein's novel – nests, grokking, water-sharing – or other SF works (Zenna Henderson's 'The People' stories are another favourite). Margot Adler makes the point: 'Science fiction has been the literature of the visionary; it has been able to challenge preconceived notions about almost everything, while at the same time attending to fundamental questions of the age.'[101] Lance Christie also comments on the importance of SF: 'Science fiction was, and is, a major vehicle for those who wish to be social critics to try out "what if" scenarios both to explore the end result of current cultural, technological, and political trends, and to explore possible solutions to contemporary or likely future problems.'[102]

In the late 1970s and early 1980s CAW turned fantasy into reality by creating a number of 'living unicorns', not from horses, as usually envisaged, but from goats.

> The two horn buds are shifted immediately after birth, before they root to the skull, and brought together symmetrically in the middle of the forehead, where they fuse together. This causes the fused horn structure to sprout as a single magnificent horn rather than as two smaller ones, and cancels out the curvatures, so the Unicorn horn arises straight and perpendicular.[103]

Some Neo-Pagans were entranced; others were critical of the surgical altering of nature to create a version of a mythological creature, especially as the 'unicorns' toured with the Ringling Brothers and Barnum & Bailey Circus.

CAW is by no means a typical Neo-Pagan group, but most of its principles, and its eclectic approach to building up a belief system, are broadly the same as those of many other Pagans, and throughout its sometimes uncertain history it has held the respect of Neo-Paganism at large.

DRUIDRY

Organised witchcraft has two major strands, Gardnerian and Alexandrian, with a smattering of other movements including Dianic Wicca, the Cochrane groups (see p. 303) and the supposedly hereditary groups. In contrast there are currently over forty different Druid organisations in the UK alone, according to the Druid Network; some of these are nationwide orders, others groves, or local groups.[104] As with Wicca and other areas of Neo-Paganism, they have very different approaches to their beliefs and practices.

The two Neo-Pagan traditions of Druidry and Wicca, though related in some ways, are quite distinct from each other; but generally their leaders and members seem to have respect for each other, and several Druid leaders are also initiated Wiccan priests. Some individuals and groups are beginning to combine the two traditions in a new synthesis known as Druidcraft.[105]

Present-day Druids have created their religion not so much from what can be surmised about the religious and philosophical beliefs of the inhabitants of the British Isles 2,000 years ago – which is practically nothing – as from Romantic ideals of the eighteenth and nineteenth centuries, coupled with folk tradition: customs such as well-dressing, May Day, Hallowe'en and decorating houses with greenery at midwinter have continued in one way or another through the centuries. Add to this a love and respect for nature, an emphasis on poetry and song and a deep study of British mythology, especially from the Celtic fringes of the country.

The traditional derivation of the word 'druid' is from the Greek *drus*, the Irish *daur* and the Welsh *derw*, each meaning 'oak', and the Indo-European word *wid* which is to do with knowing (wit, wise and wisdom are from the same root, and the Sanskrit *veda*). A Druid was one who knew or understood the oak, or perhaps the wise man of the oak – the oak standing for all trees. Interestingly, in both Irish and Welsh the words for 'tree' and 'knowledge' are etymologically connected.

It was not that the Druids worshipped the oak, or any other tree; but according to a few ancient authors they had a close relationship with nature, their worship took place in groves, and they seemed to see trees as symbolic of wisdom and solidity. 'Although the oak seems to have been favoured by the Druids of Gaul, those of Ireland certainly seem to have preferred the yew or ash as their primary sacred trees,' says Philip Shallcrass, joint Chief Druid of the British Druid Order.[106] However, most modern Druids, he says, do regard the oak as especially sacred.

Shallcrass also points out that many scholars have now discarded the 'oak' derivation of 'druid' in favour of derivations from either an early Celtic intensive prefix *dru*, which would give the meaning of Druid as 'very wise one', or from an Indo-European root, *dreo*, meaning 'true', which would give the meaning 'true [or truth] knower'.

The main problem with recreating the old religion of the Druids is that nothing was written down by the original Druids – or if it was, it is long lost. Nearly all that we know about the Druids, in itself very little, is from other writers of their time, such as Julius Caesar, Strabo, Pliny and Tacitus; their reports are likely to be antagonistic, and might well be inaccurate.

The actual evidence for the Druids as early British heroes, or even for their existence in Britain at all at the time of the Roman conquest, says Ronald Hutton, 'consists of a molehill of completely unreliable material. On this a mountain of literature was to be built'.[107] Hutton, a professor of History at Bristol University, and one of several British academics with a special interest in Neo-Paganism, has written two major scholarly studies of the Druids, *The Druids* and *Blood and Mistletoe: The History of the Druids in Britain*. In both, and in a section of his earlier work *Witches, Druids and King Arthur*, Hutton writes about the changing perception of the Druids in popular culture, including art and literature, and about their reinvention in modern times.[108]

Hutton reveals that the classic image of the long-bearded sage comes from a late fifteenth-century German writer, despite there being no evidence of any presence of the Druids in Germany. In the sixteenth century, images (and imagination) about the Druids passed from Germany to France to Scotland and then to England as part of nationalist history-writing – a form of myth-making.

The modern revival of something called Druidry can be traced to several people in the late seventeenth and eighteenth centuries. The antiquarian John Aubrey first associated Stonehenge and Avebury with the Druids in the 1690s – a completely erroneous belief still held by many today. Influenced by Aubrey, eighteenth-century antiquarian William Stukeley also studied Stonehenge seriously. John Toland's *History of the Druids* was published in 1726.

Exploding a popular misconception Hutton states that 'the Welsh came late to an incorporation of Druidry into their national self-image'[109] – and when they did in the late eighteenth century it was through the 'wayward genius' Iolo Morganwg ('Glamorgan Eddie'),[110] or more prosaically stonemason Edward Williams (1747–1826). In the spirit of his near-contemporaries Thomas Chatterton and James Macpherson he inserted his own forged poems and invented descriptions of Druid ceremonies into his translations of medieval Welsh poetry, and largely got away with it. Historian Stuart Piggott is derisory about Morganwg 'furthering his nonsense',[111] while Druid Philip Shallcrass describes him as a 'scholar, forger and genius'.[112] As well as originating many 'early' Welsh documents, Morganwg also created the 'ancient' *gorsedd*, a ceremonial meeting of Druid bards, at Primrose Hill, London, in 1792 and at the Welsh Eisteddfod in 1819, turning it from a poetry festival into a Druidic event.

Although most of Iolo Morganwg's work can justifiably be called fraudulent, it was largely responsible for inspiring nine-teenth- and twentieth-century interest – and somewhat more scholarly enquiry – into early British history and mythology. In addition it can be argued that his work should not be dismissed out of hand simply because most of it stemmed from his own fertile imagination. In all areas of Neo-Paganism the creative use of the imagination is an important part of symbolism, ritual and magic. Compare the influence on early Wicca and on the Cochranite movements (see p. 287 and p. 305) of Robert Graves's *The White Goddess*, which has much poetic but little historical merit; similarly, no one would argue that the entire Arthurian mythos should be thrown away on the grounds that the overwhelming majority of it is fictional rather than factual. Whether in religion or in orders such as Freemasonry, it is not the factual basis of mythology that is important; rather, it is the truths contained, often symbol-ically, within the myths (see p. 13 and p. 289). The same argument could be applied to Iolo Morganwg's work.

Modern Druid orders began with a philanthropic group of local worthies in Anglesey, founded in 1772, and with the Ancient Order of Druids (AOD), founded in a London pub in 1781, who celebrated drinking and music.

Moving on a full century and to Stonehenge (now insepa-rable from Druidry in the popular imagination, despite the reality), the AOD began holding ceremonies at Stonehenge around 1905, though local people had been gathering there informally in large numbers to watch the midsummer sunrise since around 1870, with pubs staying open all night for their benefit in the 1890s.[113] The problematic relationship between the authorities at Stonehenge and the spiritual counter-culture did not begin until 1913. This was with a group called the Universal Bond of the Sons of Men, which initially mixed and matched ideas from esoteric Christianity, Druidry, Kabbalah, Buddhism, Zoroastrianism and mystical Islam before settling on a Druid identity a few years later.[114] The Universal Bond was founded by a larger-than-life Scot, George Watson MacGregor Reid (the MacGregor was apparently a tribute to 'MacGregor' Mathers of the Hermetic Order of the Golden Dawn, see p. 195). Reid claimed his group's origins went back to 1717, but this is almost certainly a romantic foundation myth.

For a few years after Reid's death in 1946 there were two versions of the Universal Bond, which became known as the Druid Order, but from around 1954 only one, led by Reid's son Robert, survived. When Robert died in 1964 there was a contest for his successor, and the loser, Philip Ross Nichols (1902–75), left to found the Order of Bards, Ovates and Druids (OBOD), which is now the largest Druid group in the world. The Druid Order continues, with fortnightly public meetings in an esoteric bookshop in London, and with three ceremonies a year: Autumn Equinox at Primrose Hill, London, Spring Equinox at Tower Hill, London, and Summer Solstice at Stonehenge.

Nichols was a good friend of Gerald Gardner, the founder of modern Wicca (see p. 289f.); Gardner, who was a great eclecticist, had joined the Druid Order even before Nichols did, illustrating a closeness between these two streams of Neo-Paganism. OBOD died with Nichols, but was revived in 1988 by Philip Carr-Gomm, who edited Nichols's *Book of Druidry*, an imaginative but very spiritual exploration of Druid beliefs. OBOD has a fairly eclectic membership, which includes both Pagans and Christians.[115]

Another notable Druid group is the British Druid Order (BDO), which was founded by Philip Shallcrass in 1992, but traces its origins back to an Alexandrian Wiccan coven which, he says, 'was willingly subverted into a Druidic grove' in 1979.[116] He took the name Greywolf in 1994, and in 1995 Emma Restall Orr (known as Bobcat) became joint chief with him. The BDO is a specifically Pagan-orientated Druid group, whose teachings are based on the *Mabinogion* and other early British/Celtic texts.[117] Some of the teachings of the BDO and OBOD are discussed below.

The Secular Order of Druids was founded by poet and rock lyricist Tim Sebastion (1947–2007) in 1986. It was heavily orientated towards environmentalism, and to supporting the civil rights of Druids to meet at places like Stonehenge in the face of police opposition. (Sebastion was one of the hundreds of people arrested in the infamous 'Battle of the Beanfield' on 1 June 1985, when police in riot gear attacked the Peace Convoy heading for the Stonehenge Festival.)[118] It sought 'to enhance the modern-day relevance of Druidry by reviving folk traditions and by taking Druidry to "raves"'.[119]

The Insular Order of Druids was founded in 1993 in Portsmouth by Dylan ap Thuin (Dylan Blight, 1965–2003), again in protest at the then British government's ban on celebration at Stonehenge. Like many other small groups it died with its founder, whose ashes were scattered amongst the stones at Stonehenge.[120]

The Druid Clan of Dana, based at Clonegal Castle in Eire and in London, is a well-organised and rapidly expanding Pagan Druid movement, and part of the Fellowship of Isis (see p. 328); it 'works on the development of nature's psychic gifts' and 'has no specific religious tradition, but embraces all'.[121]

The Loyal Arthurian Warband, led by the colourful King Arthur Pendragon (born John Timothy Rothwell in 1954), campaigns for environmental and animal rights, and against new road building, nuclear and chemical weapons, and the Criminal Justice Act. Arthur, a biker and former soldier, is one of the few Neo-Pagan leaders in Britain for whom his priesthood is a full-time vocation.[122]

The Gorsedd of Bards of Caer Abiri, founded in 1993, holds open celebrations of the eight Druid festivals within the stone circles of Avebury in Wiltshire. Shallcrass describes them: 'The Gorsedd well represents the current ecumenical trend in Druidry in that it brings together members of several different

Druid orders as well as followers of other Pagan and non-Pagan faiths. Its rituals combine modern Druidic practice with the Iolo Morganwg tradition and elements from the other faiths represented among its membership.'[123]

Some groups, such as the Breton Druids and the Cornish Druids, are more cultural in their emphasis; some are more shamanic; some are closer to Wicca. Some are hierarchical, some non-hierarchical. Some are solitary Druids, effectively one-man-bands.

Terry Dobney is known as the Archdruid of Avebury, elected annually by several Druid orders as the Keeper of the Stones there; in addition to the usual eight rituals he holds thirteen full-moon rituals each year. 'The people who come to this vary from me to 40-plus people,' he says. He liaises with 'the police, National Trust, English Heritage, pub landlords, and other Pagan groups', gives talks and walks around Avebury for foreign tourists, and also organises the Sacred Sites Forum, a monthly meeting at Avebury, discussing rituals and integrating the local people and the various authorities.[124]

In London Jeremy Morgan, the self-styled Lone Druid of Wormwood Scrubs, performs his own rituals eight times a year at midday 'on the Sunday nearest the due date' on Primrose Hill; he also 'greets the dawn' in a grove in Wormwood Scrubs on the actual days, arriving 'before Sunrise and "chanting up" the Sun (an almost shamanic practice) before composing a poetic description of the event'.[125]

British Druid orders have two very different linking organisations. The Council of British Druid Orders (CoBDO) was formed when four orders came together in 1988–9 to discuss problems of access to Stonehenge. Through long and careful negotiation with English Heritage and other authorities, access at Midsummer was finally granted from 2000 onwards.[126] CoBDO broke into two rival groups in 2009, with a fluctuating membership of small local groups in each; unfortunately their infighting is often in the public eye.[127]

The other organisation, the Druid Network, was set up in 2002 by Emma Restall Orr, formerly of OBOD and then the BDO. It is 'a networking organisation, aimed to inform and support groups and individuals practising or exploring Druidry'.[128] Its website lists over forty Druid orders and individual groves in Britain, and over eighty in North America.[129] It also expresses a characteristic of Druidry, and of Neo-Paganism in general: 'It has been said that there are as many interpretations of the gods as there are druids and to this end, these pages do not aim to seek consensus. Each druid finds his or her own path into relationship with deity and here we intend to show a celebration of this diversity.'[130]

Its founder's aim was that the Druid Network would 'act as a tangible expression of the spreading web of the Druid community'. In 2010 the Druid Network gained registration as a charity furthering the religion of Druidry.[131] A savagely written opinion piece on this in a tabloid newspaper[132] prompted 120 formal complaints to the Press Complaints Commission and an online petition with over 4,000 signatures to the editor of the *Daily Mail* demanding an apology.[133]

Emma Restall Orr also set up a movement called Honouring the Ancient Dead (HAD), which seeks to persuade archaeologists, museums and government departments to treat the remains of the early inhabitants of Britain with respect. After years of groups campaigning in other countries the bones of Native Americans and Aboriginal Australians are now being returned to their peoples to be buried with honour. Because Britain does not have a readily identifiable original race or religion this poses more problems; but HAD focuses mainly on remains up to the seventh century CE, which are most likely to be pre-Christian. Its council and advisors come from a variety of Neo-Pagan and academic areas.[134]

Druidry is just as widespread, and just as diverse, in the United States. As with witchcraft, the United States has a number of Druid movements based on a supposed hereditary and largely romantic Celtic background. The Druid Heritage Society, for example, asserts that rather than being religious, 'Druidism was *secular* and denoted a Celtic social and professional class'. Its members are generally Christian rather than Neo-Pagan, and seek to 'establish and maintain within families their own hereditary Druid line; discover, reveal, and maintain the Celtic roots and traditions of the Druid's family line'.

Its foundation myth is very similar to that of Rhuddlwm ap Gawr (William Wheeler), founder of the Tribe of Dynion Mwyn and the Clan of Y Tylwyth Teg (see p. 301): the founder supposedly inherited his heritage from his great-great-grand-mother, and it was kept in the family for decades until the number of interested family members dropped too low, at which point it was opened to others. It only accepts members 'in the professional class', and is more of a Celtic study society and family genealogy society than any sort of religious group.[135]

Two more traditional Neo-Pagan Druid societies in the United States are Ár nDraíocht Féin: A Druid Fellowship (ADF), founded by the well-known American Druid Isaac Bonewits in 1983, and the Henge of Keltria, founded in 1987 by Tony and Sable Taylor. While the ADF is primarily Celtic in its focus, it also includes elements of other Indo-European spiritual traditions, including Norse and Germanic, Roman, Hellenic and Vedic. It has over a thousand members. The Henge of Keltria split away from ADF largely because its members wanted a more specifically Celtic focus, and because they wanted private rather than public rituals; it has 200 members.[136]

This selection from the Henge of Keltria's belief statement is a good indication of what many of the more modern Druid orders believe:

1. We believe in Divinity as it is manifest in the Pantheon. There are several valid theistic perceptions of this Pantheon.
2. We believe that nature is the embodiment of the Gods and Goddesses.
4. We believe that all life is sacred and should neither be harmed nor taken without deliberation or regard.

6. We believe that our purpose is to gain wisdom through experience.

8. We believe that morality should be a matter of personal conviction based upon self respect and respect for others.

10. We believe in the relative nature of all things, that nothing is absolute, and that all things, even the Gods and Goddesses, have their dark sides.

11. We believe that individuals have the right to pursue knowledge and wisdom through his or her chosen path.

12. We believe in a living religion able to adapt to a changing environment.

We recognize that our beliefs may undergo change as our tradition grows.[137]

The eight festivals celebrated by modern Druids are the same as those of modern Wicca: Samhain (Hallowe'en), Winter Solstice, Imbolc (Candlemas), Spring Equinox, Beltane (May Eve/Day), Summer Solstice, Lughnasadh (Lammas, Lady Day) and the Autumn Equinox.

Most of the Druid Orders are deeply concerned with the environment. OBOD, which offers a home learning course in Druidry, is probably speaking for most Orders when it says:

More than ever, we need a spirituality that is rooted in a love of nature, a love of the land. Druidry and the teaching programme of OBOD is based upon this love for the natural world, and offers a powerful way of working with and understanding the Self and Nature – speaking to that level of our soul and of our being which is in tune with the elements and the stars, the sun and the stones. Through the work of the Druids we are able to unite our natural, earthly selves with our spiritual selves while working, in however small a way, for the safeguarding of our planet.[138]

Many of the Druid Orders contain three grades or groupings of members; these focus on different talents and interests, and although they are not necessarily progressive levels, as in Wicca and the schools of occult science with a Golden Dawn heritage (see p. 219), those at the third level would normally have passed through the first two. In OBOD, for example, Bards are the keepers of tradition, those who remember and relate the stories, poems and myths. The Ovates are trained in prophecy and divination; they are the seers and shamans of the movement. The Druids are the teachers, counsellors and judges; they are philosophers rather than priests, and will tend to be the older, more experienced members of the Order.[139]

The British Druid Order also has three grades, roughly equivalent to those of OBOD: Bard (Poet/Seer), Ofydd (Philosopher) and Derwydd (Druid):

> The essence of the Order's teachings lies in working with the spiritual energy known to the British tradition as Awen. The feminine noun Awen literally means 'flowing spirit' or 'fluid essence'. The Bards of mediaeval Wales saw it as their primary source of inspiration, and as a gift of the ancient pagan Goddess Ceridwen, 'the Bent White One', who they referred to as Patroness of the Bardic Order.
>
> In the Bardic grade this 'flowing spirit' is directed into creativity on many levels, particularly in the traditional areas of poetry, music and storytelling, but also in all other arts and sciences.
>
> In the Ofydd grade, Awen is used to create windows, or gateways, into unseen worlds, leading to the development of the gift of seership, and knowledge of the Faery realm, the Otherworld, and its inhabitants.
>
> In the Derwydd grade, Awen is related to Earth energies, or Dragon Lines, which run through the landscape, accumulating at sacred sites. The task of the Druid is to learn to work with this energy for the benefit of the land and its inhabitants, human and animal, physical and non-physical.
>
> In all this work, we call upon the aid of the Ancestors, who are both our physical forebears who have passed on, and our spiritual Ancestors, the Druids of all past ages, and also the Gods themselves. Much of our strength and wisdom comes from them, and they give it freely and joyously, because we are part of the same golden chain of age-old tradition.[140]

In 2010 the BDO announced it was about to make available a distance learning course with six bimonthly packages of teaching material for each of the three grades of bard, ovate and druid.[141]

The academic historian Ronald Hutton estimated the total number of members of Druid orders in Britain in 1996 at roughly 6,000, and the total number of members of initiatory witch traditions at 10,000.[142] However, he also calculated that there were about another 100,000 Pagans in Britain at that time who did not belong to any formal orders or initiatory traditions. The number of Druids has certainly increased since then: OBOD alone has over 10,000 members.[143] According to Philip Carr-Gomm, 'Only a minority of the people who are inspired by Druidry actually join a Druid order or group. The majority, for reasons of time or inclination, are more likely to simply read books on the subject, informally celebrate the old festival times, and feel inspired by Druid lore.'

FELLOWSHIP OF ISIS

The Fellowship of Isis (FOI) is a movement based in Ireland which is largely Neo-Pagan but is inclusive of all Goddess worship. It was founded by the Rev Lawrence Durdin-Robertson, Baron Ruadh of Strathlock (1920–94), with his wife Pamela (1923–87) and his sister the Honourable Olivia Robertson (b.1917). It had probably the most impressive headquarters of any Neo-Pagan or esoteric movement, in Clonegal Castle in Enniscorthy, Ireland, built in 1625; the Temple of Isis, with altars and shrines to many goddesses, is still in the cellars of the castle, and open to members. 'The Fellowship of Isis itself however has been decentralized since 1999 and has many advisory boards, circles, publications and websites for its members to choose from.'[144]

Lawrence Durdin-Robertson was ordained an Anglican priest in 1948, and served as a parish priest in the Church of Ireland until 1957 when he 'discovered the feminine face of God, through researching the original Hebrew text of the Bible'.[145] With his wife and sister he founded the Huntington Castle Centre for Meditation and Study in 1963, and the Fellowship of Isis in 1976.

The FOI worships the Goddess, but differs from many other Neo-Pagan organisations in emphasising Egyptian roots as well as Celtic; its priesthood, it claims, 'is derived from an hereditary line of the Robertsons from Ancient Egypt'.[146]

Because they venerate all goddesses (and also gods), members include people from a variety of religions: 'The good in all faiths is honoured . . . The Fellowship accepts religious toleration, and is not exclusivist. Members are free to maintain other religious allegiances.' Olivia Robertson, the remaining co-founder, stated in 2002 that the FOI should not be thought of as a Pagan organisation: 'We are happy to have 1000s of Pagans among our 21,000 members in so many countries. But we also have Catholics, Protestants, Buddhists, Spiritualists and Hindus as members. All love and follow the religion of Isis of 10,000 Names.'[147] In 2010 FOI claimed a membership of 27,000 in 123 countries. The Fellowship has three 'daughter' societies, the Noble Order of Tara, 'an Order of Chivalry whose Priories promote dedicated work for our planet', the Druid Clan of Dana and the College of Isis.

The Druid Clan of Dana, which works on the development of nature's psychic gifts, 'will continue to investigate and work with ancient sites, to explore cross-cultural connections amongst ancient peoples and develop an English Druidry in the Irish tradition'.[148]

In common with esoteric Mystery Schools, the College of Isis offers a correspondence course, 'a structured Magi Degree Course in the Fellowship of Isis Liturgy. There are 32 working degrees, the 33rd relating to spontaneous mystical awakening.'[149] But in contrast with esoteric schools:

> there are no vows required or commitments to secrecy. All Fellowship activities are optional, and members are free to resign or rejoin at their own choice . . . The Fellowship reverences all manifestations of Life . . . [and] believes in the promotion of Love, Beauty and Abundance. No encouragement is given to asceticism. The Fellowship seeks to develop friendliness, psychic gifts, happiness, and compassion for all life.

The Fellowship of Isis was invited to take part in the Parliament of the World's Religions centennial session in 1993, 'the first time in which the Religion of the Goddess has been publicly acknowledged as a World Faith'.[150]

HEATHENRY/NORTHERN TRADITION

Part of the Neo-Pagan revival of the late twentieth and early twenty-first centuries has been a renewed interest in the gods and goddesses of native traditions: these include not only Celtic and Native American, but also the old Norse and Germanic religions – known today as the Northern Tradition or Heathenry.

For many people this goes little further than using runes instead of (or as well as) Tarot cards for divination, meditation and magic; but for some thousands in Britain, northern Europe and the United States the religion itself is being revived, reconstructed and reinterpreted for a modern world.

Freya Aswynn, who for many years was a Drighten (leader) in the Rune Gild and an Elder in the Ring of Troth (now known as the Troth), distinguishes Heathenry from Paganism: 'The religious organisations I represent are relatively young and modern; however, the religion itself is old, not new age as some other forms of contemporary Paganism. We therefore distinguish ourselves by naming ourselves Heathen rather than Pagan.'[151]

Heathen originally meant 'the beliefs of the people of the heath', just as 'Pagan' originally meant 'the beliefs of the country people'. Another major Heathen group, Odinshof, says:

Heathenism, or the Northern Tradition as it is alternatively known, is perhaps the most diverse of all faiths under the pagan umbrella. It has a structure unlike any other pagan religion but at the same time, a sort of nomadic looseness at worshipper level. Heathens may invoke many gods and goddesses, and yet some may worship only one, such as the shamanic wind god Odin. Heathenism is one religion or many related religions according to your point of view.[152]

Although movements such as the Rune Gild, the Troth, Odinshof and the Odinic Rite have their own different approach and emphasis, all follow versions of the Northern European traditions of the Norse, Germanic and Anglo-Saxon peoples, practised from around 2,000 years ago, and gradually supplanted by Christianity from around 1,500 to 1,000 years ago. Some Heathens today use the Norse names for the gods, others the Germanic, and many in Britain prefer to use the Anglo-Saxon names. The same applies to the runes, of which there are several versions. Different futharks ('alphabets' of runes, so named after the sound of the first six runes) have sixteen, twenty-four or up to thirty-three runes depending on their geographic origin: loosely, Scandinavian, Germanic and Northumbrian.[153]

The god most closely associated with the runes is Odin, Woden or Wotan, the Allfather. The myths tell how Odin hung upside down from the great World Tree Yggdrasil for nine days and nights, impaled on his own spear, in order to gain wisdom.

The Rune Gild, founded in the United States by Edred Thorsson in 1980, is a school of esoteric knowledge teaching rune work for divination, meditation, talismans, self-transformation and various forms of rune magic. It has a graded curriculum based on Thorsson's book, *The Nine Doors of Midgard*.[154]

The Troth is 'a religious organisation dedicated to the promotion and practice of the native heathen folk-religion of Northern Europe,' says Aswynn, whose book *Leaves of Yggdrasil* is a study of the runes, the Norse gods and magic.[155]

The Norse were a very down-to-earth people, she says; the mystical, the magical and the religious were seen as a fundamental part of everyday life. The runes were associated with wisdom and well-being, with words and deeds, with the gods and with magical power. They were both practical and mystical; if a particular combination of runes brought good luck or protection, it made sense for a warrior to carry it with him as a magical talisman. Aswynn stresses the immediacy of religion to her Norse ancestors: 'For them there was no separation between sacred and profane, spiritual and secular. Their faith was intricately interwoven into everything they did, from working in the fields to naming their children. Theirs was a life where the gods and goddesses were never any further away than their own shadow.'

These gods and goddesses include the entire Norse pantheon, known to us through the poetic or *Elder Edda*, and the prose or *Younger Edda*; the German equivalent is the *Nibelungenlied*. These myths and legends became familiar in modern times through Wagner's *Ring Cycle* and other works, and inspired J. R. R. Tolkien's *The Lord of the Rings* and related books. The Troth recognises that these gods and goddesses have always been perceived in a variety of ways, and 'affirms the right of individuals and groups to freely worship as they will, guided by the dictates of their own consciences'.[156]

British anthropologist and Heathen Jenny Blain points out that the eddas and sagas were written down after the conversion of most of northern Europe to Christianity: 'While there are claims by some Heathens (notably in Scandinavia, though there are some also in Britain) to be keepers of old traditions and customs, for the most part Heathenry is a religion constructed today from partial material.'[157]

In the United States the generic term Asatru is sometimes used for religious movements in the Northern Tradition. This comes from the Asa or Aesir, one of the two main families of Norse gods; the other family were the Vanir. According to Andrew Clifton, former Shope or editor for the Ring of Troth Europe, Asatru is an Icelandic term; 'Asatru was accepted as a legitimate religion in Iceland in 1972.'[158] The Rune Gild explains further:

Modern-day Asatru is a religion based on reconstruction from historical sources. It is a polytheistic faith encompassing belief in a multitude of different gods and goddesses. Within Asatru there is the emergence of a sister tradition named Vanatru, centring mainly on the Vanir. This branch takes especial interest in the feminine mysteries and female ancestor work. At the heart of the religion are its semi-sacred texts, the Eddas and the Runes.[159]

The religion has a strong ethical side similar to that of most Neo-Pagan movements.

Modern concerns of Asatru are environmental issues and the re-establishing of family values. Unlike many other ethnic peoples, we have lost the sense of kinship, community and extended family. Many old people are freezing or starving. Young people drift towards a life of drug abuse, crime, and general uselessness – with little but the dole queue to look forward to. We offer change. We want to give back – especially [to] the young – a pride in ancestors and their achievements. We aim to instil responsibility, respect and care for our elders, and stress the value of education for our youngsters.[160]

The Norse peoples, and their gods, lived life to the full; they were a hot-tempered bunch, but honourable within their own rules. According to Aswynn, 'The concept of Honour is the most vital element of Asatru ethics. Others are Courage, Truth, Loyalty, Self-discipline, Hospitality, Industriousness, Independence, and Endurance. We strive to express these nine virtues in our lives and dealings with people. Forgiveness, loving your enemy and turning the other cheek are tactics with no place in Asatru.'

Founded in 1973 the Odinic Rite, which claims to be the oldest Odinist or Asatru organisation in North America, also places strong emphasis on honour and self-discipline: 'Each time that we speak out against tyranny, are hospitable to guests or help to protect the environment we are performing a religious act.'[161] Like other Northern Tradition movements the Odinic Rite places great emphasis on the family and the extended

family, including close friends; it is organised in Hearths, groups
of ten to twelve people who usually meet in members' homes:

> Odinism is the organic religion of the peoples of Northern
> Europe. Our ancestors . . . reflected their awareness of a unity in
> which the cosmos is one with man and nature . . .
>
> Odinists aim at creating a restored order based on the idea of
> respect for all life and on the explicit recognition of spirituality
> within ourselves and in the world in which we live, to extend
> our views of nature so that it is seen as a true manifestation of
> the spirit.[162]

Although people might initially be attracted to Odinism by the
use of runes, there is much more to the religion than that, say
the Odinic Rite:

> Those who believe that runes and runology are the be-all and
> end-all of Odinism have a too narrow vision of the runes, a
> shallow knowledge of their mysteries and ignorance of the
> meaning of religion. The runes are the essential mystical ingre-
> dient of the Odinic Rite and are its spiritual mainstay. But they
> are not its sum total . . . The Odinist religion is our way of life,
> our inherited culture and our patrimony.[163]

As in Wicca and Druidry, a number of Heathen leaders and
writers in both the United States and Britain are academics, and
some have taken on names relevant to their faith. Edred Thorsson
(born Stephen Flowers), whose doctorate was on runes and
magic, is the author of, amongst much else, *A Book of Troth*.
Another influential academic writer is Kveldulfr Gundarsson,
author of *Teutonic Magic and Teutonic Religion*, whose doctorate
was on Odin. (His *Rhinegold* and *Attila's Treasure*, written
under his original name Stephan Grundy, are modern novelisa-
tions of portions of the Norse/Germanic sagas.)[164] Dr Jenny
Blain, of Sheffield Hallam University, is author of *Nine Worlds
of Seid-Magic: Ecstasy and Neo-Shamanism in North European
Paganism*, and co-author of books on Neo-Paganism and sacred

sites. She was one of the founders of the Association of Polytheist Traditions, whose aim was to educate people about ancient and modern polytheist traditions, increase awareness of polytheism and be a networking organisation for polytheist groups.[165]

Like most Neo-Pagan and esoteric movements, the revived Norse religions do not actively recruit new members. 'They find us,' says Aswynn. 'People join us because they want to work with others to contact the gods and goddesses. What they get out of it is a closely knit artificially constructed 'tribal family' where we support each other in everything. We are mostly bound together by personal friendships between us and our enthusiasm for our gods.'[166]

Odinshof does not limit itself strictly to the Norse religion. 'The philosophy of the 'Hof is to look back over 2,500 years or so and gain insight from most periods since then,' says Martyn Taylor, who co-founded Odinshof in 1987.[167] Its members:

> want to promote the cult of Odin (Odintru) and learn spiritual truths ('dharma'). Odinshof members do not reject anything from the past but believe strongly in the 'now' . . . The backbone of the Odinshof is its membership, whether they be working alone or attached to an official hearth or loose group (sometimes called a kindred). Some members feel the need to progress to the level of being at one with Odin – to be 'an Odin'. These are potential Grimserular, or shaman-priests . . . A Grimesruli is seen by the Odinshof as a healer, pathfinder, rune-master and teacher, all rolled into one.[168]

Odinshof's aims are to present the Northern Tradition to the general public, to train Heathen priests and priestesses, and to work with the Olgar Trust, a registered charity in Britain, to purchase woodland for conservation and ritual use.[169] It is dedicated to maintaining areas of wildwoods, and helped campaign against the proposed road through Oxleas Wood in London.

The roots of Norse religion go back at least 2,000 years. Norse/ Germanic mythology, like most others, includes creation myths and end-of-the-world myths; it has interrelated families of quarrelsome gods, who from time to time had dealings with humans, and these gods swap responsibilities to some extent over the centuries as the mythology evolves. These are a few of the major gods and goddesses:

- Odin, Woden or Wotan, sometimes known as the Allfather, was foremost among the gods. He is generally pictured with a wide-brimmed hat sloping over his blind eye, in the company of two ravens, his messengers. He was known for his wisdom, but also for his unpredictability; like many gods, he had a trickster side to his personality.
- His son Thor was the god of weather, particularly thunder, and is often seen wielding a hammer, which he frequently used to slay giants. He was also the god of the peasants and common people, which might account for the fair way in which Norse rulers treated their people.
- Tyr or Tiw was the original god of war; his prominent position was later taken on by Odin. Tyr was the god of the Thing, the people's assembly, and so of justice (see below).
- Frey, one of the most important gods, was a fertility god, and also the god of summer.
- His sister (and at one point wife) Frija or Freya was the goddess of sexuality and beauty, and also of feminine magic, which she taught to Odin.
- Often confused with Frija, especially in the Germanic versions of the myths, is Frigga, goddess of fertility, but more in the sense of motherhood; she was one of Odin's wives.
- She bore him a son, Baldur, who was the most beautiful of all the gods; he was an expert in herbal medicine, and also in the runes; he was said to have runes engraved on his tongue.
- Baldur was eventually slain through the treachery of Loki, the god of deceit and trickery – and of fire and leisure.

There are several dozen other gods and goddesses, in addition to giants, dwarves and heroic humans, entwined in Norse mythology. Four of them live on today wherever the English language is spoken around the world, in the days of the week: Tuesday is named after Tyr or Tiw, Wednesday after Woden or Odin, Thursday after Thor, and Friday after either Freya or Frigga.

As Christianity made inroads into northern Europe, the power of the old gods waned to some extent – but not entirely. For some centuries the two religions existed side by side, and there are many examples of gravestones or crosses such as the Gosforth Cross in Cumbria with the crucified Christ on one side and scenes from Norse mythology on the other. Very often the inscriptions were in runes, rather than in the Latin alphabet. Runes continued to be used for writing, and for more esoteric purposes, for many more centuries, despite the efforts of the Catholic Church to stamp out their use. As late as 1639 there was an edict in Iceland forbidding their use – which shows that they were still in use then.

Many elements of the Old Norse language survive today, obviously in the Scandinavian languages, but also in English, Dutch and German. There are still a few sheep farmers on the fells in the south of the Lake District who speak amongst them-selves a variant of Old Norse; the closest present-day language is Icelandic.[170] In English, the occasional use of 'ye' to mean 'the' (as in 'Ye Olde Tea-Shoppe') is a reminder of the rune Thorn, þ, which is pronounced as a soft 'th' but looks some-thing like a 'y'.

It is arguable that the British legal system developed in part from the Old Norse system, with defendants allowed to argue their case and be judged by a jury of their peers.

Do the modern-day successors to Sigismund and the other great Norse heroes actually believe in Odin, Thor, Baldur, Frija and the rest of the gods? 'We have no fixed doctrine at all,' says Aswynn. 'Most of us believe on the whole in an objective existence of our gods as spiritual beings, whereas others in our religion perceive the gods more as Jungian Archetypes. Most people have a favourite god or goddess they are devoted to in particular.' Thus there are Odinists, Thorians, Tyrians and others. The Odinic Rite explain it a different way:

> We know that our gods exist: we can see, feel and sense them. They are manifested in various forms: in the summer and the winter, sunshine and storm, hill and river and plain. Because it is in keeping with our culture and our tradition Odinists give names to the gods who show themselves to us in this way: Thor, Frey, Balder, Odin and many others . . . There is nothing unusual or illogical in this Odinist use of an ancient mythology. All religions are mythical in their development. It is not the myth that we believe in but the gods whom the myth helps us to understand.[171]

Like Wiccans and Druids, Heathens have sometimes been accused of being too much in love with a rose-tinted past. The Odinic Rite disagrees: 'It is not a spare-time religion providing an escape route from the problems of modern life by invoking visions of the romantic past but an opportunity for the individual to grow in self-reliance, to grow closer to nature in the practice of the ancient rituals of our ancestors and to secure the future.'[172]

Odinshof also stress the practical, everyday nature of its beliefs:

> There is a danger of members becoming too reliant on written texts and not spending time being involved with hearth activities or out of door rituals. 'Armchair Heathens' do not change society for the better. Again, Tacitus said, 'The Germanic-speaking tribes do not think it is in keeping with the divine majesty to confine gods within walls or to portray them in the likeness of any human countenance. Their holy places are woods and groves, and they apply the names of deities to that hidden presence which is seen only by the eye of reverence.'[173]

Believers in the Norse/Germanic religions are conscious that their symbolism has been appropriated by the extreme right wing. In the 1930s and 1940s Hitler deliberately drew on Norse/Germanic sources to provide a religious, mystical and magical basis for Nazism. The SS used the rune Sig, Sigel or

Sowulo as their symbol. (The swastika, one of the oldest religious symbols in the world, and signifying well-being, has probably been irreparably polluted by its adoption by Nazism; see p. 137–8). Aswynn comments:

> Unfortunately, some in the past have sought to use the revival of our native folk religion to advance their racial and political agendas. Such activity is not tolerated in the Ring of Troth. The peoples of the North did not achieve great things by fearing, distrusting or hating everyone unlike themselves; rather they attained greatness through their ability, where necessary, to learn from others and to borrow, adapt and improve ideas and technologies which suited their own needs. If the Germanic peoples had hated and feared all that was new and different they may not have achieved all that they have.

A Rune Gild press release on Asatru looks at it from a different angle: 'Attempts to call and control the Northern gods were made in the 1930s and 1940s. However the gods had their own agenda, and seeing the subversion of the runes and other sacred signs, extracted the penalties of the perpetrators – who lost!'[174]

The efforts of Heathens to distance themselves from Nazism and the far right are made more difficult by two things: the fact that the Norse/Germanic/Anglo-Saxon religion *is* an ethnic tradition, and the rise of Neo-Nazism, which is once again appropriating some of the symbols and which lays claim to the same ethnic heritage. In Britain this is not a great problem; in parts of North America, and also in parts of Scandinavia, it can be.

It is difficult to say how many followers of the Northern Tradition there are. As well as the several different organisations, many Heathens pursue an essentially solitary path, keeping in touch with others through, for instance, the UKHeathenry email list.[175]

The Troth, which has around 500 members, estimates that there may be as many as 10,000 Heathens in the English-speaking world, depending on how one defines Heathens: 'Do we count Norse Wiccans? Do we count dual-tradition folks, or ADF Druids [Ár nDraíocht Féin: A Druid Fellowship; see p. 324] with a Norse cultural focus, or assorted other eclectic types? Do we want to include the Wotanist white supremacists in the same religious tally as ourselves? Deciding who gets counted as Heathen could be contentious'.[176]

Another member of the Troth points out that as well as Britain, Europe and North America, there are also Heathen individuals, networks and groups in Australia and New Zealand – 'and South America, where there are pockets of families with northern European backgrounds too'.[177]

PAGAN FEDERATIONS

In general, Neo-Paganism glories in its diversity. Shamans, witches, Druids, Heathens and others have different approaches, based on different mythological traditions; and within each broad group there are many varieties, many different aims and emphases. This is both a strength and a potential weakness; the lack of any central organisation prevents the movement becoming dogmatic and authoritarian, both of which are alien to the Neo-Pagan way of thinking, but it also means a lack of a centralised cohesive voice. (It can also mean that groups with a strong or maverick leader might wander off in unusual directions; but this can be seen as part of the colour in the rich tapestry of Neo-Paganism.)

Various umbrella organisations have arisen over the years to give Neo-Paganism a clearer and stronger voice in wider society. Three British ones will be mentioned here.

In 1981 the Pagan Federation (PF) grew out of the former Pagan Front, which had begun in 1970. The PF 'works to make Paganism accessible to people genuinely seeking a nature-based spiritual path'.[178] It has three major aims:

- To seek to support all Pagans in their personal and public life, to help ensure that they have the same rights as the followers of other beliefs and members of other religions.
- To promote a positive profile for Pagans and Paganism and to provide information on Pagan paths and beliefs to the media, official bodies and the greater community.

- To facilitate effective communication, education and dialogue within and between Pagan communities and with non Pagans, through publications and events.[179]

A large part of its work is informational, and it has become effectively the official mouthpiece of British Paganism to the outside world; it has established links with the Home Office, the police, social services, the press, libraries, teachers and Members of Parliament. Amongst other things it works towards establishing an acceptance of Pagan hospital and prison chaplains, and Pagan weddings and funerals.

Initially the Pagan Federation was almost exclusively Wiccan, but by the late 1980s, according to one Wiccan authority, it was 'facing increased criticism for its lack of democracy, and its inability to cater adequately for members who followed other paths than Wiccan'.[180] It was also very much centred on the south-east of England, which was a source of irritation to Pagans elsewhere in the country. From around 1991, recognising these weaknesses, it expanded its work to give more emphasis to non-Wiccan Paganism, and made efforts to become more democratic. Its magazine *The Wiccan* was relaunched as *Pagan Dawn*. Its annual conferences, established in 1989, attract Neo-Pagans from a wide variety of traditions.

Far from being focused exclusively on the south-east, the Pagan Federation now has fourteen districts – the north-west, the north-east, Scotland and Ireland, Devon and Cornwall, London, etc. – each of which is divided into regions; each district has its own website highlighting local events, including conferences, workshops and moots.

A newer and smaller organisation, the Pagan Network, also grew out of a Wiccan group, WiccaUK, which was founded in 2000; it changed its name and focus in 2005. Its aims overlap with those of the Pagan Federation: 'Pagan Network is a networking organisation set up to promote the acceptance and tolerance of Paganism as a faith system within the UK, and to provide a safe and informative social network both on and offline for Pagans in the UK.'[181]

It is more socially focused than the Pagan Federation, and initially had a younger membership with its leaders and members in their twenties; by 2010 'members are now older, but tend towards the more eclectic end of Paganism'.[182]

Recognising a specific need, Pebble, the Public Bodies Liaison Committee for British Paganism, was set up in 2005 to encourage and facilitate 'positive and productive interaction between the growing communities of modern British Paganisms and British government departments, bodies and institutions'.[183] Again it has some overlap with the Pagan Federation, which is one of its partner organisations, along with the Druid Network, the Pagan Network and others; but its specific task is to liaise with national and local government, including the police and the armed forces, on behalf of the Pagan community.

One of its successful campaigns was to introduce, in 2006, a non-faith-specific Pagan oath for use in British courts: 'I swear by all that I hold sacred that the evidence I shall give shall be the truth, the whole truth and nothing but the truth.'

It also supported a campaign originated by Pagan magazine editor Jon Randall for a coordinated approach to the UK 2011 Census, encouraging Neo-Pagans of all varieties to write in their faith as 'Pagan – Wiccan', 'Pagan – Druid', etc. Known as PaganDASH, this will ensure that the Census is an accurate measure of the number of Neo-Pagans in Britain, while not losing the specific path identity of individuals.[184] A similar campaign has been mounted by leaders of the New Age community in Britain to use the umbrella label 'Holistic' (see p. 144).

Umbrella groups, federations and networks serve a number of functions: exchange of views, mutual support, general friendship, central information point for the media and official bodies, centralised research and publication, and so on. The Neo-Pagan movement in general is still quite young, and much of its vigour seems to come from its diversity. A possible danger, which the leaders of such federations and networks are

What I Believe . . .
After Death?

Consciousness continues to develop.
Dr William Bloom
Author and educator in a holistic and modern
approach to spirituality

When you're dead you're dead.
Terry Dobney, Keeper of the Stones at Avebury
Retired motorcycle restorer

Another life, life in another dimension, in another body.
And reincarnation. Certainly continuing. In terms of
reincarnation, a modification obviously each time. I am
me; I was somebody else, but I am me, essentially me as
I am now, but there is a little bit of that somebody else
in me, in fact many somebody elses, not just one.
Jack Gale, Magician
Retired school teacher

Individual consciousness becomes non-corporeal.
According to one's personal inclinations and
expectations, one's experiential realm may
become that of any of the various afterlives,
dreamworlds, astral planes, etc. envisioned by
various religions and philosophies – including
merging into a collective subconscious (of
humanity, the planet, or even the cosmos). If one's
training and spiritual discipline instils sufficient
ability to maintain coherent focus, and one is
powerfully motivated by love to return, one may
even achieve reincarnation of one's identity in a
new body.
Oberon Zell-Ravenheart, Co-founder,
Church of All Worlds

The real me is an immortal spirit, whereas the me which is more obvious is simply a mortal body, so obviously the immortal spirit is more important. You continue as an individual being. You might reincarnate as someone who seems different, but nevertheless there is continuity in the same way that when you're fifty you're the same person you were when you were five, but different.

Gareth J. Medway, Priest Hierophant of the Fellowship of Isis
Writer and assistant psychic

I don't worry about it. In the Universe nothing gets lost, it is just transformed. The physical body will go in the earth, and the consciousness will melt into the All.

Ina Cüsters-van Bergen, Magister, Hermetic Order of the Temple of Starlight

I don't know. If there is any justice, then I have nothing to worry about; If there isn't any justice, there's nothing I can do about it.

Steve Wilson, Thelemite
Civil Servant

Who knows? I have a firm belief in the life-after-death thing. I think our bodies stop; I think our bodies in the end are a bit like a comfortable pair of shoes, that however much we love them and however familiar they are, eventually we have to throw them away . . .

But I do think that we do carry on. Maybe it is only for as long as people remember us as us. But if we don't have a body to stop us inhabiting other people and other things then maybe we don't stop inhabiting other people and other things.

Geraldine Beskin, third-generation esoteric witch and eclectic occultist
Co-owner of the Atlantis Bookshop, London

clearly aware of, could be a shift from what is essentially a
mutual support group to a structured, centralised authority
that decides who may join and who may not, with a too-rigid
codifying of what is or is not a valid and acceptable form of
Paganism;[185] if this were to occur, most would see it as being
against the overall free spirit of Neo-Paganism.

NOTES FOR PART THREE

1   Oberon Zell, founder of Church of All Worlds, in corres-
    pondence with the author, 14 June 1995.
2   See a large number of books by R. J. Stewart, John and Caitlín
    Matthews and others.
3   Waite 1888: x, xi.
4   Leo Rutherford, of the Eagle's Wing Centre for Contemporary
    Shamanism, course leaflet: *Elements of Shamanism*, 1995.
5   Jonathan Horwitz, 'All Life is Connected: The Shaman's Journey',
    at http://www.shamanism.dk/Artikel%20-%20All%20life%20
    is%20connected.htm.
6   Dr Michael York in conversation with the author, 9 June 2010.
7   http://www.lodg.org.uk.
8   http://www.shamanism.dk/Artikel%20-%20All%20life%20
    is%20connected.htm.
9   See http://www.thefourgates.com.
10 http://www.dailymail.co.uk/news/article-1276921/Pagan-
    police-win-right-time-festivals.html.
11 Barrett 2006a: 44–5; Stobart 2006, http://www.education.gov.
    uk/research/data/uploadfiles/RR750.pdf.
12 Compare the more recent and equally fictional concept of
    Satanism with its black masses (see p. 249–50) and the very
    recent myth of Satanic Ritual Abuse (see p. 255).
13 Briggs 1996: 6.
14 Kramer and Sprenger 1971: 116.
15 Centuries earlier, before the Inquisition began, the Cistercian
    abbot St Bernard of Clairvaux wrote in the Rule of the Knights
    Templar: 'The company of women is a dangerous thing, for by it
    the old devil has led many from the straight path to Paradise . . .
    We believe it to be a dangerous thing for any religious to look
    too much upon the face of woman. For this reason none of you

may presume to kiss a woman, be it widow, young girl, mother, sister, aunt or any other; and henceforth the Knighthood of Jesus Christ should avoid at all costs the embraces of women, by which men have perished many times'. Sections 70–71 of the Rule of the Templars: Upton-Ward 1992, quoted at http://www.the-orb.net/encyclop/religion/monastic/t_rule.html; cf. Burman 1986: 32, Newman 2007: 39–40, Barrett 2008a: 21; http://www.sacred-texts.com/sro/hkt/hkt04.htm#fn_20.

16 Kramer and Sprenger 1971: 267–8.

17 House of the Goddess leaflet, n.d.

18 See Briggs 1996 for a sensible and thorough historical analysis of 'witches and neighbours'.

19 Barker 1992: 145; Barrett 2001: 24.

20 Murray 1962: 12.

21 Hutton 1999: 142.

22 Ibid: 144–8.

23 The standard 971-page one-volume abridged edition was published in 1922.

24 Whether the archaeologist Lord Dorwin in Isaac Asimov's classic SF novel *Foundation* was intended as a parody of Frazer is not known, but he bears some comparison. When asked why he doesn't go out and conduct his own study on the ground Lord Dorwin replies: '"Why, whatevah foah, my deah fellow?" "To get the information first hand, of course." "But wheah's the necessity? It seems an uncommonly woundabout and hopelessly wigmawolish method of getting anywheahs. Look heah now, I've got the wuhks of all the old mastahs – the gweat ahchaeologists of the past. I wigh them against each othah – balance the disagweemcnts – analyse the conflicting statements – decide which is pwobably cowwect – and come to a conclusion. That is the scientific method. At least" – patronisingly – "as *I* see it. How insuffewably cwude it would be to go to Ahctuwus, oah to Sol, foah instance, and blundah about, when the old mastahs have covahed the gwound so much moah effectually than we could possibly hope to." Hardin murmured politely, "I see." Scientific method, hell! No wonder the galaxy was going to pot.' Isaac Asimov, *Foundation* (London: Panther, 1951), 52–3.

25 Cavendish 1987: 159.

26 Murray 1970 (1931).

27 Simpson 1994: 89–96.
28 Adler 1986: 59.
29 Matilda Joslyn Gage, *Woman, Church and State* (Chicago, IL, 1893), 106–7, cited in Hutton 1999: 141.
30 Hutton 1999: 343.
31 Briggs 1996: 8.
32 Ibid.
33 See, for example, Hutton 1999; Waldron 2008.
34 Weston 2009: 132.
35 Ethan Doyle-White, 'The Origins of Wicca and "Traditional Witchcraft"', at The Moot With No Name, London, 22 September 2010; this talk was based on research for his forthcoming book.
36 Hutton 1999: 211.
37 Ibid: 214–16.
38 Heselton 2001; Heselton 2003.
39 Gardner 1954: 137.
40 Waldron 2008: 88.
41 Weston 2009: 141.
42 Hutton 2003: 194. The essay, 'A Modest Look at Ritual Nudity', examines the topic in the historical context of other religions, including naked baptism in very early Christianity, and accusations of sexual misconduct in later Christian 'heretical' movements.
43 Hutton 1999: 214.
44 Ibid: 238.
45 http://en.academic.ru/dic.nsf/enwiki/989734; http://www.sacred-texts.com/bos/bos258.htm.
46 Weston 2009: 149.
47 Hutton 1999: 329.
48 Farrar and Farrar 1981:12.
49 Shan 1985: 75.
50 Excerpted from Farrar and Farrar 1971 (1991 edition): 172–3; other versions can be found at http://www.sacred-texts.com/bos/bos058.htm; http://www.fortunecity.com/greenfield/deer-creek/248/101/charge1.html.
51 http://www.witchcraft.org.
52 Children of Artemis in correspondence with the author, 30 September 2010.

53   http://www.hern-tribe.org, and Mani Navasothy in corres-
      pondence with the author, 13–14 October 2010.

54   Ethan Doyle-White. He cites Michael Dietler, '"Our Ancestors
      the Gauls": Archaeology, Ethnic Nationalism, and the manipu-
      lation of Celtic Identity in Modern Europe', *American
      Anthropologist*, 96: 3 (September 1994), 584–605; and Simon
      James, 'Celts, politics and motivation in archaeology', *Antiquity*,
      72: 275 (1998), 200–209.

55   Gawr et al. 2002: 21–2. Note: Rhuddlwm ap Gawr sent the
      author print-outs of two chapters of the 1986 edition of this
      book in 1995–6. Original publisher unknown. It was reissued in
      2002 from self-publishing company iUniverse.

56   See Clifton 2006: 116.

57   http://www.pagan.com/Plagiarized/Aidan%20Kelly.html;
      http://web.archive.org/web/20050227170720/http://www.geoc-
      ities.com/ferigold/yttfiles/index.html; http://web.archive.org/
      web/20050420161650/www.angelfire.com/wv/clanndroen/
      nithings.html.

58   See the 'Frauds and Fakes' page on http://www.dynionmwyn.
      net/association/cymry.html; http://www.dynionmwyn.net/
      camelot/cotw.html; http://www.tylwytheg.com/ufp.html.

59   http://www.sacredwheel.org.

60   http://www.sacredwheel.org/nal.html.

61   Barrett 2007a: 139.

62   Shani Oates in correspondence with the author, 18 and 21 October
      2010. The 'horns worn by Moses' are in fact an old mistranslation
      of Exodus 34:29, which actually says that Moses's face shone.

63   Clifton 2006: 21.

64   Ronald Hutton, 'The History of Pagan Witchcraft', in Blécourt
      et al. 1999: 57.

65   Oates in correspondence with the author.

66   Valiente 1989: 136.

67   *Pentagram* (August 1965), at http://www.cyberwitch.com/
      bowers/faith.pdf.

68   All of Cochrane's articles and letters are available at http://
      www.cyberwitch.com/bowers/.

69   Graves 1961, Chapter 16: 'The Holy Unspeakable Name of God'.

70   Dave Finnin, co-founder of the Roebuck Tradition, in conver-
      sation with the author, 11 September 2010.

71　Letter from Evan John Jones to Ann and David Finnin, 18 June 1987, at http://ancientkelticchurch.org/CTubalCain/. Despite Jones writing 'This is not open to negotiation, arbitration, civil liberties, uncivil liberties or anything else', the interpretation of this letter is disputed by Shani Oates.

72　Ann Finnin, 'The Rest of the Story', talk hosted by *Esoteric Source* magazine, London, 10 September 2010.

73　Shani Oates and Robin the Dart at http://www.clanoftubalcain. org.uk/luxveritatis.html.

74　See details of Shani Oates's book *Tubelo's Green Fire* (Oxford: Mandrake 2010) at http://www.mandrake.uk.net/shanioates.htm.

75　Carol Stuart Jones and Blackthorn at http://clanoftubalcain. co.uk/html/clan_history.html.

76　Ibid.

77　See http://www.clanoftubalcain.org.uk; also, in long and detailed correspondence from Shani Oates to the author, 18 and 21 October 2010, she argues vehemently against Carol Stuart Jones's right to call herself Maid.

78　Ann Finnin in correspondence with the author, 17 October 2010.

79　http://clanoftubalcain.co.uk/blog/.

80　http://ronaldchalkywhite.org.uk/articles/the-regency-the-cochrane-coven-by-john-of-monmouth/. Queen's Wood is still used by both small and large groups of London Pagans for public seasonal rituals.

81　See Chapter 17, 'Schism in a Sect', Barrett 2001: 479–518; see also the author's forthcoming work, *The Fragmentation of a Sect: Schism in the Worldwide Church of God* (New York: Oxford University Press 2012).

82　Unless otherwise stated, all quotations are from Oberon Zell in correspondence with the author, 14 June 1995.

83　For convenience he is referred to as Oberon Zell throughout.

84　http://www.earthfirst.org.

85　G'Zell 1994: 4.

86　Ibid: 41.

87　Melton et al. 1990: 84.

88　Zell, correspondence, 1995.

89　Ibid.

90　Bylaws of the Church of All Worlds, Inc., Article 7.1, as amended 8 August 1998.

91　Oberon Zell in conversation with the author, 21 March 2000.

92　http://original.caw.org/bod/CAWterminationByBoD.html.

93　http://original.caw.org/articles/ReportToWaterKin.html.

94　Lance Christie, post on the CAW-Phoenix Yahoo group, 13 December 2005.

95　http://www.greyschool.com.

96　See Chapter 6, 'After the Prophet Dies: How Movements Change', in Barrett 2001: 58–69.

97　Oberon Zell-Ravenheart, in correspondence with the author, 30 September 2010.

98　G'Zell 1994: 4.

99　Ibid: 11.

100　Zell, correspondence, 1995.

101　Adler 1986: 285.

102　Article: Lance Christie on 'CAW/ATL Origins, Influences and History', n.d., supplied by Zell-Ravenheart, 2 October 2010.

103　Oberon Zell-Ravenheart, in correspondence with the author, 30 September 2010.

104　http://druidnetwork.org/en/directory/list.

105　Carr-Gomm 2002; http://www.druidcraft.de; http://www.druidry.org/modules.php?op=modload&name=PagEd&file=index&topic_id=0&page_id=67.

106　Unless otherwise stated, quotations by Philip Shallcrass are from correspondence with the author, 9 September 1995 and 25 November 2000.

107　Hutton 2007: 6.

108　Hutton 2007; Hutton 2009; there is also a relevant chapter in Hutton 2003. I am grateful to Professor Ronald Hutton for allowing me to summarise aspects of his work here. This section also makes use of material previously published in my reviews of these books in the *Independent* newspaper: Barrett 2004; Barrett 2007b; Barrett 2009.

109　Hutton 2009: 241.

110　Hutton 2009: 154.

111　Piggott 1968: 143.

112　Letter to *Odinism Today*, no. 18, May 1995: 22.

113　Worthington 2004: 15–16.

114　Hutton 2007: 173ff.

115　http://www.druidry.org.

116 Philip Shallcrass in correspondence with the author.

117 http://www.druidry.co.uk.

118 Worthington 2004: 129–34; Worthington 2005.

119 'Druid Directory' in *The Druids' Voice*, 9 (Winter 1998/9), 39.

120 http://www.lugodoc.demon.co.uk/Druids/IOD.htm.

121 Fellowship of Isis in correspondence with the author, 11 October
     2010; http://www.fellowshipofisis.com/druidclanofdana.html;
     http://lotuspharia.freeyellow.com/thecircleofisis/id2.html.

122 http://www.warband.org.uk.

123 Philip Shallcrass in correspondence with the author.

124 Terry Dobney in conversation with the author, September 2010.

125 Jeremy Morgan, correspondence with the author, 2 October 2010.

126 http://www.cobdo.org.uk.

127 http://www.dailymail.co.uk/news/article-1127430/Druid-wars-
     How-drunken-row-4-000-year-old-bones-causing-chaos-
     pagan-circles.html.

128 Emma Restall Orr, correspondence with the author, 3 October
     2010.

129 http://druidnetwork.org.

130 http://druidnetwork.org/en/deity.

131 'Druidry to be classed as religion by Charity Commission',
     http://www.bbc.co.uk/news/uk-11457795. At one point this
     story quotes King Arthur Pendragon, delightfully referring to
     him as 'Mr Pendragon, of Stonehenge'.

132 http://www.dailymail.co.uk/debate/article-1317490/Druids-
     official-religion-Stones-Praise-come.html.

133 See Sieveking and Barrett 2010.

134 http://www.honour.org.uk.

135 http://www.druidism.info.

136 Henge of Keltria, in correspondence with the author, 2 October
     2010; http://www.adf.org/about/; http://www.keltria.org;
     http://www.neopagan.net/OriginsKeltria.html.

137 http://www.keltria.org/acrobat/Beliefs.pdf.

138 The Order of Bards, Ovates and Druids, introductory leaflet.

139 Summarised from Carr-Gomm 1991: 43–64.

140 British Druid Order introductory leaflet.

141 http://www.druidry.co.uk/bdocourse.html.

142 Hutton 1999: 400; Hutton 2003: 258.

143 Professor Ronald Hutton in correspondence with the author, 7 October 2010.

144 FOI in correspondence with the author, 11 October 2010.

145 http://www.fellowshipofisis.com/durdinrobertson.html.

146 Quotations are from the Fellowship of Isis *Manifesto* unless otherwise stated.

147 http://www.fellowshipofisis.com/olivia11b_2002.html.

148 'Druid Directory' in *The Druids' Voice*, 9 (Winter 1998/9), 38.

149 *The Handbook of the Fellowship of Isis*, n.d.: 8.

150 Ibid.

151 Quotations from Freya Aswynn are from correspondence with the author, 5 February 1995, confirmed by her on 7 November 2010.

152 *Odalstone*, the news sheet of Odinshof, 10: 1 (1993).

153 Most commercial sets have twenty-four runes. The occasional blank twenty-fifth rune, representing the Wyrd (fate or destiny), is a very modern addition; being blank it cannot be considered a rune, which by definition is a carved letter and symbol.

154 http://runegild.org/intro.html.

155 Aswynn 1990; a revised edition, *Northern Mysteries and Magick*, was published by Llewellyn in 1998. See http://www.aswynn.co.uk.

156 http://www.thetroth.org.

157 Jenny Blain, 'Heathenry, the past, and sacred sites in today's Britain', in Strmiska 2006.

158 Andrew Clifton, former Shope/editor for the Ring of Troth Europe, in conversation with the author, 14 March 2000.

159 Rune Gild press release: 'Asatru – Ancient to Modern', n.d.

160 Ibid.

161 Odinic Rite leaflet. *Odinists say Yes to Life!*, n.d.

162 Ibid.

163 Leaflet: *Welcome to the Odinic Rite*, n.d.

164 *Rhinegold* (London: Michael Joseph, 1994); *Attila's Treasure* (London: Michael Joseph, 1996).

165 http://www.manygods.org.uk.

166 Correspondence with Freya Aswynn, 1995.

167 Martyn Taylor, Odinshof, in correspondence with the author, 4 August 1995.

168 Odinshof *Members' Handbook*, n.d.

169 http://www.gippeswic.demon.co.uk/odinshof.html.

170 The author grew up in Westmorland (now south Cumbria) with these farmers as neighbours.

171 Odinic Rite leaflet: *Odinists say Yes to Life!*, n.d.

172 Ibid.

173 Odinshof *Members' Handbook*, n.d.

174 Rune Gild press release: 'Asatru – Ancient to Modern', n.d.

175 http://groups.yahoo.com/group/ukheathenry/.

176 Ben Waggoner, Shope/editor of the Troth, in correspondence with the author, 5 October 2010.

177 Blade, Australia/New Zealand Steward for the Troth, in correspondence with the author, 6 October 2010.

178 Pagan Federation introductory leaflet.

179 http://www.paganfed.org.

180 Farrar, Farrar and Bone 1995: 167.

181 http://www.pagan-network.org.

182 Jon Randall in correspondence with the author, 15 October 2010.

183 http://www.pebble.uk.net.

184 http://www.pagandash.org.

185 This occurred in Christianity with the World Council of Churches (WCC) and its UK equivalent, Churches Together in Britain and Ireland (CBTI). Although the Unitarian Church was in the forefront of ecumenical dialogue, it is not granted even observer status at the WCC and CTBI because it is not Trinitarian.

Coda

THE CHURCH OF SCIENTOLOGY:
AN ESOTERIC MOVEMENT?

Note: This entry does not present a detailed account of either the history or the beliefs and practices of Scientology; that has been done, with varying degrees of objectivity and subjectivity, by a large number of scholars, journalists, former members and the Church itself, over the years.[1] This entry is also not suggesting that the Church of Scientology is in any way an occult religion. What it is doing is drawing a number of comparisons and indicating a number of resemblances between some aspects of Scientology and some of the other religious movements in this book: a short exercise in comparative religion.

A collection of twenty-two academic essays about Scientology published in 2009 includes one by Andreas Grünschloß entitled 'Scientology: A "New Age" Religion?'[2] This mentions that founder L. Ron Hubbard (1911–86) himself wrote a short article entitled 'Scientology: The Philosophy of a New Age'.[3] In this Hubbard says 'We are the heralds of a New Age' and 'We are the prime movers in this, the new age.' In his 1955 poem 'Hymn of Asia' Hubbard also referred to himself as the 'Metteyya' or Maitreya (see p. 38 and p. 41–3).[4]

This is, of course, not the same as saying that Scientology is a New Age movement in the sense of Part One of this book. It is easy to see that it is not a Neo-Pagan movement (Part Three). However, it may be instructive to consider very briefly the Church of Scientology in the context of some aspects of both

New Age movements (Part One) and Hermetic movements (Part Two).

An essay by sociologist Bryan R. Wilson, in a book published by the Church of Scientology, discusses the 'exoteric and esoteric elements of Scientology': 'The restricted corpus of esoteric literature, which is made available only to advanced students of Scientology, presents both a fuller account of the metaphysics of the religion and more advanced techniques of auditing.'[5] Roy Wallis, who made one of the first major scholarly studies of Scientology, wrote:

> The theory itself became differentiated into what we may refer to as an esoteric and an exoteric ideology. The exoteric ideology is presented in most of the movement's publications, the works for publication by Scientologists other than Hubbard, and sympathisers of the movement . . .
>
> The esoteric ideology develops a cosmological doctrine of the origin and development (or degeneration) of the thetan [see below], and manifests far greater concern with past lives, and the supernatural abilities that the individual can acquire through the practice of Scientology.[6]

Wallis explains the esoteric nature of the religion in terms redolent of Hermetic movements:

> The belief system of the movement became increasingly esoteric, and a 'hierarchy of sanctification' emerged. Members could locate themselves on levels of initiation into the movement's mysteries through 'the grades', 'clear' and the 'OT levels'.
>
> The charismatic nature of the revelation, the gnosis, is evident in the power which it is conceived to have. Viewing the materials of a higher level than one has yet achieved, even by accident, is held to be dangerous. Hence the 'advanced materials' are kept secret from the uninitiated.[7]

Scientology is certainly esoteric (or Hermetic) in the specific sense that most of its teachings are not freely available to non-members, as they would be in an exoteric religion such as

Christianity. (In reality most of the teachings are now widely available, just as the details of masonic rituals and recognition signs, Golden Dawn teachings and the Wiccan *Book of Shadows* are available both in books and on the internet.) Neither are they freely available to most members, but only to those who have worked their way up the 'spiritual career path' represented by the 'Bridge to Total Freedom', the 'Scientology Classification Gradation and Awareness Chart of Levels and Certificates'.[8] In that sense it is an initiatory religion, with different levels of knowledge at different levels of membership.

Scientology has also been classified as a Gnostic religion, partly because of the secret knowledge at its heart, known only to initiates, and partly because it teaches that humans are immortal beings (Thetans) within mortal human bodies. Bryan R. Wilson wrote of religious movements like the Church of Scientology 'emphasising their monopoly of special, and sometimes secret knowledge as the way of salvation'; their members 'are seeking a short-cut to knowledge of greater power than is available in secular systems'.[9] In a later work he called it 'a privatised religion which relies hardly at all on communal expression or community activity.'[10] All of these descriptions apply equally to many of the Hermetic movements in Part Two of this book.

Although its members are not sworn to secrecy about the doctrines, as they might be in an occult group, they are strongly discouraged from telling others, including new recruits, about them; using Scientology's own terminology Roy Wallis writes: 'Talking whole track to raw meat is frowned upon.'[11] Not only former members but scholars and journalists frequently find themselves put under pressure, sometimes with threats of legal action, not to reveal details about the religion.

The teachings of the Church of Scientology come from its founder, L. Ron Hubbard, and the Church itself is clear that the teachings must be followed precisely. Wallis writes:

> Hubbard is accepted as possessing privileged access to the truth with regard to matters of doctrine and administration.

His revelations are final and complete. Hence there can be no ground upon which they could be challenged or criticised . . .

The 'hierarchy of sanctification' that has been erected within the movement is a further institutional barrier to criticism. The member is made to realise that there is a graded progression of enlightenment and insight into the gnosis. Those on the lower rungs of this hierarchy therefore shortly realise that much information is not yet available to them and come to believe that as more is revealed in the progression upwards, so any lingering queries, doubts and criticisms will be dealt with.[12]

Like several other movements in this book Scientology has a number of science fictional elements to it (see p. 117). Founder L. Ron Hubbard was best known as an SF writer before creating the therapeutic system of Dianetics, the first major article about which was published in the magazine *Astounding Science Fiction* (April 1950). Fellow American SF writer A. E. Van Vogt initially ran the Los Angeles Dianetic Research Foundation, but split away early on to run his own version, firmly based on Dianetic principles but without Hubbard's later religious ideas, with which he openly disagreed. British SF writer and editor George Hay, as secretary of the British Dianetics Association in the early 1950s, was the first to invite Hubbard to Britain, and spoke of 'Hubbard's extraordinary powers (I can vouch for it that he could read minds as a matter of routine)'.[13] Like Van Vogt, Hay was no longer interested 'when Dianetics was being transmogrified into Scientology'.

As for the beliefs of Scientology, the first major goal is to go Clear: 'Clearing represents the attainment of Man's dreams through the ages of attaining a new and higher state of existence and freedom from the endless cycle of birth, death, birth . . . Clear is the total erasure of the Reactive Mind from which stems all the anxieties and problems the individual has.'[14]

Hubbard's book *Dianetics: the Modern Science of Mental Health* (first published in 1950) claims that someone who has reached Clear will have better health, better eyesight and hearing, will be able to deal with any psychosomatic illness, and will have greatly increased intelligence. He (or she) will have become the optimum man (or woman) – a superman: 'A clear, for instance, has complete recall of everything which has ever happened to him or anything he has ever studied. He does mental computations, such as those of chess, for example, which a normal [sic] would do in half an hour, in ten or fifteen seconds'.[15] The description is not dissimilar to that of the possible benefits of membership of the Builders of the Adytum (see p. 224).

Hubbard's early science fiction, say SF authorities John Clute and Peter Nicholls, 'often came to haunt his readership, and its canny utilisation of superman protagonists came to tantalise them with visions of transcendental power.' They continue:

> The vulnerability of the SF community . . . to this lure of transcendence may help account for the otherwise puzzling success first of Dianetics, then of Scientology itself, which gained many early recruits from SF; for, both as technique and as religion, these very US bodies of doctrine centrally posited a technology of self-improvement, a set of instructions to follow in order to liberate the transcendent power within one.[16]

Deeper into the religion comes a text that could also be seen as science fictional, but is presented as a factual account of extra-terrestrial beings (see p. 117). It is an open secret that at one of the higher levels, the Operating Thetan III course, is a short story involving the evil dictator of a Galactic Federation; this could be seen as the central myth at the heart of the religion.[17] This account is also the religion's version of theodicy, i.e. an explanation of why there is evil in the world.

There is also a small link between Scientology and flying saucer groups; two of the leaders of the UFO group written up in the classic sociological work *When Prophecy Fails* (see p. 114) had previously been involved in Dianetics.[18]

Psychologist Christopher Evans wrote of 'black box' technology in certain religions, including the Spiritual Energy Battery of the Aetherius Society (see p. 125) and the E-Meter, the device used in Scientology 'which helps the auditor and

preclear locate areas of spiritual distress or travail': 'The
E-Meter measures the spiritual state or change of state of a
person and thus is of enormous benefit to the auditor in helping
the preclear locate areas to be handled. The reactive mind's
hidden nature requires utilisation of a device capable of regis-
tering its effects – a function the E-Meter does accurately.'[19]
The E-Meter measures electrical skin conductivity and
resistance in a similar way to a polygraph or lie-detector –
though the Church claims it bears no resemblance to this, and
that it measures instead 'the movement of mental masses';
'mental image pictures . . . have weight and mass'.[20]

According to Evans:

> When a Scientologist, an Aetherian or a radionics expert
> twiddles knobs on his particular gadget, he is on one plane
> performing a routine act of diagnosis, psychic defence or what
> have you, in yet another plane he is reminding himself and his
> colleagues of the most important single fact motivating all reli-
> gious thought – man is both flesh *and* soul, the latter as real and
> measurable as the former.[21]

L. Ron Hubbard apparently had a fascinating, mysterious,
adventurous youth. In a number of glossy A4 booklets the
Church of Scientology tells us that Hubbard could ride horses
at the age of three-and-a-half; that he was made a blood brother
of the Blackfoot Indians at the age of six; that he visited Guam,
Hawaii, Japan, Hong Kong and Shanghai when he was sixteen,
and the Great Wall of China, various temples, palaces and the
Forbidden City at seventeen; that he 'studied with the last in
the line of royal magicians from the court of Kublai Khan'; that
he gained 'admittance to the fabled Tibetan lamaseries in the
Western Hills of China'; that 'in addition to the local Tartar
tribes, he spent time with nomadic bandits originally from
Mongolia'; and much more.[22]

The point of mentioning this is not to question either
Hubbard's truthfulness or his Church's public relations on his

biography, but to draw a parallel with the founders of several other religions. Hubbard's astonishing youth, including his journeys to the mysterious East, has much in common with the early years of Madame Blavatsky (see p. 23), G. I. Gurdjieff (see p. 44–5), Raymond Armin ('Leo', see p. 100) and others. The founders of many religions enjoy such myths – using the word in its technical sense, which implies no judgement on factual veracity (see p. 13). On the other hand no one reading the lives of early saints believes all the fantastical stories they contain. For their medieval authors, the factuality of such stories was never the point; these are hagiographies, wonder stories showing great men in a glorious light. It may be considered that what applies to saints might perhaps also apply to founders of religions.[23]

Details of Hubbard's early life and naval career have frequently been challenged, and the challenges have been met with forthright rebuttals by the Church of Scientology. But Hubbard is in good company with George King, founder of the Aetherius Society (see p. 119), and Gerald Gardner, founder of Wicca (see p. 291), in claiming a fake doctorate; in Hubbard's case it was 'awarded' in 1953 by 'Sequoia University', an unaccredited 'degree mill' in Los Angeles, which was eventually shut down by a court order in 1984.[24]

Hubbard's name has been linked with Aleister Crowley. The two men never met, though in his Philadelphia Doctorate Course lectures in 1952, crucial to the development of Scientology, Hubbard referred to Crowley as 'my very good friend' and said his writing on magic was 'a trifle wild in spots but is a fascinating work in itself'.[25]

One of the most controversial and contentious episodes in Hubbard's life was his involvement in a major magical ritual known as the Babalon Working, in January and March 1946. Hubbard stayed for some months in 1945–6 at the home of Jack Parsons, a brilliant rocket scientist and the acting head of the Agape lodge of the Ordo Templi Orientis (see p. 212) in Pasedena, near Los Angeles. In a letter to Crowley at the time Parsons said of Hubbard:

> Although he has no formal training in Magick, he has an extraor-
> dinary amount of experience and understanding in the field.
> From some of his experiences I deduce that he is in direct contact
> with some higher intelligence, possibly his Guardian Angel. He
> is the most Thelemic person I have ever met, and is in complete
> accord with our own principles.[26]

Although Hubbard did not join the OTO, Parsons referred to
him as his 'magical partner'. According to Parsons, in January
1946 they performed a series of rituals over several days to
summon a 'scarlet woman', the future actress Marjorie
Cameron. Then in March 1946 Parsons performed a sex-magic
ritual with her, with Hubbard acting as 'the clairvoyant seer
describing the happenings on the astral plane',[27] in an attempt
to conceive a 'moonchild' as described by Crowley in his novel
Moonchild (1929).

The Church of Scientology is very sensitive about this story.
It challenges this account, saying in a 1969 statement that
'Hubbard was working as an undercover agent for the US
Navy to break up black magic in America.'[28] According to
Graeme Wilson, Public Affairs Director of the Church of
Scientology in the UK, 'Mr Hubbard was indeed involved
with Aleister Crowley – in order to break up Crowley's black
magic ring!'[29] This may be completely genuine, or it may not;
even occult writer Paul Weston, who writes favourably of
Hubbard, says the Church's 1969 statement on this 'was obviously not true in any literal sense'.[30] There is unlikely ever to be
incontrovertible evidence for or against either Jack Parsons' or
the Church of Scientology's version of events. Hubbard's true
role in the Second World War, says the Church, was highly
classified because of his intelligence work, and so could never
be proved by official documentation.[31]

Although Kenneth Grant, who worked with Crowley in
the mid-1940s and later founded the Typhonian OTO (see
p. 217), implied that Hubbard had 'grown wealthy and famous
by a mis-use of the secret knowledge which he had wormed

out of Parsons',[32] it must be emphasised that there are no resemblances between the teachings of Scientology and those of the OTO and Thelema.

Some esoteric movements are coy about giving out their membership numbers. As a general rule it seems that when organisations are reluctant to give their membership figures the actual numbers are far smaller than they wish people to think. Other movements inflate them, sometimes wildly: 'It is well established in the social scientific literature that religious movements of all types – both established and new – regularly inflate membership and attendance figures, sometimes by an order of magnitude or more.'[33]

The Rosicrucian group AMORC (see p. 186) claimed 250,000 members in 1990,[34] far more than any other Rosicrucian groups. That number pales into insignificance compared to the Church of Scientology, which for some years claimed 8 million members worldwide. By 2006 it was claiming 10 million, a number that was repeated unquestioned in newspaper articles and radio and TV news items. In Britain it claimed 120,000 members.

For the Church, size matters; it is a very public indicator of its power and position. Wallis writes: 'The social reality of Scientology can also be legitimated by reference to its powers, its size, its ability to achieve results and its success as a movement in terms of its wealth.'[35]

Census returns on religious affiliation may not always be reliable, especially when dealing with small numbers (see p. 252). But the 2001 Census returns revealed a very different picture from the Church's figures. In England and Wales 1,781 people said they were Scientologists, less than 1.5 per cent of the number the Church claims. The 2001 Census figures for other English-speaking countries were similarly low: in Australia, 2,032 people said they were Scientologists; in Canada, only 1,525; and in New Zealand, just 282. In the same year the American Religious Identification Survey estimated that there were just 55,000 Scientologists in the United States, Scientology's home country, which would suggest a worldwide membership of less than 100,000.[36]

The 100:1 disparity between 10 million and 100,000 may partly be explained by the fact that according to its president, Heber Jentzsch, the Church of Scientology claims as a member every person who has ever taken even a single introductory Scientology course since the Church was founded in 1954, whether they are now alive or dead.[37] More recent figures from former senior members suggest that even 100,000 is an over-estimate; around 2002 a member of the elite Sea Organisation at the heart of the Church 'estimated maybe 40,000 or 50,000 max'.[38] In 2010, now a former member, he put worldwide membership somewhere between 25,000 and 40,000,[39] and falling as increasing numbers of members leave the Church to become 'Freezone' Scientologists, still practising the religion but outside the Church of Scientology.[40] As with Thelemites outside the OTO (see p. 218), it may soon be the case that there are more Scientologists outside the Church of Scientology than inside it.

NOTES FOR CODA

1   Barrett 2001: 446–78; Lewis 2009; Evans 1973: 17–134; Lamont 1986; Atack 1990; Duignan 2008; Hawkins 2010; Church of Scientology International 1994, 1998a, 1998b.
2   Lewis 2009: 225–43.
3   First published in *Ability – the Magazine of Dianetics and Scientology*, 60 (1957); this is available at http://www.blog scientology.com/2007/03/12/the-philosophy-of-a-new-age/.
4   Andreas Grünschloß, 'Scientology: A "New Age" Religion?', in Lewis 2009: 233; Wallis 1977: 250.
5   Church of Scientology International 1998a: 141.
6   Wallis 1977: 124.
7   Ibid: 125.
8   Church of Scientology International 1994: 81, and many other Church of Scientology publications.
9   Wilson 1970: 44–5.

10   Wilson 1990: 278.

11   Wallis 1977: 106.

12   Ibid: 228, 229.

13   George Hay in correspondence with the author, 8 August 1995.

14   *The Auditor: the Journal of Scientology*, 21 (14 February 1967), 2.

15   Hubbard 1981: 171.

16   Clute and Nicholls 1993: 593.

17   From past conversations and correspondence the author is aware that the Church of Scientology strongly objects to this story being related. To avoid any potential unpleasantness – and so that Scientologists below OTIII may read this section without being 'enturbulated' – the story is not told here.

18   Andreas Grünschloß, 'Scientology: A "New Age" Religion?', in Lewis 2009: 240.

19   Church of Scientology International 1998b: 83.

20   Ibid: 539.

21   Evans 1973: 180.

22   The booklets include *Ron: Letters and Journals: Early Years of Adventure* (1997); *Ron: Adventurer/Explorer: Daring Deeds and Unknown Realms* (1996); *L Ron Hubbard: A Profile* (1995). The final quote is from *What is Scientology?* (Los Angeles, CA: Bridge Publications, 1998b), 32.

23   See Barrett 2000 for a more detailed look at this topic.

24   Evans 1973: 22; http://en.academic.ru/dic.nsf/enwiki/1754307.

25   The relevant text is given in Lamont 1986: 21; Weston 2009: 374; Atack 1990: 91. Graeme Wilson, Public Affairs Director of the Church of Scientology in the UK, in correspondence with the author in 1999–2000, said that Hubbard's remark was 'clearly facetious', but that assessment is not supported by the context. Hubbard went on to say: 'Now a magician – getting back to cause and effect and Aleister's work – a magician postulates what his goal will be before he starts to accomplish what he is doing' (Philadelphia Doctorate Course, lecture 18).

26   Atack 1990: 92; Miller 1988: 153. See also *Fortean Times*, 132 (March 2000: 34–8), and Carter 1999.

27   The Church of Scientology's Graeme Wilson says in a letter to the author that Hubbard was absent from this ritual, while providing a copy of the academic paper by J. Gordon Melton from which this quotation is taken (J. Gordon Melton, 'Thelemic

Magic in America: The Emergence of an Alternative Religion', Conference on Alternative Religions: Research and Study, Loyola University, 7–10 May 1981).

28   In support of this Graeme Wilson cites a December 1969 article in the London *Sunday Times*: 'L. Ron Hubbard was still an officer of the US Navy [and] because he was well known as a writer and a philosopher and had friends amongst the physicists, he was sent in to handle the situation. He went to live at the house and investigated the black magic rites and the general situation and found them very bad.' In fact, this passage is from a statement sent to the *Sunday Times* by the Church of Scientology, which was quoted verbatim by the newspaper as a result of legal action.

29   Graeme Wilson in correspondence with the author in 1999–2000.

30   Weston 2009: 367.

31   The evidence supplied to the author by the Church of Scientology consists largely of assertions by the Church and does not constitute proof of its version of events.

32   Kenneth Grant, *The Magical Revival* (London: Muller, 1972), 107, cited in Wallis 1977: 111.

33   Douglas E. Cowan, 'Researching Scientology: Perceptions, Premises, Promises and Problematics', in Lewis 2009: 56.

34   Philip Charles Lucas, in Melton and Baumann 2002: 47, gives figures of 250,000 members of AMORC in 1990, falling to 200,000 in 1998.

35   Wallis 1977: 238.

36   Barrett 2006b.

37   Heber Jentzsch, president of the Church of Scientology, on *Nightline*, ABC, 14 February 1992, http://www.solitarytrees. net/racism/howmany.htm. See also Douglas E. Cowan, 'Researching Scientology: Perceptions, Premises, Promises and Problematics', in Lewis 2009: 56.

38   Hawkins 2010: 261.

39   http://leavingscientology.wordpress.com/2010/03/27/so-how-big-is-the-church-of-scientology-really/. The 2008 figures from the American Religious Identification Survey show a drop from 55,000 in 2001 to 25,000 in 2008. See further figures at http:// www.lermanet.com/howmany.htm.

40   http://scientologistsfreezone.com; http://internationalfreezone. net; http://independentscn.zzl.org.

BIBLIOGRAPHY

Adler, Margot, *Drawing Down the Moon: Witches, Druids, Goddess Worshippers and Other Pagans in America Today* (Boston, MA: Beacon Press, 1986).

Alexander, Pat and David Alexander (eds), *The New Lion Handbook to the Bible* (Oxford: Lion, 1999).

Annett, Stephen, *The Many Ways of Being: A Guide to Spiritual Groups and Growth Centres in Britain* (London: Abacus, 1976).

Anson, Peter F., *Bishops at Large* (London: Faber and Faber, 1964).

Aswynn, Freya, *Leaves of Yggdrasil* (St Paul, MN: Llewellyn, 1990).

Atack, Jon, *A Piece of Blue Sky: Scientology, Dianetics and L. Ron Hubbard Exposed* (New York, NY: Lyle Stuart, 1990).

Bailey, Alice, *The Unfinished Autobiography of Alice A. Bailey* (New York, NY: Lucis Trust, 1951).

— —, *The Externalization of the Hierarchy* (New York, NY: Lucis Trust, 1957).

Bain, Alan, *Bishops Irregular: An International Directory of Independent Bishops* (Bristol: A. M. Bain, 1985).

Barker, Eileen, *New Religious Movements: A Practical Introduction* (London: HMSO, 1992).

Barkun, Michael, *A Culture of Conspiracy: Apocalyptic Visions in Contemporary America* (Berkeley, CA, Los Angeles, CA, and London: University of California Press, 2003).

Barnstone, Willis (ed.), *The Other Bible* (San Francisco, CA: Harper & Row, 1984).

Barrett, David V., *Sects, 'Cults' & Alternative Religions* (London: Blandford/Cassell, 1996).

— —, 'Eastern Promise: Foundation Myths in Religions', *Fortean Times* (December 2000).

— —, *The New Believers: A Survey of Sects, Cults and Alternative Religions* (London: Cassell, 2001).

— —, 'Witches, Druids and King Arthur by Ronald Hutton. In the shadowlands of magic and ritual', *Independent* (7 January 2004).

— —, 'Possession and Exorcism', *Fortean Times* (November 2006a).

— —, 'How many members do they really have?' *Church Times* (1 December 2006b), http://www.churchtimes.co.uk/content. asp?id=29766.

— —, *A Brief History of Secret Societies* (London: Robinson, 2007a).

— —, 'The Druids: A History, by Ronald Hutton. White robes, mistletoe, and heroes from ancient times to the present day', *Independent* (21 June 2007b).

— —, 'City of Secrets', *Fortean Times* (August 2007c).

— —, *The Atlas of Secret Societies: The Truth Behind the Templars, Freemasons and Other Secretive Organisations* (London: Godsfield Press/Octopus, 2008a).

— —, 'How Scientologists pressurise publishers' *Guardian* (4 December 2008b), http://www.guardian.co.uk/books/booksblog/2008/ dec/04/religion-scientology-books.

— —, 'Blood and Mistletoe: a history of the Druids in Britain, by Ronald Hutton', *Independent* (15 May 2009).

— —, 'I'm not the Messiah', *Fortean Times* (April 2010a).

— —, 'Patrice Chaplin: The Portal', *Fortean Times* (November 2010b).

Barton, John and John Muddiman (eds), *The Oxford Bible Commentary* (Oxford and New York, NY: Oxford University Press, 2001).

Beekman, Scott, *William Dudley Pelley: A Life in Right-Wing Extremism and the Occult* (Syracuse, NY: Syracuse University Press, 2005).

Beit-Hallahmi, Benjamin, *Despair and Deliverance: Private Salvation in Contemporary Israel* (New York, NY: State University of New York Press, 1992).

— —, *The Illustrated Encyclopedia of Active New Religions, Sects, and Cults* (New York, NY: Rosen Publishing Group, 1998).

Blavatsky, H. P., *The Secret Doctrine: the Synthesis of Science, Religion and Philosophy* (Pasadena, CA: Theosophical University Press, 1977).

Blécourt, Willem de, Ronald Hutton and Jean La Fontaine, *The Athlone History of Witchcraft and Magic in Europe. Volume 6: The Twentieth Century* (London: Athlone Press, 1999).

Bloom, William (ed.), *The New Age: An Anthology of Essential Writings* (London: Rider, 1991).

Bloom, William, Judy Hall and David Peters (eds), *The Encyclopedia of Mind, Body, Spirit* (London: Godsfield Press/Octopus, 2009).

Bogdan, Henrik, *Western Esotericism and Rituals of Initiation* (New York, NY: State University of New York Press, 2007).

BOTA, *The Great Adventure* (Los Angeles, CA: Builders of the Adytum, n.d.)

— —, *The Open Door* (Los Angeles, CA: Builders of the Adytum, 1989).

Brandreth, Henry R. T., *Episcopi Vagantes and the Anglican Church* (London: Society for Promoting Christian Knowledge, 1947).

Briggs, Robin, *Witches & Neighbours: The Social and Cultural Context of European Witchcraft* (London: Harper Collins, 1996).

Bromley, David G. and J. Gordon Melton (eds), *Cults, Religion & Violence* (Cambridge: Cambridge University Press, 2002).

Burman, Edward, *The Templars: Knights of God* (Wellingborough: Crucible, 1986).

Butler, W. E., *Magic and the Magician: Magic – Its Ritual, Power and Purpose, and The Magician – His Training and Work* (London: Aquarian, 1991).

Cabot, Laurie and Tom Cowan, *Power of the Witch: A Witch's Guide to her Craft* (London: Michael Joseph, 1990).

Campbell, Eileen, and J. H. Brennan, *The Aquarian Guide to the New Age* (Wellingborough: Aquarian, 1990).

Carlson, Shawn and Gerald A. Larue, *Satanism in America (Committee for Scientific Examination of Religion)* (San Francisco, CA: Gaia Press, 1989).

Carr-Gomm, Philip, *The Elements of the Druid Tradition* (Shaftesbury: Element, 1991).

— —, *Druidcraft: The Magic of Wicca and Druidry* (Illustrated edition, London: Thorsons, 2002).

Carroll, Peter J., *Liber Kaos* (York Beach, ME: Weiser Books, 1992).

— —, *Psybermagick: Advanced Ideas in Chaos Magic* (Tempe, AZ: New Falcon, 2000).

Carter, John, *Sex and Rockets: The Occult World of Jack Parsons* (Venice, CA: Feral House, 1999).

Case, Paul Foster, *The Book of Tokens: Tarot Meditations* (14th edition, Los Angeles, CA: Builders of the Adytum, 1989).

Cavendish, Richard, *Encyclopedia of the Unexplained: Magic, Occultism and Parapsychology* (London: Routledge & Kegan Paul, 1974).

——, *The Magical Arts: Western Occultism and Occultists* (Original edition 1967. London: Arkana, 1984).

——, *A History of Magic* (Original edition 1987. London: Arkana, 1990).

Chaplin, Patrice, *City of Secrets* (London: Robinson, 2007).

——, *The Portal* (Wheaton, IL: Quest Books, 2010).

Christensen, Karen and David Levinson (eds), *Encyclopedia of Community: From the Village to the Virtual World* (Thousand Oaks, CA, London, New Delhi: Sage, 2003).

Church of Scientology International, *A Description of the Scientology Religion* (Los Angeles, CA: Bridge Publications, 1994).

——, *Scientology: Theology & Practice of a Contemporary Religion* (Los Angeles, CA: Bridge Publications, 1998a).

——, *What is Scientology?* (Los Angeles, CA: Bridge Publications, 1998b)

Church Universal and Triumphant, *Keepers of the Flame: A Fraternity* (Livingston, MT: Summit Lighthouse, 1986).

——, *Profile: Elizabeth Clare Prophet/Teachings of the Ascended Masters* (Livingston, MT: Summit University Press, 1992).

——, *Climb the Highest Mountain: A Profile of the Church Universal and Triumphant* (Livingston, MT: Summit University Press, 1994).

Clarke, Peter B., *Encyclopedia of New Religious Movements* (Abingdon, Oxford: Routledge, 2006).

Clifton, Chas S., *Her Hidden Children: The Rise of Wicca and Paganism in America* (Lanham, MD: Alta Mira Press, 2006).

Clute, John and Peter Nicholls (eds), *The Encyclopedia of Science Fiction* (London: Orbit, 1993).

Creme, Benjamin, *The Ageless Wisdom Teaching: An Introduction to Humanity's Spiritual Legacy* (London, Amsterdam, Los Angeles, CA: Share International Foundation, 1996).

Davis, Morgan, 'From Man to Witch: Gerald Gardner 1946–1949' (n.d.), http://www.geraldgardner.com/Gardner46-49.PDF.

DeHaan, Richard W., *Satan, Satanism and Witchcraft* (Grand Rapids, MI: Zondervan, 1972).

Deveney, John Patrick, *Paschal Beverly Randolph: A Nineteenth-century Black American Spiritualist, Rosicrucian, and Sex Magician* (New York, NY: SUNY Press, 1997).

Douglas, J. D., *The New Bible Dictionary* (London: Inter-Varsity Fellowship, 1962).

Drury, Nevill, *The History of Magic in the Modern Age: A Quest for Personal Transformation* (London: Constable, 2000).

Duignan, John, *The Complex: An Insider Exposes the Covert World of the Church of Scientology* (Dublin: Merlin, 2008).

Ehrman, Bart D., *Misquoting Jesus: The Story Behind Who Changed the Bible and Why* (San Francisco, CA: Harper San Francisco, 2005).

Evans, Christopher, *Cults of Unreason* (London: Harrap, 1973).

Evans, Dave, *The History of British Magick after Crowley* (London: Hidden Publishing, 2007).

Evans, Dave and David Sutton, 'The Magical Battle of Britain', *Fortean Times* (October 2010).

Faivre, Antoine, *Access to Western Esotericism* (New York, NY: State University of New York Press, 1994).

Farrar, Janet and Stewart Farrar, *Eight Sabbats for Witches* (London: Robert Hale, 1981).

——, *Spells and How They Work* (London: Robert Hale, 1990).

Farrar, Janet, Stewart Farrar and Gavin Bone, *The Pagan Path* (Custer, WA: Phoenix Publishing, 1995).

Farrar, Stewart, *What Witches Do: A Modern Coven Revealed* (Original edition 1971. London: Robert Hale, 1991).

Festinger, Leon, *A Theory of Cognitive Dissonance* (Palo Alto, CA: Stanford University Press, 1957).

Festinger, Leon, Henry W. Riecken and Stanley Schachter, *When Prophecy Fails* (New York, NY: Harper & Row, 1956).

Fortune, Dion, *The Mystical Qabalah* (Original edition 1935. Wellingborough: Aquarian, 1987).

——, *The Esoteric Orders and their Work* (Wellingborough: Thorsons, 1994).

Frazer, J. G., *The Golden Bough*. Abridged (Original edition 1922. London: Macmillan, 1974).

Gardner, Gerald, *Witchcraft Today* (London: Rider, 1954).

Gawr, Rhuddlwm ap, Taliesin enion Vawr, Sarah Llewellyn and Merridin Gawr, *The Word: The Grail Mysteries of Welsh Witchcraft* (Original edition 1986. Bloomington, IN: iUniverse, 2002).

George, Leonard, *The Encyclopedia of Heresies and Heretics* (London: Robson, 1995).

Gilbert, R. A., *The Golden Dawn Companion: A Guide to the History, Structure and Workings of the Hermetic Order of the Golden Dawn* (Wellingborough: Aquarian, 1986).

——, *The Golden Dawn and the Esoteric Section* (London: Theosophical History Centre, 1987a).

——, *A. E. Waite: Magician of Many Parts* (Wellingborough: Crucible, 1987b).

——, *Casting the First Stone: The Hypocrisy of Religious Fundamentalism and its Threat to Society* (Shaftesbury: Element, 1993).

——, *Revelations of the Golden Dawn: The Rise & Fall of a Magical Order* (Slough: Quantum/Foulsham, 1997).

Graves, Robert, *The White Goddess* (London: Faber and Faber, 1961).

Greer, John Michael, *The Element Encyclopedia of Secret Societies and Hidden History* (London: Element, 2006).

G'Zell, Otter, *Church of All Worlds Membership Handbook* (Ukiah CA: Church of All Worlds, 1994).

Harpur, Patrick, *Daemonic Reality: A Field Guide to the Otherworld* (London: Viking, 1994).

Harvey, Graham, 'Satanism in Britain Today', *Journal of Contemporary Religion*, 10: 3 (1995), 283–96.

——, *Listening People, Speaking Earth: Contemporary Paganism* (London: Hurst & Co, 1997).

Harvey, Graham and Charlotte Hardman (eds), *Paganism Today: Wiccans, Druids, the Goddess and Ancient Earth Traditions for the Twenty-First Century* (Wellingborough: Thorsons, 1996).

Hawkins, Jefferson, *Counterfeit Dreams* (Clackamas, OR: Hawkeye, 2010).

Heelas, Paul, *The New Age Movement: The Celebration of the Self and the Sacralisation of Modernity* (Oxford: Blackwell, 1996).

Heindel, Max, *The Rosicrucian Cosmo-Conception* (Oceanside, CA: Rosicrucian Fellowship, 1909).

Heindel, Mrs Max, *The Birth of the Rosicrucian Fellowship: An Account of Max Heindel's Preparation and Work on the Occult Field* (Oceanside, CA: Rosicrucian Fellowship, n.d.).

Heselton, Philip, *Wiccan Roots: Gerald Gardner and the Modern Pagan Revival* (Freshfields, Berks: Capall Bann, 2001).

——, *Gerald Gardner and the Cauldron of Inspiration: An Investigation into the Sources of Gardnerian Witchcraft* (Milverton, Somerset: Capall Bann, 2003).

Howe, Ellic, *The Magicians of the Golden Dawn: A Documentary of a Magical Order 1887–1923* (London: Routledge & Kegan Paul, 1972).

Hubbard, L. Ron, *Dianetics: the Modern Science of Mental Health* (Original edition 1950. Copenhagen: New Era Publications, 1981).

Hutton, Ronald, *The Stations of the Sun: A History of the Ritual Year in Britain* (New York, NY: Oxford University Press, 1996).

— —, *The Triumph of the Moon: A History of Modern Pagan Witchcraft* (Oxford: Oxford University Press, 1999).

— —, *Witches, Druids and King Arthur* (London and New York, NY: Hambledon & London, 2003).

— —, *The Druids* (London: Hambledon Continuum, 2007).

— —, *Blood and Mistletoe: The History of the Druids in Britain* (New Haven, CT, and London: Yale University Press, 2009).

Jackson, Keith B., *Beyond the Craft: The Indispensable Guide to Masonic Orders Practised in England and Wales* (Addlestone, Kent: Lewis Masonic, 1994).

Kenny, Anthony, *A Stylometric Study of the New Testament* (Oxford and New York, NY: Oxford University Press, 1986).

Kick, Russ (ed.), *Everything You Know About God is Wrong* (New York, NY: Disinformation Company, 2007).

King, Francis, *Sexuality, Magic & Perversion* (Los Angeles, CA: Feral House, 2002).

King, Francis and Isabel Sutherland, *The Rebirth of Magic* (London: Corgi, 1982).

King, George, *You Are Responsible!* (London: Aetherius Press, 1961).

— —, *The Nine Freedoms* (Hollywood, CA: Aetherius Society, 1963).

King, George and Richard Lawrence, *Contacts With the Gods from Space: Pathway to the New Millennium* (Hollywood, CA: Aetherius Society, 1996).

Knight, Gareth, *Dion Fortune and the Three Fold Way* (London: Society of the Inner Light, 2002).

Kramer, Heinrich and James Sprenger, *Malleus Maleficarum* (London: Arrow Books, 1971).

Lachman, Gary, *Politics and the Occult: The Left, the Right and the Radically Unseen* (Wheaton, IL: Quest Books, 2008).

La Fontaine, Jean, *Speak of the Devil: Tales of Satanic Abuse in Contemporary England* (Cambridge: Cambridge University Press, 1998).

Lamont, Stewart, *Religion Inc.: The Church of Scientology* (London: Harrap, 1986).

LaVey, Anton, *The Satanic Bible* (London: W. H. Allen, 1969).

Lawrence, Richard, *UFOs and the Extraterrestrial Message* (London and New York, NY: Cico Books, 2010).

Leo, *Dear Dragon* (4th edition, Ma'ale Tzvia, Israel: Topaz Publications, 1992).

Lévi, Eliphas, *Transcendental Magic: Its Doctrine and Ritual*, trans. A. E. Waite (Original edition, *Le Dogme et Rituel de la Haute Magie*, 1855–6. London: Bracken Books, 1995).

Lewis, James R. (ed.), *The Gods Have Landed: New Religions from Other Worlds* (New York, NY: State University of New York Press, 1995).

— — (ed.), *Encyclopedic Sourcebook of UFO Religions* (Amherst, NY: Prometheus Books, 2003).

— — (ed.), *Scientology* (Oxford: Oxford University Press, 2009).

Lewis, James R. and J. Gordon Melton (eds), *Church Universal and Triumphant in Scholarly Perspective* (Stanford, CA: Centre for Academic Publication, 1994).

Lottes, Günther, Eero Medijainen and Jón Višar Siguršsson (eds), *Making, Using and Resisting the Law in European History* (Pisa: Plus-Pisa University Press, 2008).

Lurie, Alison, *Imaginary Friends* (London: William Heinemann, 1967).

Lyle, Robert, *Subud* (Tunbridge Wells: Humanus, 1983).

Martin, Lois, *Witchcraft: A Brief History of Demons, Folklore and Superstition* (London: Robinson, 2010).

Matthews, Caitlín and John Matthews, *The Western Way: A Practical Guide to the Western Mystery Tradition. Vol. 1: The Native Tradition* (London: Arkana, 1985).

— —, *The Western Way: A Practical Guide to the Western Mystery Tradition. Vol. 2: The Hermetic Tradition* (London: Arkana, 1986).

Maxwell-Stuart, P. G., *Witch Hunters: Professional Prickers, Unwitchers & Witch Finders of the Renaissance* (Stroud: Tempus, 2003).

Medway, Gareth J, *Lure of the Sinister: The Unnatural History of Satanism* (New York, NY, and London: New York University Press, 2001).

— —, 'Beyond the Reality Barrier', *Magonia*, 94 (January 2007).

Melton, J. Gordon, 'Spiritualisation and Reaffirmation: What Really Happens When Prophecy Fails', *American Studies*, 26 (1985), 17–29.

— — (ed.), *Encyclopedic Handbook of Cults in America* (New York, NY: Garland, 1992).

Melton, J. Gordon and Martin Baumann (eds), *Religions of the World: A Comprehensive Encyclopedia of Beliefs and Practices*, 4 vols (Santa Barbara, CA: ABC-Clio, 2002).

Melton, J. Gordon, Jerome Clark and Aidan A. Kelly (eds), *New Age Encyclopedia* (Detroit, MI: Gale Research, 1990).

— —, *New Age Almanac* (Detroit MI: Visible Ink, 1991).

Miller, Russell, *Bare-Faced Messiah* (London: Sphere, 1988).

Moore, James, *Gurdjieff: A Biography* (Shaftesbury: Element, 1999).

Murray, Margaret A., *The God of the Witches* (London: Sampson Low, Marston & Co, 1931).

— —, *The Witch-Cult in Western Europe* (Original edition 1921. Oxford: Oxford University Press, 1962).

Newcomers' Guide to Essential Paganism, Witchcraft, Shamanism (Leeds: Sorcerer's Apprentice Press, 1994).

Newman, Sharan, *The Real History Behind the Templars* (New York, NY: Berkley Books, 2007).

New Testament in Basic English, The (Cambridge: Cambridge University Press, 1944).

Occult Census: Statistical Analyses & Results, The (Leeds: Sorcerer's Apprentice Press, 1989).

Olp, Susan, 'In memoir, daughter of CUT leader comes to grips with where church went wrong', *Billings Gazette* (28 October 2008).

O'Shea, Stephen, *The Perfect Heresy: The Life and Death of the Cathars* (London: Profile Books, 2000).

Pagan Index, The (London: House of the Goddess, 1993).

Parker, John, *At the Heart of Darkness: Witchcraft, Black Magic and Satanism Today* (London: Sidgwick & Jackson, 1993).

Partridge, Christopher (ed.), *UFO Religions* (London: Routledge, 2003).

— — (ed.), *Encyclopedia of New Religions: New Religious Movements, Sects and Alternative Spiritualities* (Oxford: Lion, 2004).

Pendergrast, Mark, *Victims of Memory: Incest Accusations and Shattered Lives* (London: Harper Collins, 1996).

Petersen, Jesper Aagaard (ed.), *Contemporary Religious Satanism: A Critical Anthology* (Farnham: Ashgate, 2009).

Pfeiffer, Charles F. and Everett F. Harrison (eds), *The Wycliffe Bible Commentary* (London: Oliphants, 1963).

Pickering, W. S. F., *Anglo-Catholicism: A Study in Religious Ambiguity* (London and New York, NY: Routledge, 1989).

Piggott, Stuart, *The Druids* (Original edition 1968. London: Penguin, 1974).

Poesnecker, Gerald E., *One Flesh* (Quakertown, PA: Humanitarian Publishing Company, 1996).

Pollack, Rachel, *The New Tarot: Modern Variations of Ancient Images* (Wellingborough: Aquarian, 1989).

Prophet, Elizabeth Clare, *Saint Germain on Alchemy: Formulas for Self-Transformation* (Livingston, MT: Summit University Press, 1985).

— —, *The Lost Years of Jesus: Documentary Evidence of Jesus' 17-year Journey to the East* (Livingston, MT: Summit University Press, 1987).

Prophet, Elizabeth Clare, Patricia R. Spadaro and Murray L. Steinman, *Kabbalah: Key to your Inner Power* (Livingston, MT: Summit University Press, 1997).

Rabelais, François, *The Histories of Gargantua and Pantagruel* (London: Penguin, 1955).

Raël, *The Message Given to Me by Extra-Terrestrials/They Took Me to Their Planet* (Tokyo: AOM Corporation, 1986).

— —, *The Final Message: Humanity's Origins and Our Future Explained* (London: Tagman Press, 1998).

— —, *The Maitreya: Extracts from his Teachings* (Vaduz, Liechtenstein: Raelian Foundation, 2004).

— —, *Intelligent Design: Message from the Designers* (Geneva: Nova Distribution, 2005).

Rawlinson, Andrew, *The Book of Enlightened Masters: Western Teachers in Eastern Traditions* (Chicago, IL: Open Court, 1997).

Regardie, Israel, *Foundations of Practical Magic* (Wellingborough: Aquarian, 1979).

— —, *The Golden Dawn* (6th edition, St Paul, MN: Llewellyn, 1989).

Religious Systems of the World: A Contribution to the Study of Comparative Religion (Original edition 1889. 9th edition, London: Swann Sonnenschein & Co, 1908).

Richardson, Alan, *A Theological Word Book of the Bible* (London: SCM Press, 1957).

Richardson, James T., Joel Best and David G. Bromley (eds), *The Satanism Scare: Social Institutions & Social Change* (New York, NY: Aldine Transaction, 1991).

Ritchie, Jean, *The Secret World of Cults: Inside the Sects that Take Over Lives* (London: Angus & Robertson, 1991).

Roberts, Andy, 'Peter Caddy, Contactees and the Findhorn Community', *Magonia* (August 2005).

— —, 'Saucers Over Findhorn', *Fortean Times* (December 2006).

Rothstein, Mikael, 'The Family, UFOs and God: A Modern Extension of Christian Mythology', *Journal of Contemporary Religion*, 12: (1997), 353–62.

Servants of the Light, *Introductory Booklet* (n.d.).

Shan, *Which Craft? An Introduction to the Craft* (London: House of the Goddess, 1985).

Sieveking, Paul and David V. Barrett, 'Druids finally recognised', *Fortean Times* (December 2010).

Simpson, Jacqueline, 'Margaret Murray: Who Believed Her and Why?', *Folklore*, 105 (1994), 89–96.

Smith, Andrew Phillip, *A Dictionary of Gnosticism* (Wheaton, IL: Quest Books, 2009).

Smith, William, *Smith's Bible Dictionary* (New York, NY: Pyramid, 1967).

Stobart, Eleanor, 'Child Abuse Linked to Accusations of "Possession" and "Witchcraft"' (London: Department for Education and Skills, 2006), http://www.education.gov.uk/research/data/uploadfiles/RR750.pdf.

Storm, Rachel, *In Search of Heaven on Earth* (London: Bloomsbury, 1991).

Stoyanov, Yuri, *The Other God: Dualist Religions from Antiquity to the Cathar Heresy* (New Haven, CT: Yale University Press, 2000).

Strmiska, Michael (ed.), *Modern Paganism in World Cultures: Comparative Perspectives* (Santa Barbara, CA: ABC-Clio, 2006).

Taylor, Eric S., *The Liberal Catholic Church: What Is It?* (3rd edition, London: St Alban Press, 1987).

Thomas, Keith, *Religion and the Decline of Magic* (London: Weidenfeld & Nicolson, 1971).

Thompson, Damian, *The End of Time: Faith and Fear in the Shadow of the Millennium* (London: Random House/Minerva, 1996).

Todd, Douglas, 'Leader left Divine Light behind him', *Vancouver Sun* (29 September 2003).

Upton-Ward, Judith, *The Rule of the Templars* (Woodbridge: Boydell Press, 1992).

Valiente, Doreen, *The Rebirth of Witchcraft* (London: Robert Hale, 1989).

Waite, A. E., *Elfin Music: An Anthology of English Fairy Poetry* (London: Walter Scott, 1888).

— —, *The Pictorial Key to the Tarot* (London: Rider, 1911).

— —, *The Brotherhood of the Rosy Cross* (London: William Rider & Son, 1924).

— —, *Shadows of Life and Thought* (London: Selwyn and Blount, 1938).

— —, *Devil Worship in France; with Diana Vaughan and the Question of Modern Palladianism* (Original edition 1896. Boston, MA: Weiser Books, 2003).

Waldron, David, *The Sign of the Witch: Modernity and the Pagan Revival* (Durham NC: Carolina University Press, 2008).

Wallis, Roy, *The Road to Total Freedom: A Sociological Analysis of Scientology* (New York, NY: Columbia University Press, 1977).

Weber, Eugen, *Apocalypses: Prophecies, Cults and Millennial Beliefs throughout the Ages* (London: Hutchinson, 1999).

Weiss, René, *The Yellow Cross: The Story of the Last Cathars 1290–1329* (London: Viking, 2000).

Weston, Paul, *Aleister Crowley and the Aeon of Horus* (Glastonbury: Avalonian Aeon, 2009).

Wilson, Bryan R., *Religious Sects: A Sociological Study* (London: Weidenfeld & Nicolson, 1970).

— —, *The Social Dimensions of Sectarianism: Sects and New Religious Movements in Contemporary Society* (Oxford: Oxford University Press, 1990).

Wilson, Stephen, *The Magical Universe: Everyday Ritual and Magic in Pre-Modern Europe* (London and New York, NY: Hambledon & London, 2000).

Wilson, Steve, *Chaos Ritual* (London: Neptune Press, 1994).

Woodman, Justin, 'Psychologising Satan: Contemporary Satanism, Satanic-Abuse Allegations, and the Secularisation of Evil', *Scottish Journal of Religious Studies*, 18: 2 (1998), 134.

Worthington, Andy, *Stonehenge: Celebration and Subversion* (Loughborough: Heart of Albion Press, 2004).

— — (ed.), *The Battle of the Beanfield* (Teignmouth: Enabler Publications, 2005).

Yates, Frances A., *The Rosicrucian Enlightenment* (London and New York, NY: Routledge, 1972).

Zain, C. C., *The Sacred Tarot* (Los Angeles, CA: The Church of Light, 1987).

Zeller, Benjamin E., *Prophets and Protons: New Religious Movements and Science in Late Twentieth-Century America* (New York, NY: New York University Press, 2010).

INDEX